On-Line Cognition
in Person Perception

On-Line Cognition
in Person Perception

Edited by

John N. Bassili
Scarborough Campus
University of Toronto

1989

LAWRENCE ERLBAUM ASSOCIATES, PUBLISHERS
Hillsdale, New Jersey   Hove and London

BF
323
.S63
O5
1989

Copyright © 1989 by Lawrence Erlbaum Associates, Inc.
All rights reserved. No part of this book may be reproduced in any form, by photostat, microform, retrieval system, or any other means, without the prior written permission of the publisher.

Lawrence Erlbaum Associates, Inc., Publishers
365 Broadway
Hillsdale, New Jersey 07642

Library of Congress Cataloging in Publication Data

On-line cognition in person perception / edited by John N. Bassili
   p.   cm.
  Bibliography: p.
  ISBN 0-8058-0423-4
  1. Social perception.   I. Bassili, John N.
BF323.S6305   1989
153.7′5 – dc20   89-11630
                                                                         CIP

Printed in the United States of America
10 9 8 7 6 5 4 3 2 1

To Susan

Contents

List of Contributors xi

Preface xiii

1 Notes on the Distinction Between Memory-Based Versus On-Line Judgments 1
Reid Hastie and Nancy Pennington

Basic Experimental Paradigms 2
Theoretical Concepts and Confusions 5
What Inferences are Made When? 9
A Speculation About
  Task-Strategy Relationships 11

2 Procedural Efficiency and On-Line Social Judgments 19
Eliot R. Smith

Implications of General Practice Effects
  for On-Line Social Judgments 24
Specificity of Practice Effects 29
Implications of a Procedural View
  of Social Judgments for Stereotyping 32
Conclusions 35

3 Trait Attributes as On-Line Organizers in Person Impressions 39
Bernadette Park

The Fan Effect Paradigm and Integrated
  Knowledge Structures 43
Trait Attributes as Organizing Elements 45
Eliminating On-Line Organization
  of Person Impressions 49
Conclusion 53

4 Traits as Action Categories Versus Traits as Person Attributes in Social Cognition 61
John N. Bassili

Traits as Action Categories Versus
  Traits as Person Attributes 62
Evidence Supporting the
  Traits-as-Action-Categories Notion 67
Evidence Based on Reaction Times 67
Discussion 77
Conclusion 84

5 The Relation Between Opinion and Memory: Distinguishing Between Associative Density and Structural Centrality 91
Shinobu Kitayama and Eugene Burnstein

Associative Density and Structural Centrality 92
An Experiment on the Effects of Opinion
  Formation on the Probability of Recall
  and Priority of Entry in Recall 97
Method 98
Results 100
Discussion 108
On-Line Versus Memory-Based
  Opinion Formation 109
Opinion as a Recall Cue 112
Implications for Opinion Change 114
Summary and Conclusion 117

6 The Multiple Roles of Context in Dispositional Judgment   123
Yaacov Trope

The Two-Stage Model of Dispositional Judgments   *124*
The Contextual and Inferential Effects of Situational Inducements   *126*
Relevant Research   *127*
The Order of Situational and Behavioral Information   *130*
Types of Nondiagnostic Behavior   *134*
The Role of Behavior as Disambiguator of Situations   *136*
Concluding Remarks   *136*

7 On-Line Processes in Category-Based and Individuating Impressions: Some Basic Principles and Methodological Reflections   141
Susan T. Fiske and Janet B. Ruscher

Some Principles of On-Line Impression Formation   *142*
Methodological Reflections   *158*
Conclusion   *168*

8 Functional Memory and On-Line Attribution   175
Norman H. Anderson

Life is On-Line   *176*
Functional Memory: A Case History in Cognitive Theory   *177*
Social Memory   *187*
Social Attribution   *196*
Issues in Functional Memory   *204*
Social Cognition   *214*

Author Index   221

Subject Index   227

List of Contributors

Norman H. Anderson
*University of California,
San Diego*

John N. Bassili
*Scarborough Campus
University of Toronto*

Eugene Burnstein
University of Michigan

Susan T. Fiske
*University of Massachusetts
at Amherst*

Reid Hastie
University of Colorado

Shinobu Kitayama
University of Michigan

Bernadette Park
University of Colorado

Nancy Pennington
University of Colorado

Janet B. Ruscher
*University of Massachusetts
at Amherst*

Eliot R. Smith
Purdue University

Yaacov Trope
New York University

Preface

This book focuses on cognitive processes that occur during the initial acquisition of information about others rather than later when stimulus information is retrieved from memory. The distinction between these two classes of processes has recently been emphasized by Reid Hastie and Bernadette Park who referred to the first as *on-line* processes and the second as *memory-based* processes. The issue is not new in social psychology and has had other incarnations, most notably in research by Norman Anderson and his collaborators. Still, the distinction is particularly relevant at a time when the cognitive modeling of social information processing has become of primary concern in social psychology.

It is not the aim of this book to suggest that on-line processes are more common, more natural, or more important in social functioning than memory-based processes. This would miss the point. It is also not the aim of this book to suggest that on-line cognition dispenses with memory phenomena altogether. Our general knowledge of the world, without which no interpretation of stimulus input would be possible, is necessarily stored in memory. Moreover, on-line cognition requires a buffer or a work space to operate, and this work space can best be conceptualized as a working memory. What is important about on-line cognition is that it relies on cognitive dynamics that are distinct from those of memory-based processes and that the understanding of these dynamics can shed new light on phenomena of person perception.

There is an important difference in emphasis between processes responsible for memory-based cognition and those responsible for on-line cognition. In the former case, the encoding and retrieval of person information are of primary importance, whereas in the latter case it is the initial interpretation and integration of the stimulus information that are central. One important consequences of the focus of on-line cognition on the here-and-now is that the pivotal role played by long term storage in memory-based phenomena is replaced by an equally pivotal role for working memory. Given recent successes in exploring the episodic storage of person information, it would now be fruitful to focus more on the cognitive mechanisms that are responsible for processing immediate stimulus input.

This book originated as a symposium that took place at the Scarborough Campus of the University of Toronto in the spring of 1988. The symposium had three themes—to approach person perception as a diversified set of social judgments, to explore the cognitive underpinnings of these judgments, and to focus on judgments that occur at the time that information is initially encoded. The three themes were nicely addressed by the talks at the symposium. It became apparent, however, that it was the notion of on-line processing as it relates to person perception that generated the most interest and excitement among the contributors. This, therefore, has become the driving theme for the book.

Because of the relative novelty of the on-line approach, it would be helpful to begin by considering some of what is distinctive about on-line cognition. The contributors to this book have in many places addressed the matter with insight, so a brief compendium of their statements is an excellent way to start. Here is some of what they had to say:

- "On-line processes intrinsically involve limits on time and other resources. The information is before the perceiver mere moments, and new information is constantly available." (Eliot Smith)

- "When we consider social inference processes that are likely to occur on-line as opposed to being memory-based, one of the most likely candidates is a personality impression of an acquaintance." (Bernadette Park)

- "People possess on-line strategies for impression formation that prove to be quite functional for social purposes." (Susan Fiske and Janet Ruscher)

- "In memory-based opinion formation, less elaboration is performed on arguments than in on-line opinion formation." (Shinobu Kitayama and Eugene Burnstein)

- "Such factors as instructions, task demands, and the perceiver's own need to predict the target's behavior in the future may encourage perceivers to make dispositional inferences on-line." (Yaacov Trope)

- "The essential notion of an on-line task is that inferences made on-line and stored in memory are subsequently the subject of a judgment about another person." (Reid Hastie and Nancy Pennington)

- "Life is on-line." (Norman Anderson)

I would like to express my gratitude to the Life Sciences Division of the Scarborough Campus, University of Toronto, for sponsoring and hosting the symposium on on-line cognition and for the opportunity to prepare this volume. I would also like to thank my colleagues for the support they have given me and for the interest they have shown for this project. I hope that what they have learned about social cognition will lighten my debt to them. Special thanks are also due to John Racine whose helping hand remained extended for the entire period of this project and who is responsible for the indexes of this book. Finally, I would like to thank the contributors who submitted their chapters on time. I would also like to thank those who did not.

Notes on the Distinction Between Memory-Based Versus On-Line Judgments

Reid Hastie
Nancy Pennington
University of Colorado

When we observe other people, we make many inferences about them; inferences about hidden characteristics, intentions, their future behavior, the causes of their behavior, and generalizations about the essence of their personalities and temperaments. We also make inferences about our own reactions to another person and relationships with them. Do we like them? Are we superior or inferior, the same or different on various comparative dimensions? The flood of information, much of it inferred, that is tapped when we reflect on our memories of almost any acquaintance or public figure is compelling evidence of our proclivity to make "on-line" inferences.

We have selected the label "on-line" to indicate that many inferences are made during the processes of perception, when the other person is still present to the senses. There is a contrasting case that occurs when we think about a person in their absence and, at this later time, when we are not engaged "on-line" in perceiving them, make inferences about them. We have labeled this type of inference "memory-based" to distinguish it from active, on-line processing and to emphasize that it depends on retrieval from memory for "premises" from which to derive inferences about the other person.

Hastie and Park cited several intellectual precursors to the distinction made in their 1986 paper. Norman Anderson's experiments and theoretical analysis were the most significant influence on their treatment of memory-judgment relationships. Anderson, in a classic study of impression formation (Anderson & Hubert, 1963; see also Dreben, Fiske, & Hastie, 1979), introduced the "two memory hypothesis"; namely that in the typical on-line impression formation task, memory for the "raw" trait adjective stimulus items is independent (not necessarily correlated or uncorrelated) with memory for the impression that has been extracted from the items (Anderson, 1981; see chap. 8 of this volume for further comments on the relation between the two memory hypothesis and the Hastie & Park analysis).

Watts and McGuire (1964) had also reached a conclusion much like the two memory hypothesis in their research on attitude organization and change. What they found was that a person's memory for an attitude was not closely linked to the arguments that had initially produced it. Thus, they concluded that the attitude and supporting arguments were independently stored in long-term memory. Their methods and theoretical interpretation were also a major consideration in the design and interpretation of the Hastie & Park experiments.

In the early stages of the Hastie and Park research on memory–judgment relationships, important distinctions were also emerging or had crystallized in papers by members of "The Person Memory Research Club" (see Hastie et al., 1980), by McArthur (1980), and by Taylor and her students (Taylor & Fiske, 1975; Taylor & Thompson, 1982). Some experimental conditions were interpreted as reflecting on-line inference processes (e.g., Anderson & Hubert, 1963; Watts & McGuire, 1964), whereas others were interpreted as exhibiting memory-based processes (e.g., Taylor, 1982; Tversky & Kahneman, 1973). However, no single experiment had included conditions that compared on-line versus memory-based tasks within a single design.

BASIC EXPERIMENTAL PARADIGMS

For the past several years, Bernadette Park and Reid Hastie (Hastie & Park, 1986) have been trying to create experimental conditions that would distinguish between on-line and memory-based inferences. The goal of that research was to find one set of conditions of a judgment task that would induce an on-line inference and a second set of conditions that would induce a memory-based version of the same inference. As it turned out, Hastie and Park invented two pairs of conditions that achieved this goal.

The first method utilized the factor of surprise to create the two conditions. In the *on-line procedure*, subjects were exposed to an experimental task that was simple and straightforward. First, they were told they were participating in an experiment on social judgment. Next, they were told they would be playing the role of a personnel officer and making occupation suitability judgments of candidates for a position in their company. Then, they were given detailed instructions about the nature of the position and a description of the attributes of a good candidate for the job. For example, they might have been told that they would be evaluating a candidate for the job of a computer programmer and that good computer programmers typically were precise, quantitative thinkers, moderate to low in gregariousness, and so forth. Then, *with their judgment task in mind*, the subjects listened to a tape-recorded conversation between two men, Phil and Frank (who did most of the talking). The conversation was scripted so that five of Frank's statements clearly implied (at least in our subjects' minds) that he would make a good computer programmer (e.g., "I did quite well on the GRE quantitative aptitude test," "I've got a personal computer and have been teaching my son to use it," "I'm a real bridge buff, a 'life master' ") and five implied that he was unsuitable for the job (e.g., "I can't stay still indoors, I really get restless inside," "When I was younger I majored in creative writing and wanted to be a poet," "I've changed jobs three times in the past 2 years"). These statements were distributed evenly and unsystematically throughout the conversation to avoid confoundings with serial position and type of statement. After listening to the tape recording, the subjects were given the personnel officer judgment instructions again and rated Frank's suitability for the computer programmer job.

Finally, the subjects recalled everything they could remember hearing in the taped conversation (actually, half of the subjects recalled before rating job suitability). The memory test results were used to determine whether there was a relationship between subjects' ratings and what they could recall from the interview. A failure to find a relationship between what was remembered from the interview and the subjects' judgments was interpreted as evidence for an on-line inference when making the job suitability judgment. In contrast, if subjects who remembered more favorable statements also made higher suitability ratings, it would support the conclusion that they were relying on recall of the statements to make the ratings. However, note that Hastie and Park believed that the present conditions induce an *on-line* judgment strategy for the job suitability judgment and, thus, they would *not* expect there to be a correlation between recall and the judgments.

In a second experimental procedure, paired with the one just described, Hastie and Park attempted to induce a *memory-based judgment process*. Everything was identical, with one change: The subjects were told nothing about the job suitability judgment *before* they heard the taped conversation. Rather, they were given a nebulous instruction that the experiment was concerned with "social psychology" and that they should listen to a taped conversation and then they would be asked "some questions." No one would suspect that the particular questions they would be asked would have to do with computer programming job aptitude. The subjects would be surprised by the request for a job suitability judgment and forced to rely on what they could remember from the conversation to generate a response to the post-conversation task. Here, Hastie and Park expected a *memory-*

based judgment strategy and a correlation between the recall measure and subjects' ratings.

As predicted, surprising the subject with an unexpected judgment did produce a memory-based strategy as evidenced by reliable and sizeable correlations between the proportion of statements recalled that favored suitability (median correlation of +.46 across three replications of the experiment) versus non-significant memory-judgment correlations in the "no surprise" on-line judgment condition (median correlation of +.09). This pattern of correlations has been replicated in several experiments with judgments about another person's daily activities, chances of surviving a serious illness, and other job suitability questions. Closely related research by Lichtenstein and Srull (1987), Srull (1988) has also obtained similar results. The conclusion that subjects were engaged in memory-based processing in the second condition and on-line processing in the first condition is further supported by tape recordings of subjects' "think aloud protocols" collected while they were listening to the taped conversations and making ratings. Subjects in the memory-based conditions consistently referred to efforts to retrieve facts from long-term memory (at least half of their protocols comprised such comments), whereas most subjects in the on-line conditions never mentioned efforts to retrieve "raw" facts from the conversations.

Hastie and Park constructed a second pair of experimental conditions to produce the on-line versus memory-based contrast. In this pair of procedures, they attempted to use *interference*, rather than surprise, to prevent subjects from making the relevant judgments on-line. In the *on-line procedure*, subjects were first instructed that they would be hearing tape-recorded descriptions of behaviors that another person had performed. They were to make judgments, based on these descriptions, about the person's personality and how much they thought they would like the person if they were to meet him or her. Then they listened to 50 tape-recorded sentences describing actions selected to have implications (in the subjects' minds) for the to-be-judged person's character. Four personality traits had been used to generate 10 behaviors for each of the traits hostile, friendly, intelligent, and stupid. They were presented in a scrambled sequence to avoid confounding with serial position, and 10 additional sentences describing personality-irrelevant behaviors were placed at the beginning and end of the list to block primacy and recency influences on the results (see Hastie & Kumar, 1979, for a detailed description of the method used to generate these materials). At the end of the tape, subjects were distracted from the judgment task by 10 minutes of Miller Analogy items. Following the analogy task, subjects were asked to rate the person described on the tape on scales labeled with personality trait adjectives and on likeability. Then subjects were asked to recall as many of the behaviors from the tape as they could remember.

This procedure is exactly parallel to the on-line condition from the first pair of treatments. It functioned in the same manner, and correlations between recall and ratings were low and non-significant (median correlation of +.15 in this on-line treatment). Similarly, think-aloud subjects did not frequently refer to long-term memory during the rating phase of the task.

The partner, *memory-based procedure*, used a method of interference to prevent subjects from making spontaneous personality and likeability judgments. Subjects were initially instructed that they were participating in a psycholinguistics experiment and that their task would be to make judgments of the grammaticality of sentences they would hear. No mention was made that the sentences should be integrated to form an impression of the personality or likeability of a single individual. As the subjects in this condition heard each sentence, they rated its apparent grammaticality on a response form. Then, only after all the sentences had been presented and rated and a 10-minute stint of analogy problems had been completed, subjects were surprised by a request to make judgments of a person described by all of the sentences taken together, on the same set of personality and likeability rating scales used by subjects in the on-line condition. Finally, subjects attempted to recall the original set of sentences. Again, the correlations fit the expected pattern, relatively large, significant correlations in this memory-based condition (median correlation of +.67), and subjects' think-aloud comments reflected their efforts to retrieve the original sentences from long-term memory in order to perform the personality-rating task.

THEORETICAL CONCEPTS AND CONFUSIONS

Hastie and Park spelled out some alternate information-processing accounts of what subjects might be doing when performing on-line and memory-based judgment tasks (Hastie & Park, 1986). The purpose of the present chapter is to clarify and extend that analysis and to eradicate some confusions that have arisen.

Three Types of Judgments

There are several confusions about the events that are hypothesized to occur in on-line judgment tasks. Our assumption is that in on-line tasks, subjects are encoding information about the person they are observing (and the circumstances in which he or she is behaving). Much of this information involves the creation of relatively "direct" memory representations of the events actually observed. We often refer to these memory traces, recordings of the events perceived, as "raw memories." In addition, the perceiver is undoubtedly making some inferences that take him or her away "from the information given" and involve more extensive elaborations, additions, or transformations of the stimulus information.

These on-line inferences are the focus of the present theoretical analysis, and we assume that they are also stored in long-term memory. For example, the perceiver might combine elements of the stimulus information to judge the observed person's personality (e.g., "he's very pushy," "he's self-centered"), abilities (e.g., "he must be an accomplished sailor," "he's good at math"), future actions (e.g., "he's going to drop out of college," "he'll be at the party tonight"), group affiliations (e.g., "he must be in a fraternity," "he's an engineer"), and so forth. We think it is important to distinguish between the "raw," relatively direct representations of stimulus events in memory and the "inferred," more remote ideas (derived from the original stimulus events) that are also stored in long-term memory.

The essential notion of an on-line task is that inferences made on-line and stored in memory are subsequently the subject of a judgment about another person. At this later time, the original inferences are retrieved from long-term memory or retained in active working memory and serve as the basis of a judgment response. (Thom Srull [1988] prefers the label "retrieved" for this judgment condition to emphasize that at the time of judgment [in his experiments], an inference that was made previously and stored in memory is *retrieved* and is the basis of the later response.)

In memory-based tasks, the original stimulus events that serve as evidence for the memory-based judgments are in the past. When the stimulus events were initially perceived, no judgment-relevant inference was made. The subject refers to long-term memory to retrieve representations of the original events to use at that time as input into a judgment or inference process. (Srull prefers the label "computational" for this situation to emphasize that, at the time of judgment, "raw" evidence information is the input to a computational process that generates an inference to serve as the basis of a response.)

In previous discussions of these processes, we have restricted our use of the label "memory-based" to conditions under which the information retrieved from memory is from the relatively direct, "raw" category. This has created some confusion, probably because to most readers it is obvious that there are three plausible types of judgment process—although Hastie and Park only provided two labels: First, there is the immediate on-line judgment based on inferences made earlier in time while observing or interacting with another person. Second, there is the first type of memory-based judgment; inferences are made after the observations and based on "raw" memory traces; this is the type labeled "memory-based." Third, there is a second type of *inference*-memory-based judgment, in which the inferences are made some time after the observations and do not rely on "raw" memories, but rather on previously made inferences (possibly made on-line or perhaps made at an intermediate time between the original stimulus event and the final judgment).

A concrete example should help clarify these distinctions. First, in an on-line task, imagine two college students, Peter and Oliver, who meet one another while waiting to talk to a teacher about a term paper assignment. While they are talking, Peter infers that Oliver is a member of a fraternity. Perhaps this inference is based on references by Oliver to a party, a charity drive, and living in a "house," all associated with fraternity life in the college that both students attend. This conclusion, "Oliver is a fraternity member," is stored in Peter's long-term memory. Later in time, a third student, Quintin, asks Peter if Oliver belongs to a fraternity. Peter retrieves the fact, "Oliver is a fraternity member," from his long-term memory and answers the question, "Yes, I think so."

Now, consider a second example, where the two students meet, have the same conversation, but where Peter does *not* make an inference about Oliver's social group affiliations. Now, when the subsequent conversation occurs between Quintin and Peter, Peter retrieves information about his conversation with Oliver — recalls the party, and the reference to living in a "house" — and at this later point in time makes the inference and responds that he thinks Oliver belongs to a fraternity. This would be the memory-based condition.

The third condition, the inference-memory-based task, would be an intermediate condition. Peter meets Oliver and makes several inferences about his social life — he lives "on campus," he is very sociable, he does not live in a dormitory — but does not reach the conclusion that Oliver belongs to a fraternity. Peter stores these inferences in long-term memory. Later, when Quintin asks him whether Oliver belongs to a fraternity, Peter retrieves these inferences from memory and makes a further inference, that Olivers belongs to a fraternity.

Other researchers did not get bogged down in the issue of distinguishing between the two types of memory-based task. Although they recognized the difference between inference- and "raw"-memory-based judgments, they deliberately lumped the two types together. Thus, Srull (1988) refers to this category as "computational" and includes both inferences based on "raw" stimulus traces and based on more elaborate intermediate inferences. Lingle and Ostrom (1979), Schul (1983), and others have also recognized the difference but have stayed with the usual two-case system.

Why do we now think it is important to separate the three cases? It is because the primary operations that Hastie and Park used to distinguish memory-based from on-line are sensitive to the difference between "raw" -memory-based and inference-memory-based cases. They depended on the presence or absence of a correlation between memory and judgment to identify the judgment strategy. Those memory measures were calculated by counting the numbers of "raw" stimulus items recalled (both for the decision and opposing it), and so the measures are bound to the concept of the memorability of "raw" stimulus traces. The same is true of the other researches. The implication of this disagreement and confusion is that we need more and better operations to distinguish the theoretically important cases. Think-aloud protocols are a step in this direction, but not a final solution.

We have been involved in research on the third category of *inference-memory-based judgments*; our studies of *explanation-based decision making* provide a prime example of such judgments (Pennington & Hastie, 1986, 1988). Here, we have found that mock-jurors performing a realistic legal judgment task construct a mental structure summarizing the credible evidence in the case. This summary (we call it a story or an explanation) is retrieved from memory or reconstructed as the penultimate basis for a decision about the proper verdict. The juror's story is primarily composed of inferences that he or she made from the original stimulus trial events; thus, this is a clear case of the third inference-memory-based strategy.

Judgment Task Versus Judgment Strategy

A second collection of confusions seems to have arisen from Hastie and Park's efforts to make another distinction, this time between the task that the subject performs and the mental strategy that the subject pursues to perform the task. Many researchers, over the last century of experimental psychological research, have found it useful to separate theoretical statements about the task environment from those about the organism behaving in the environment (Brunswik, 1956; Dawes, 1975; Simon, 1969).

In the Hastie and Park (1986) paper, we attempted to separate descriptions of the task—memory-based versus on-line—and the strategy (we identified five strategies) employed by the subject to achieve the experimenter-defined goals of making valid judgments about another stimulus person. Our notion was that the *task* referred to relatively objective circumstances of the situation concerned with the sources (memory or external environment) of the evidence that was the basis of judgment, the nature of the evidence (independent pieces of evidence versus inter-dependent pieces of evidence), the response alternatives available for the expression of the judgment, and the temporal relations between evidence presentation and the response. The *strategy* referred to the timing of *mental events*, primarily under deliberate control of the perceiver, such that most task conditions could be associated with several alternate strategic "solutions." As we noted in 1986, not all strategies could be performed under each particular task condition, yielding some predictions for differences in behavior in memory-based versus on-line tasks.

One way to elucidate the confusions that have arisen from this terminology is to consider the theoretical entities about which the labels "memory-based" and "on-line" might be predicated. First, we might refer to memory-based and on-line *tasks*; this was the usage proposed by Hastie and Park (1986). Second, we might refer to the judgment *strategy*; the systematic sequence of mental processes and events that occur in a subject's mind when performing an experimental task. Hastie and Park avoided this usage because we thought it was important to distinguish between the *two* types of task and the *five* (or more) judgment strategies. Third, and perhaps most felicitous, we might refer to an *inference* as memory-based or on-line, and include both task characteristics and mental processes as elements of the definition of each category.

We would like to amend the terminology in the Hastie and Park (1986) paper to shift the reference of the on-line versus memory-based distinction from the task to the properties of a particular inference. Thus, on-line inferences are made while the evidence or premises for the inference are perceptually available, whereas memory-based inferences are made when the evidence was perceived in the past and must be retrieved from memory to serve as input to the inference computation process. We still think that it is useful to separate theoretical descriptions of the task and of the mental processes that are deployed in the task situation. But, for the moment, we give up the attempt to distinguish between on-line and memory-based *tasks* and follow the more natural usage of applying the labels to inferences. Now, when we use the terms on-line or memory-based, we refer to a particular inference. We occasionally talk loosely about an on-line or memory-based task, and here, we mean that (specified) inferences are drawn by subjects under the task conditions that have an on-line or memory-based character.

WHAT INFERENCES ARE MADE WHEN?

The primary significance of the on-line versus memory-based distinction derives from the importance of determining when people make inferences, what inferences they make, and what sources of evidence are the bases for the inferences. The answers to these questions are essential ingredients in an information-processing theory of social judgment, and the theory's capacity to generate predictions about the nature and timing of inferences will determine if it is useful and testable. Furthermore, answers to practical questions about judgment task performance are also dependent on whether underlying inferences are on-line or memory-based: What biases are likely to be present in a judgment? How confident will a person be in his or her judgments? How easy will it be to reconsider and modify a judgment?

During the course of normal social interaction, we probably make a great variety of inferences about other people. This means that it is not a trivial theoretical task to predict which inferences will be made on-line and which will be memory-based. Predictions are especially difficult because a number of poorly understood factors influence which inferences are made and when, including subtle characteristics of the social environment and the invisible goals and moods of the people engaged in social interaction.

Recently, some progress has been made on the problem of determining when some socially significant inferences are made by applying methods developed by psycholinguists studying text comprehension (Bargh, 1984; Bassili, chap. 4 in this volume; Smith & Miller, 1983; Watkins & Peynircioglu, 1984). We have reached some preliminary conclusions about when *trait* inferences are made about other people (Winter & Uleman, 1984), but we are far from having a comprehensive analysis of the natural social contexts that elicit the full range of social inferences.

An important message can be extracted from the text comprehension literature, crystallized in the conclusions reached by Gail McKoon and Roger Ratcliff concerning on-line inferences in the comprehension of written narrative discourse. McKoon and Ratcliff (1986) have injected an attitude of cautiousness into the realm of theoretical claims about on-line inferences. Intuitions and previous theoretical conclusions had suggested that readers make many inferences on-line to produce a complex, richly interassociated memory structure summary of a narrative text. However, McKoon and Ratcliff, using sensitive priming reaction-time measures of memory contents, concluded that only a few low-level inferences (e.g., anaphoric inferences to instantiate the references of pronouns) were made by the typical reader. The message for researchers interested in social judgment is that we must not be too quick to assume that an on-line inference has been made.

On the other hand, there is a related message, pointing in the other direction: We must not allow a principle of minimal inference-making deter us from identifying theoretically unexpected on-line inferences. For example, Shedler and Manis (1986) have provided convincing evidence that inferences about the frequency of occurrence of many types of social events are made spontaneously, on-line, in judgment tasks that did not obviously require such inferences. The Shedler and Manis results are interesting because they link research on on-line versus memory-based inferences to the experimental literature on automatic inference processes (Hasher & Zacks, 1984). Furthermore, their judgment tasks are similar to the tasks used by

Tversky and Kahneman (1973) to show memory-based frequency-of-occurrence judgments as an illustration of the operation of their "availability heuristic." But, in the Shedler and Manis tasks, the judgments are almost certainly not memory-based.

The essential message is that we must not trust our intuitions or simple generalizations from past research about the nature and timing of social inferences. At present, because we lack theoretical principles to predict the conditions that instigate various types of inferences, we must conduct empirical research to explore every new case.

A SPECULATION ABOUT TASK–STRATEGY RELATIONSHIPS

Our lack of knowledge about the conditions of occurrence of various inferences implies that a useful orientation for current research involves the quest for principles that relate the judgment task to the nature of the mental strategy selected or learned by the judge to "solve" the task. The concept of strategy includes a prescription for on-line or memory-based inferences, but it goes further and specifies the type of combination rule that is used to integrate evidence. We already have some useful taxonomies of strategies in Norman Anderson's (1981) family of cognitive algebra integration rules; Amos Tversky and Daniel Kahneman's (1973) judgment heuristics; and John Payne's (1982) contingent processing models. But, work on a systematic taxonomy of tasks is in its infancy.

Most current theories of judgment make almost no a priori predictions of which task conditions will elicit one or another processing strategy. For example, Norman Anderson has labeled his Information Integration Theory approach "inductive" to emphasize that the power of its empirical analysis is primarily in post hoc model-testing. Tversky and Kahneman have addressed the issue of predicting when reasoning underlying a judgment will be heuristic ("intuitive") or extensional, but in very general terms (Tversky & Kahneman, 1983, p. 308). And, researchers in the Lens Model tradition, have implemented Brunswik's precept that an analysis of the task is as important as a model of the organism by proposing a "Task Continuum Index" to assess the tendency of task conditions to elicit intuitive reasoning (represented by linear and non-linear regression models) or analytical reasoning (involving configural relationships in cue utilization or other complex interactions in cue-judgment interdependencies; Hammond, Hamm, Grassia, & Pearson, 1987).

We suggest that two aspects of the task definition are the key elements in predicting judgment strategy: the subject's foreknowledge about whether a judgment will be required after he or she has been exposed to information that may be relevant to the judgment *and* the structure of the relevant evidence (interdependent elements versus independent elements). These two "variables" can be combined to yield four task conditions, each associated with a distinct set of judgment strategies (Fig. 1.1).

The first aspect of the predictive table, foreknowledge of the judgment task, comprises two components: an expectation that a judgment will be required later in time or no such expectation; and, if a judgment is expected, beliefs about the nature of the judgment. What are the relevant underlying dimensions of meaning (e.g., likeability, job suitability, responsibility for an accident, etc.)? And, what are the associated payoff and loss functions (e.g., it is more important to acquit a guilty defendant than convict an innocent man; it is more costly to hire a lousy programmer than to delay hiring for a few months, etc.)?

Foreknowledge of the judgment is not necessarily a highly controlled, deliberative state of mind. The explicit instruction, by an external agent, to make a judgment is not the only condition that instigates the judgment process. Expectations of an impending judgment will arise virtually automatically, with little or no conscious anticipation as byproducts or substages in larger sequences of cognitive processes. Individuals also vary in their propensity to make judgments spontaneously, to maintain characteristic, chronic goals through many social encounters. Some people seem to be constantly assessing the intelligence, or athletic ability, or sexual availability, or religiosity of each person they encounter.

The distinction between independent and interdependent sets of evidence items is also complex. Under some conditions, sets of evidence items or premises for an inference are *perceived* as separate, independently meaningful inputs for a judgment. Our claim is that this perception has an influence on the nature of the judgment strategy selected or "constructed" to perform the judgment task. For example, when the evidence items are perceived as independent, a sequential adjustment judgment strategy like the anchor-and-adjust heuristic or averaging model operator may be used to make the judgment. But, when the evidence is perceived as interdependent,

	EVIDENCE STRUCTURE	
	INDEPENDENT ITEMS	INTER-DEPENDENT ITEMS
JUDGMENT EXPECTATION — FOREKNOWLEDGE	ANCHOR-AND-ADJUST HEURISTIC	REPRESENTATIVENESS HEURISTIC
JUDGMENT EXPECTATION — NO FOREKNOWLEDGE	POISSON CRITICAL EVENT AND RACE PROCESSES	EXPLANATION-BASED "MENTAL MODELING"

FIG. 1.1. A framework to predict the relationship between task conditions (judgment foreknowledge and evidence structure) and common judgment strategies.

a process more like the explanation-based "mental modeling" operations proposed by Pennington and Hastie (1986) will be selected.

The *common sense* notion of independence that we have in mind corresponds to the subject's perception that the implications of one piece of evidence for a judgment are not dependent on the nature of the context of another piece of evidence relevant to the judgment. This concept of independence is closely related to the notion of *conditional independence* of evidence sources as formalized by Bayesian statisticians (Schum & Kelly, 1973) or *additivity* of values of two sources of information in an algebraic model of judgment implications (e.g., Anderson, 1981, pp. 12–21). However, we want to restrict the current application to the *subject's* (not the scientist's) perception of independence.

There may be many conditions under which the subject does not perceive two sources of information as "dependent," but in which the pattern of his or her judgments violates the formal conditions for conditional independence or additivity. For example, subjects in impression formation experiments may not be aware that the valuation and weighting of one trait adjective is affected by the immediately preceding context of other trait adjectives. Such a situation would be one where the subject's behavior revealed a "dependence" between the two evidence sources, but without the subject's awareness. In the present context, we are concerned only with when the subject believes there is a dependency. Our claim is that this belief (that the evidence will be independent or interdependent) influences the manner in which the subject samples and combines evidence to make a judgment.

One class of cues that a subject utilizes to infer evidence interdependence involves perceptions of causal dependencies between sources of evidence. So when two people describe an event both experienced together, or when one person hears another person's report before speaking, or when the two people share a bias to exaggerate a description in the same manner, a third person making a judgment based on the reports will perceive them as redundant or interdependent. This means the impact of each report on the final judgment will be different than it might have been, had only one report been received. Furthermore, we are speculating that the larger judgment strategy will vary as a function of whether the reports are perceived as independent or interdependent.

A second class of cues is based on a judge's sensitivity to the possibility that the meaning of one piece of evidence will condition the implications of another piece of evidence. For example, people reasoning about another person's character will draw one implication from an action if other evidence implies that the action will lead to personal profit but another implication about character if the action leads to a personal loss. It is beyond the scope of the present chapter to attempt to identify all of the types of evidence relationships that are perceived by a person making a social judgment. But, these illustrations should suffice to communicate the basic ideas of evidence independence and interdependence.

Our speculation is that certain judgment strategies are associated with each of the four task conditions. When the evidence comes in independent pieces and the ultimate judgment is expected, incremental on-line operators, exemplified by the ubiquitous anchor-and-adjust integration rule are the most common strategies (Einhorn & Hogarth, 1985; Lopes, 1982; Tversky & Kahneman, 1973). When the evidence comes in independent pieces, but the judgment is unexpected, the family of race models and critical event models described by random walk and Poisson stochastic processes receiving raw memory-based input will be the most common strategies (Ratcliff, 1978; Thomas & Hogue, 1976). When the evidence elements are interdependent and the judgment is expected, similarity-based representativeness heuristic strategies will be common (Tversky & Kahneman, 1983). And, when the evidence is conditionally interdependent and the judgment is unexpected, the inference memory-based mental summary strategies studied by Pennington and Hastie (1986, 1988) will be used. (N.B., as Pennington & Hastie, 1981, have pointed out, jurors in typical criminal cases are surprised by the nature of the specific legal judgments they are instructed to make *at the end of the trial,* after they have heard the evidence.)

In addition to our substantial intellectual debt to Norman Anderson's cognitive algebra approach, our analysis has benefited from Tversky and Kahneman's (1973) treatment of judgment under uncertainty in terms of a "mental toolbox" filled with useful heuristics that are pulled out and applied to judgment tasks as they are encountered. We have tried to go a bit further than Tversky and Kahneman in our speculations about the task conditions that are associated with the reliance on one judgment strategy or another. We have also included only two of their heuristics, anchor-and-adjust and representativeness, in our collection of strategies, and we include strategies described by other judgment processes (stochastic processes and the "explanation-based" mental modeling). Furthermore, we move their availability heuristic from consideration as a strategy in its own right to a role as a characteristic of a strategy and elaborate on it by distinguishing between raw memory-based and inference memory-based judgments.

We emphasize that the four-cell taxonomy and our hypotheses about judgment strategies are highly speculative. But, because we think that an important direction for current social judgment research involves the development of a useful theory of task–strategy relationships, we have presented the hypothesis to get the ball rolling on the "Contextualist" program (McGuire, 1983) of establishing the task–strategy relationships in naturally occurring social judgments.

ACKNOWLEDGMENTS

The preparation of this paper was supported by funds from NSF Grant BNS-8717259. The authors are grateful to the other authors of the present volume and the faculty and students of the University of Toronto for constructive comments on early versions of the paper and to Bernadette Park for her major contributions to the theory and research that is the subject of this essay.

REFERENCES

Anderson, N. H. (1981). *Foundations of information integration theory.* New York: Academic Press.

Anderson, N.H., & Hubert, S. (1963). Effects of concommitant verbal recall on order effects in personality impression formation. *Journal of Verbal Learning and Verbal Behavior, 2,* 379–391.

Bargh, J. A. (1984). Automatic and conscious processing of social information. In R. S. Wyer, Jr. & T. K. Srull (Eds.), *Handbook of social cognition* (Vol. 3, pp. 1–43). Hillsdale, NJ: Lawrence Erlbaum Associates.

Brunswik, E. (1956). *Perception and the representative design of psychological experiments.* Berkeley, CA: University of California Press.

Dawes, R. M. (1975). The mind, the model, and the task. In F. Restle, R. M. Shiffrin, N. J. Catellan, H. R. Lindman, & D. F. Pisoni (Eds.), *Cognitive theory* (pp. 66–82). Hillsdale, NJ: Lawrence Erlbaum Associates.

Dreben, E. K., Fiske, S. T., & Hastie, R. (1979). The independence of item and evaluative information: Impression and recall order effects in behavior-based impression formation. *Journal of Personality and Social Psychology, 37,* 1758–1768.

Edwards, W. (1968). Conservatism in human judgment. In B. Kleinmuntz (Ed.), *The formal representation of human judgment* (pp. 17–52). New York: Academic Press.

Einhorn, H. J., & Hogarth, R. M. (1985). Ambiguity and uncertainty in probablistic inference. *Psychological Review, 92,* 433–461.

Hammond, K. R., Hamm, R. M., Grassia, J., & Pearson, T. (1987). Direct comparison of the efficacy of intuition and analytical cognition in expert judgment. *IEEE Transactions on Systems, 17,* 753–770.

Hasher, L., & Zacks, R. (1984). Automatic processing of fundamental information: The case of frequency of occurrence. *American Psychologist, 39,* 1372–1388.

Hastie, R., & Kumar, A. P. (1979). Person memory: Personality traits as organizing principles in memory for behavior. *Journal of Personality and Social Psychology, 37,* 25–38.

Hastie, R., Ostrom,. T. M., Ebbesen, E. B., Wyer, R. S., Jr., Hamilton, D. L., & Carlston, D. E. (1980). *Person memory: The cognitive basis of social perception.* Hillsdale, NJ: Lawrence Erlbaum Associates.

Hastie, R., & Park, B. (1986). The relationship between memory and judgment depends on whether the judgment task is memory-based or on-line. *Psychological Review, 93,* 258–268.

Lichtenstein, M., & Srull, T. K. (1987). Processing objectives as a determinant of the relationship between recall and judgment. *Journal of Experimental Social Psychology, 23,* 93–118.

Lingle, J. H., & Ostrom, T. M. (1979). Retrieval selectivity in memory-based impression judgments. *Journal of Personality and Social Psychology, 37,* 180–194.

Lopes, L. L. (1982). *Toward a procedural theory of judgment* (Tech. Rep. No. 17). Wisconsin

Human Information Processing Program. 1-49.

McArthur, L. Z. (1980). Illusory correlation and illusory causation: Two epistemological accounts. *Personality and Social Psychology Bulletin, 6,* 507-519.

McGuire, W. J. (1983). A Contextualist theory of knowledge: Its implications for innovation and reform in psychological research. In L. Berkowitz (Ed.), *Advances in experimental social psychology* (vol. 16, pp. 1-47). New York: Academic Press.

McKoon, G., & Ratcliff, R. (1986). Inferences about predictable events. *Journal of Experimental Psychology: Learning, Memory, and Cognition, 12,* 82-91.

Payne, J. W. (1982). Contingent decision behavior. *Psychological Bulletin, 92,* 382-402.

Pennington, N., & Hastie, R. (1981). Juror decision making models: The generalization gap. *Psychological Bulletin, 89,* 246-287.

Pennington, N., & Hastie, R. (1986). Evidence evaluation in complex decision making. *Journal of Personality and Social Psychology, 51,* 242-258.

Pennington, N., & Hastie, R. (1988). Explanation-based decision making: Effects of memory structure on judgment. *Journal of Experimental Psychology: Learning, Memory, and Cognition, 14,* 521-533.

Ratcliff, R. (1978). A theory of memory retrieval. *Psychological Review, 85,* 59-108.

Schul, Y. (1983). Integration and abstraction in impression formation. *Journal of Personality and Social Psychology, 44,* 45-54.

Schum, D., & Kelly, C. W. (1973). A problem in cascaded inference: Determining the inferential impact of confirming and conflicting reports from several unreliable sources. *Organizational Behavior and Human Performance, 10,* 404-423.

Shedler, J., & Manis, M. (1986). Can the availability heuristic explain vividness effects? *Journal of Personality and Social Psychology, 51,* 26-36.

Simon, H. A. (1969). *The sciences of the artificial.* Cambridge, MA: MIT Press.

Slovic, P., & Lichtenstein, S. (1971). A comparison of Bayesian and regression approaches to the study of information processing in judgment. *Organizational Behavior and Human Performance, 6,* 649-744.

Smith, E. R., & Miller, F. D. (1983). Mediation among attributional inferences and comprehension processes: Initial findings and a general method. *Journal of Personality and Social Psychology, 44,* 492-505.

Srull, T. K. (1988, March). *On-line cognition in person perception.* Paper presented at Cognition and Judgments We Make About People conference, University of Toronto, Scarborough campus.

Taylor, S. E. (1982). The availability bias in social psychology. In D. Kahneman, P. Slovic, & A. Tversky (Eds.), *Judgment under uncertainty: Heuristics and biases* (pp. 190-200). Cambridge, England: Cambridge University Press.

Taylor, S. E., & Fiske, S. T. (1975). Point-of-view and perceptions of causality. *Journal of Personality and Social Psychology, 32,* 439-455.

Taylor, S. E., & Thompson, S. C. (1982). Stalking the illusive "vividness" effect. *Psychological Bulletin, 89,* 155-181.

Thomas, E. A. C., & Hogue, A. (1976). Apparent weight of evidence, decision criteria, and confidence ratings in juror decision making. *Psychologidal Review, 83,* 442-465.

Tversky, A., & Kahneman, D. (1973). Availability: A heuristic for judging frequency and probability. *Cognitive Psychology, 5,* 207-232.

Tversky, A., & Kahneman, D. (1983). Extensional versus intuitive reasoning: The conjunction fallacy in probability judgment. *Psychological Review, 90,* 293-315.

Tversky, A., & Kahneman, D. (1986). Rational choice and the framing of decisions. *Journal of Business, 59,* 251-278.

Watkins, M. J., & Peynircioglu, Z. F. (1984). Determining perceived meaning during impression formation: Another look at the meaning change hypothesis. *Journal of Personality and Social Psychology, 46,21 1005-1016.*

Watts, W. A., & McGuire, W. J. (1964). Persistence of induced opinion change and retention of the inducing message contents. *Journal of Abnormal and Social Psychology, 68,* 233–241.

Winter, L, & Uleman, J. S. (1984). When are social judgments made? Evidence for the spontaneousness of trait inferences. *Journal of Personality and Social Psychology, 47,* 237–252.

2
Procedural Efficiency and On-Line Social Judgments

Eliot R. Smith
Purdue University

In the "real world," as in the social-psychological laboratory, social interaction and person perception often depend on on-line judgments. These are judgments and inferences that a perceiver computes while stimulus information is immediately available, rather than those that a perceiver might formulate after the fact based on information retrieved from memory. One goal of my recent research has been to identify some factors that might influence the social judgments people make in on-line processing situations.

My starting point for this research program is the deceptively obvious fact that cognitive processes become more efficient with practice. Everyone is aware of the dramatic and robust effects of practice on cognitive and motor skills, and they have been well documented in the literature on nonsocial cognitive processes. For example, Kolers (1976) had people practice the skill of reading text in novel orientations (right to left, backwards, reversed letter-by-letter, etc.). He observed that the readers improved with practice, cutting the time taken to read a page from over 15 minutes to about 2 minutes. As long as a year later, his subjects were still significantly faster than unpracticed people. Different measures showed that 60–80% of the practice effect was retained over the year. Thus, as is generally known, the effects of practice are long-lasting as well as large in magnitude.

In another study of a high-level, complex skill, McKendree and Anderson (cited in Anderson, 1987) found that people increased their accuracy in solving problems in computer programming from 58% to 85% over 4 days of practice, while decreasing their average time from over 18 sec per problem to 10 sec. Just a few days of practice, then, cut the error rate by more than half and the time per problem by almost half. The generality of practice effects with nonsocial judgments and other processes has been addressed by Newell and Rosenbloom (1981). The effects are ubiquitous, applying to nonsocial cognitive tasks ranging from proving geometry theorems to learning text-editing skills to scanning for visual targets. Newell and Rosenbloom also show that time per trial generally decreases with practice in a power-function curve; in this chapter, this functional specification is assumed.

Do social judgments increase in efficiency with practice in the same way as nonsocial judgments or cognitive processes? Social judgments are more complex and may differ in other ways from nonsocial judgments (cf. Ostrom, 1984), making this question nontrivial. In this chapter, I focus on the decrease in time per judgment that occurs with practice. Several experiments have focused on these issues (Smith, 1988, Smith, Branscombe, & Bormann, 1988; Smith & Lerner, 1986), and one illustrates their general approach. In this study (Smith et al., 1988, Experiment 2), people made 200 yes/no judgments concerning whether or not a particular behavior implies a trait. (In other experiments, such as Smith & Lerner, 1986, I have used other types of social judgments, but behavior-to-trait inferences are theoretically central to person perception and much of my research has focused on their properties.) A sample judgment would be, "Is hitting friendly?" The behavior stimulus, presented as a single verb on a computer screen, was different on each of the 200 trials (except for systematic repetitions of behaviors, described later). The target trait in different conditions (between subjects) was friendly, intelligent, or dominant, chosen to represent major dimensions of social judgment. The dependent variable is the time taken to make each judgment, measured from the onset of the behavior on the screen until the press of a response key.

This study (and others using similar methods) have produced several significant findings. For one, people speed up as they practice making the judgments. Over 200 trials, the average reduction in response time (RT) in one study was from the initial 2400 msec to about 1000 msec, approximately two thirds of the way down to the estimated asymptotic value, 500 msec. Figure 2.1 shows the actual data points and the fitted power function.

Another finding is that the speedup is long-lasting. In another study with a similar design (Smith, 1988), I had subjects return to the experiment 24 hr after the first session and resume their work at the task for another 200 trials. As Fig. 2.2 shows, their speed after the delay was about what it had been at the *end* of the first session, rather than at the beginning, demonstrating that the increased efficiency lasted without notable loss for at least a day.

How can these changes induced by practice be accounted for in theoret-

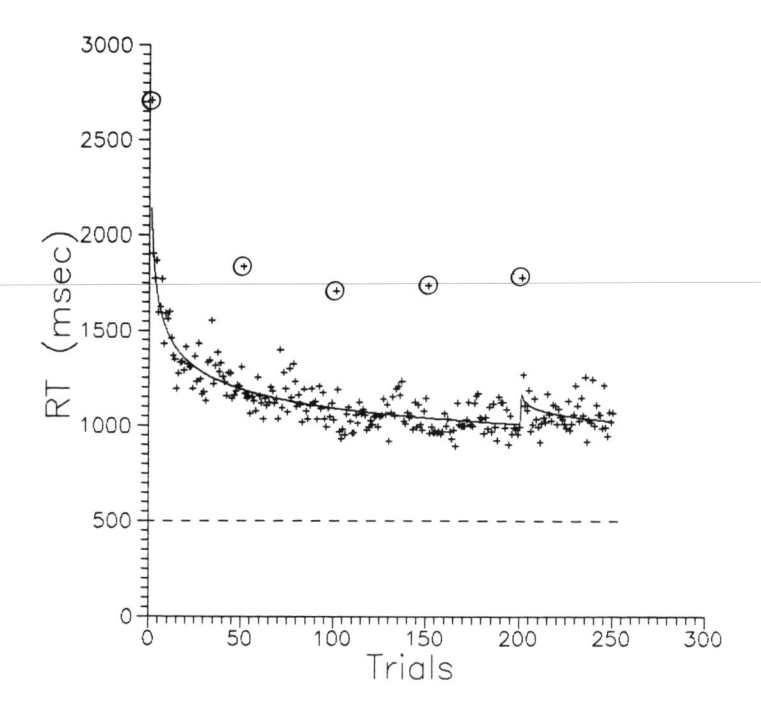

FIG. 2.1.

ical terms? I borrow from J. R. Anderson's ACT* (1983) cognitive model the representation of cognitive procedures as productions (see Smith, 1984). A production is an if-then pair; when its "if" component (pattern) is matched to information in working memory, the "then" part (an action) may occur. Productions are a flexible theoretical language that can be used to represent all kinds of cognitive skills (see Anderson's work), including social inferences. Inference productions would typically include the preconditions for the inference among the pattern elements, and would have an action that deposits a representation of the conclusion of the inference into working memory. For example, a production to infer the trait of hostility from behavioral features such as causing harm to another might be represented as follows:

If (actor performs behavior)

and (behavior is intentional)

and (behavior harms another person)

then (conclude actor is hostile).

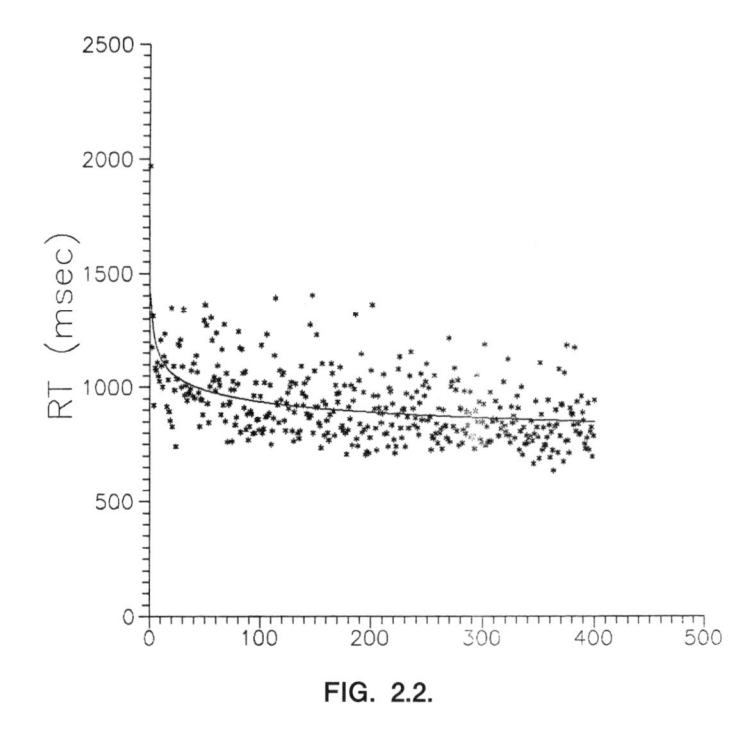

[Figure 2.2: Scatter plot of RT (msec) on y-axis (0 to 2500) vs. x-axis (0 to 500), showing a decreasing curve fitted through data points.]

FIG. 2.2.

The theoretical predictions I present in this chapter do not depend on the details of Anderson's (1983) theory, just on three basic principles:

1. Each production has a *strength* value that increases with practice, that is, with each successful execution of the production. Production strength decays over time when the production is not used, but quite slowly.
2. The strength influences the speed of firing when the pattern is matched, the completeness of the pattern match that is necessary for firing, and the probability of the production's firing (in competition with others that also may match). Specifically, a stronger production will execute more rapidly, will require a less complete or exact pattern match, and will have a higher probability of "winning" the competition with other productions that also match available information.
3. Productions exist at different levels of specificity. As Anderson (1987) described, when a general production incorporating variables in its pattern is executed with specific values filled in for those variables, a more specific version will be formed.

For example:

If (actor hits another person)
then (conclude actor is hostile)

might be formed as a specialization of the foregoing, more general, hostility inference production. This principle allows for the coexistence of general rules with specific exceptions, and also for general and specific productions that reach the same conclusion, as in this example. The specific version could, in principle, execute faster than the general one if it is strengthened by further practice with the same information content.

In combination, these principles yield several predictions. First, general practice will strengthen the practiced production, making it execute faster, and Anderson (1982) has shown that his quantitative assumptions predict the observed power-function form of the speedup curve. Second, the strengthened general production is not content-specific. It will execute even on new unpracticed content, but only when the same *task* is performed (Anderson, 1987). That is, the size of practice effects on a target task depends on the similarity of the procedures performed during practice and those used by the target task — if there is no procedural overlap, the practice will not influence this particular task. Third, the effects of practice should be long-lasting, because procedural strength decays slowly.

I attribute the changes in efficiency induced by practice to procedural strengthening, rather than to the increased accessibility of a trait construct in memory (Higgins & King, 1981) or to a schema's position in a Storage Bin in memory (Wyer & Srull, 1986). Some of the evidence for this conclusion can be seen in Fig. 2.1. For the last block of 50 trials in that study, we changed the target trait for each subject. A subject might be told, for example, that he or she would now be judging behaviors for intelligence rather than friendliness. As the figure shows, subjects kept most of their increased efficiency, so that the decrease of speed between the fourth and fifth block is quite small. This pattern is inconsistent with trait-accessibility interpretations. Although the first 200 trials might increase the accessibility of the first target trait, they should have no effect on the accessibility of the changed target. On the other hand, some of the practice effect was target-specific, and the increase in RT from block 4 to block 5 was statistically reliable. This component of the practice effect could be due to the increased accessibility of trait information or to the formation of procedures specific to the target trait (the interpretation we prefer). However, it is clear that some of the speedup applies when the *same procedure* (behavior–trait judgments) is used even on new content (a new target trait). This pattern (process specificity without strong content specificity) is the signature of procedural efficiency (see Smith, in press).

IMPLICATIONS OF GENERAL PRACTICE EFFECTS FOR ON-LINE SOCIAL JUDGMENTS

It is clear that practice increases the efficiency (speed) of social judgment processes. Does this effect have any implications for the *content* of social judgments? The mere fact that a perceiver could make a judgment a few hundred msec faster would not appear to have major implications for social interaction or on-line impression formation. However, my thesis is that the efficiency of judgment processes can influence the content of on-line social judgments, through several different mechanisms. I describe three of them in this section.

The basic argument in all three cases can be summarized as follows. A judgmental procedure that is more efficient (because it has been practiced) will be *more likely to execute,* and can *execute with a less precise pattern match,* than a less-efficient procedure. This means that practice can influence whether or not a particular inference is drawn and thus whether it enters into the contents of the perceiver's judgments. Efficiency may have particularly important effects in the context of on-line (rather than memory-based) judgments, for two reasons. First, by definition, on-line judgments are those that occur spontaneously to the perceiver, rather than those that are demanded by external task constraints. An externally provided goal of making a certain judgment could certainly override differences in efficiency among judgmental processes that would be evident in the absence of such a goal. Second, on-line processes intrinsically involve limits on time and other resources. The information is before the perceiver for mere moments, and new information is constantly becoming available. In such a context, an inference that is not made quickly may well not be made at all. For these reasons, efficiency differences may have particularly strong effects in an on-line context, compared to a setting where an inference is to be based on information stored in memory, without strong limitations on the time taken to compute the inference.

Efficiency of Attitude Access

One mechanism by which procedural efficiency can shape the contents of social judgment has been elucidated by Fazio and his colleagues. They have demonstrated in several elegant experiments that a manipulation of repeated attitude access (i.e., practice accessing one's attitude toward a target object) causes attitude access to become more efficient and even spontaneous. Fazio, Chen, McDonel, and Sherman (1982) caused subjects to repeatedly express their attitude, finding that it increased the attitude's accessibility (as measured by RT). They also observed an increase in attitude-behavior consistency when subjects had a chance to act in an attitude-relevant way. Fazio, Sanbonmatsu, Powell, and Kardes (1986) used the same manipulation and showed that practice caused subjects to access their attitude spontaneously upon encountering the attitude object (i.e., when reporting the attitude was not part of the subjects' task). Finally, Fazio and Williams (1986) showed that more accessible attitudes (those that could be reported faster) lead to greater consistency between the attitude and the person's perceptions of the object's attributes. Presumably, when the attitude is readily accessible it colors or biases perceptions of the object. This, Fazio (1986) argued, is one mechanism by which greater attitude-behavior consistency is produced, if behavior depends to some extent on the (attitude-biased) immediate or on-line perceptions of the object.

Put in my theoretical terms, here is evidence for the judgmental consequences of the efficiency of attitude access (considered as a sort of inference process, deriving the attitude from the object). Efficiency decreases the time taken to activate the attitude and hence (a) increases the probability of spontaneous activation of the attitude when the object is encountered, (b) gives the attitude a chance to color perceptions of the object, and (c) increases attitude-behavior consistency. Fazio (1986) has summarized the evidence for the various links in this theoretical chain.

Efficiency of Behavior-to-Trait Inference Processes

A given behavior often—even usually—has implications for several different traits. For example, "sat in the library studying for the psychology test" may be perceived to have implications for such relatively independent dimensions as the actor's intelligence, conscientiousness, and even sociability. When such a behavior is observed, which trait is accessed may be important in determining the content of the impression the perceiver will form. And the relative efficiency of the perceiver's procedures for drawing inferences about the various possible traits may influence which trait is accessed. Practice making inferences about one trait may tip the balance, making the perceiver more likely to draw the practiced inference in preference to potential alternatives. As Carlston (1980) has shown, perceivers under many circumstances may not think through *all* the potential trait implications of a behavior, but may content themselves with a single, highly accessible inference. As I argued earlier, this tendency may be particularly marked under the time pressures that are characteristic of on-line processing situations.

To test this hypothesis, I used (for experimental convenience) behaviors that had evaluatively opposite implications on two different traits. In one study described heretofore (Smith, 1988), recall that people in some conditions made 400 judgments over two sessions concerning whether behaviors were intelligent or friendly. Subjects received a questionnaire after the experiment was ostensibly complete, asking for their overall liking of a hypothetical person who performed each of 20 different behaviors. This questionnaire was presented as a pilot, intended to secure ratings of materials for an unrelated study. Included among a number of evaluatively mixed filler behaviors were four unfriendly but intelligent behaviors (e.g., "won the political argument with his roommate," "refused to help his classmate with the homework even though he had understood it all perfectly") and four friendly but unintelligent behaviors (e.g., "tried to fix his friend's refrigerator but ended up making it worse," "stopped on the street and picked up the hitchhiker"). I predicted that practice judging intelligence would cause perceivers to derive the target behavior's implications for intelligence more fluently, and thus to base their overall liking ratings relatively more on intelligence than on friendliness. Those who judged friendliness would do the opposite.

This prediction was supported by a significant interaction, depicted in Fig. 2.3. Intelligent/unfriendly behaviors were rated more positively by people who had practiced judging intelligence than by those who had judged friendliness (M = 3.63 and 3.08 respectively, on a 7-point scale), whereas the reverse was true for unintelligent/friendly behaviors (M = 4.25 vs. 5.42).

Thus, the practice-induced increase in the efficiency of a particular trait judgment procedure makes that trait inference *more likely to occur spontaneously* when people evaluate the questionnaire behaviors in a

Behavior Ratings by Practiced Judgment

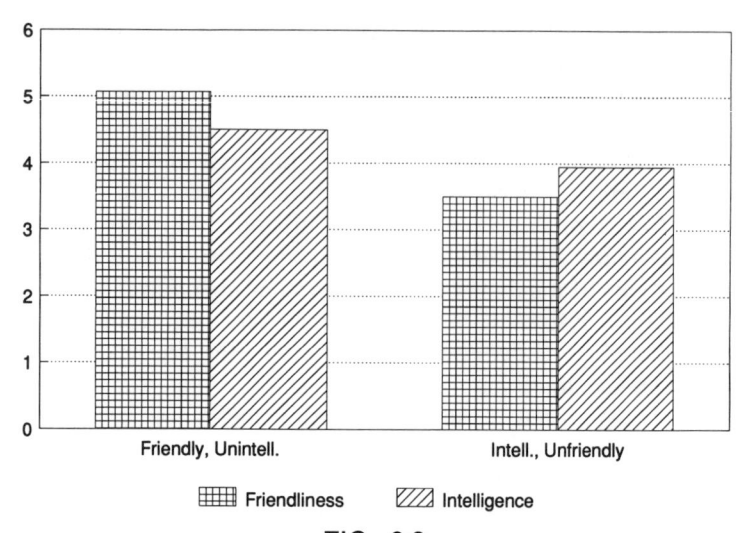

FIG. 2.3.

relatively unconstrained way, and therefore gives that trait increased weight in an overall evaluative judgment. It is tempting to speculate that a similar process could affect judgments in real social interaction. For example, if a perceiver repeatedly judges people's clothes for fit and stylishness (perhaps because of occupational demands), the processes involved in that judgment will become quite efficient and will be likely to be used whenever the perceiver encounters and observes someone. Liking and other interpersonal reactions are likely to be more heavily influenced by attributes of the target's clothing (and hence less responsive to the person's other attributes) than are the reactions of a perceiver who lacks this type of practice. In general, then, practice can increase the efficiency and therefore the likelihood of a particular inference being made within the limited time available in on-line interaction. This may increase the weight of particular attributes in social judgments (including affective and evaluative judgments).

Efficiency of social inference processes may also have implications for individual differences in personality. As Sorrentino and Higgins (1986) have suggested within a somewhat different theoretical framework, individuals may have particular attributes to which they characteristically respond in other persons or in social situations. An authoritarian will be particularly attuned to personal characteristics like strength and weakness, for instance, and to situational factors like the expectations of authorities. A person who is high on n Achievement will be especially likely to draw inferences about standards of excellence that are implicit in a situation as points of comparison for personal performances. It is intriguing to think that personality differences may rest at least in part on systematic differences in the efficiency of processes of social inference and interpretation that result from a lifetime of experience.

Procedural Efficiency and Category Accessibility

Procedural efficiency may influence social judgments in a third way, by shaping the perceiver's interpretation of relatively ambiguous behaviors. It has long been known that "priming" (exposure to information related to a trait category) can influence people's judgments about behaviors that are ambiguous exemplars of the trait (Higgins, Rholes, & Jones, 1977; Srull & Wyer, 1979). Generally, the effect is assimilative, with the target behaviors being seen as more strongly indicative of the trait after priming. Various theoretical interpretations of these "category accessibility" effects have been proposed. I have suggested a novel interpretation: The effect may be due in some cases to an increase in efficiency for a procedure for behavior–trait judgments due to practice (Smith, 1984, p. 405; Smith & Branscombe, 1987, 1988).

The procedural mechanism may operate as follows. In the paradigm used by Srull and Wyer, the priming manipulation for a target trait like *hostile* involves subjects reading a number of scrambled sentences describing hostile behaviors. I assume that the subject implicitly categorizes the behaviors as hostile (not necessarily at a conscious level), repeatedly applying a procedure for inferring hostility based on behavioral features, like the one illustrated earlier in this chapter. The subject is then tested with a description of a target person's ambiguously hostile behaviors, and these are more likely to activate the strengthened procedure. As discussed earlier, the stronger a procedure is, the less exact or complete a pattern match is needed to invoke it. This could account for the increase of category accessibility with practice, for ambiguous behaviors are theoretically behaviors that have some but not all of the features of the trait category, or that have those features only to a limited extent.

In three experiments (Smith & Branscombe, 1987, 1988), results were consistent with the hypothesis that the Srull and Wyer priming manipulation affects category accessibility through this type of procedural mediating mechanism. The results did not show the patterns that would be expected if alternative mediators, such as a general increase in the accessibility of the trait construct, were responsible for the effect. Space does not permit a description of the full method and results of these experiments, but one finding is briefly summarized. In Smith and Branscombe (1988), we found that two priming manipulations (reading the trait word versus generating the trait from behavior descriptions) had opposite patterns of effects on two different dependent measures. These were a test of subjects' ability to complete the trait word presented in fragmented form (e.g., H_ _ T_ _ E) and a category-accessibility measure assessing perception of an ambiguous behavior. Reading the word had a larger effect than generating on the word-fragment completion test, whereas generation had a larger effect than reading on the category-accessibility test.

If both manipulations simply increased the accessibility of the trait construct, one would expect them to have parallel effects. Instead, as predicted by the procedural hypothesis, the effect of performing a particular process (considered as a priming manipulation) on a particular dependent measure depends on the extent to which the manipulation and dependent measure share similar cognitive procedures. Reading the word exercised a process that *accesses the word from visual information,* and thus made the same process more likely to occur when the word is encountered a second time on the later test, even with fragmented visual information. Generating the trait word from behavioral cues, in contrast, used a *trait-inference process* (like the hypothetical productions shown before), and therefore increased the subject's ability to use that process later: Generation increased the likelihood that the target word would be inferred from an ambiguous behavior on the category-accessibility test.

In summary, increases in the efficiency of cognitive procedures due to practice may influence on-line social judgments in at least three ways. With practice, attitude access may occur spontaneously, allowing the attitude to color perceptions and behavioral tendencies. Particular trait inferences about behaviors with multiple implications may become more likely to occur at the expense of other, equally possible but nonpracticed inferences. And practiced procedures may have a higher probability of matching relatively ambiguous behavioral stimuli, categorizing them within the target trait category. The relative efficiency of a multitude of social inference procedures thus represents a significant residue of the perceiver's past experiences that, along with explicit memories and the accessibility of constructs in declarative memory, can influence future social judgments and behavior in a long-lasting way.

SPECIFICITY OF PRACTICE EFFECTS

The effects that have just been discussed are all *general* effects of practice. For example, reading inverted text increases one's ability to read all such material, and judging some behaviors on friendliness increases the speed with which other behaviors can be judged. I have argued that such increases in efficiency can have effects on the *content* (not just the speed) of social judgment in several different ways.

But practice effects also have a strikingly specific component. If I practice for weeks until I can play a particular Mozart piano sonata, this practice will make me a better pianist in general, but it will increase my ability to play this particular piece much more than other, unpracticed pieces. In the Kolers (1976) study, some of the speedup of people's ability to read inverted text was specific to particular practiced pages of text. That is, subjects were significantly faster at reading pages that they had practiced a year earlier than equivalent new pages in the same typographical orientation. This effect was not related to their ability to recognize the pages as having been seen before. Thus, practice effects may have a specific component that is amazingly long-lasting and that does not depend on conscious recognition of the practiced items.

Results from my studies with behavior–trait judgments also show specific effects of practice in facilitating judgments that have been made before, above and beyond the general effect that makes subjects more efficient on nonpracticed materials. In Smith (1988) and Smith et al. (1988), I examined the specificity of the increase in efficiency resulting from making a judgment concerning a particular stimulus behavior. Some randomly selected behaviors among a subject's several hundred trials were repeated after varying lags. Lags ranged from 1 (an immediate repetition) to 16 (15 unrelated behaviors intervening) within a block of 50 trials. Other behaviors were repeated from one block to the next (with an average lag of 50) and, in Smith (1988), between sessions with 24 hours in between. One can ask, therefore, whether repeated behaviors are judged more quickly than new ones.

They are, and the effect, not surprisingly, is quite large for immediate repetitions. What may be surprising is that the benefit of repetition does not diminish beyond lag 4 within a session, being constant from lag 4 up to lag 50, as Fig. 2.4 shows.

In Smith (1988), judgments on behaviors that had been presented 24 hr earlier were still significantly facilitated, although the size of the effect had declined somewhat. Further, the facilitation on between-session repetitions was as large when the subject did not even recognize that the word had been presented earlier as when the word was recognized. In log units, the effect was -.051 for words where the recognition question was not asked, -.050 for old words that were recognized, and -.058 for old, unrecognized words.

Thus, like other types of implicit memory performance (Schacter, 1987; Smith & Branscombe, 1988), the facilitation of social judgments from repetition can be dissociated from explicit memory measures (such as recognition). A long-lasting trace of the judgment process, not accessible to conscious recognition, must be established by making a single judgment about the stimulus, and the trace enables people to respond more quickly

RT Facilitation for Repeated Behaviors

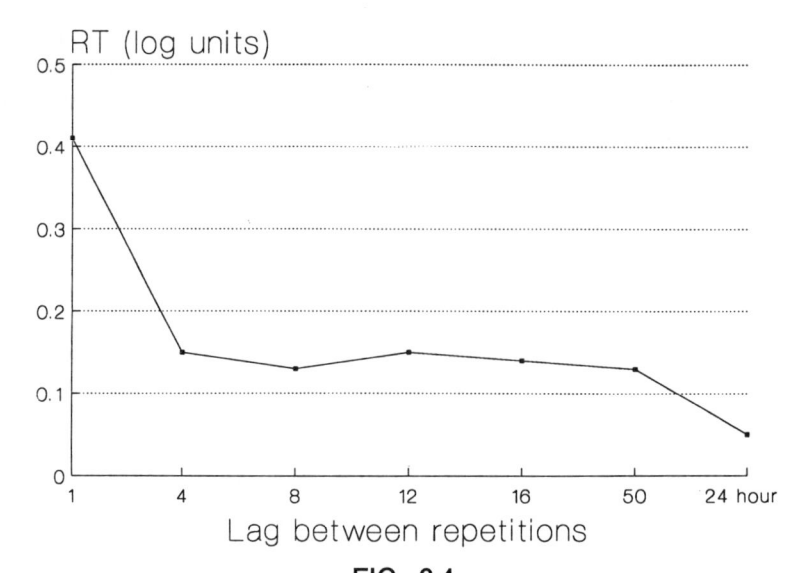

FIG. 2.4.

when the stimulus is repeated. Mitchell and Brown (1988) recently provided a striking demonstration of these points in an experiment involving a picture-naming task. When subjects spoke the names of simple line drawings as fast as possible, naming of previously named pictures was facilitated for as long as 6 weeks after the initial exposure, and the facilitation was independent of subjects' recognition of those pictures as previously seen. Based on the Kolers (1976) result and others, then, it appears that the specific effect of practice (i.e., the facilitation of processing of a particular practiced item) (a) is long-lasting, perhaps lasting as long as the general practice effect, and (b) is generally independent of the ability to consciously recognize that the practiced materials have been previously seen.

The repeated behaviors that were incorporated in the study designs also serve a methodological purpose, allowing us to assess changes in speed-accuracy tradeoff as an artifactual explanation for the observed speedup with practice. Because social behavior-to-trait judgments are subjective, it is impossible to examine "errors" in judgments in the usual sense, although several indirect arguments persuade us that subjects do not speed up in these studies by changing their accuracy criterion over trials (cf. Smith & Lerner, 1986, p. 249). With the repeated behaviors, we can examine changes of response as one type of error that should reveal whether subjects are changing their criterion. The overall error rate was around 7%, and it did increase somewhat over blocks of trials. However, "error" responses were *slower* than unchanged ones to repeated behaviors. This is the reverse of the pattern that would be predicted from a speed-accuracy tradeoff effect, which implies an association of errors with higher speed. The observed pattern is consistent with the hypothesis that subjects can use their memory trace of the earlier response to respond quickly when a particular behavior is repeated. If the previous response is not accessible for some reason, a new judgment must be computed, resulting in (a) some probability of giving a different response, and (b) a response that is as slow as that to an unrepeated behavior. In fact, this model fits the data precisely, for repeated behaviors were only judged more quickly than new ones when the response remained the same; that is, repeated behaviors with changed responses were not faster than new behaviors at any lag.

Specific Practice Effects and Social Judgments

The specific increase in efficiency for practiced judgments also has implications for the content of social judgment. Although I have not yet collected data on this particular point, it is a direct extension of the findings on facilitation of judgments about repeated behaviors after a time lag (Smith, 1988). For example, imagine that I meet a person who often quotes from literary classics, and that I infer that she is well educated. Encountering her at a later time, I may be unable to recall her earlier behavior, my conclusion about her, or even the fact that I have previously met her. But increased efficiency of specific judgment processes may remain as a trace of the incident. Thus, if she repeats the behavior, I may make the same inference more rapidly and with greater probability, just as people were able to make judgments about a specific behavior more rapidly if they had encountered it once among hundreds of trials a day earlier.

Will the increased facility of a once-practiced judgment process be specific not only to the target behavior but also to the target person? That is, will the trait inference be made more efficiently when this person repeats her previous behavior, compared to the same behavior performed by a different person? This amounts to a question about the context-specificity of the practice effect, considering the identity of the actor as a sort of context for the behavior that is to be judged. I have no data directly relevant to this question, but results in other paradigms underline the extreme specificity of many repetition or practice effects (e.g., Brooks, 1987). My tentative prediction is that the facilitation would be largely specific to the target person, although some facilitation might be observed if the same behavior is performed by a different person. Obviously, the concrete implications of this specific practice effect for everyday social judgments differ somewhat depending on its degree of person-specificity.

Specific judgments and inferences that we have made before are particularly easy for us to make again, even in the absence of conscious memory for the earlier occurrence. This constitutes a form of implicit memory (Schacter, 1987; Smith & Branscombe, 1988) for our impressions or inferences about others—an influence on later judgments that occurs without any intentional search of memory and can be independent of conscious recollections (explicit memories).

IMPLICATIONS OF A PROCEDURAL VIEW OF SOCIAL JUDGMENTS FOR STEREOTYPING

A procedural view of social inference processes, including the postulates about increasing efficiency with practice and the other assumptions drawn from Anderson (1983, 1987), has implications for many areas within social cognition and social psychology. Here, I briefly outline some implications for one particular area that is central to person perception: stereotyping. In common with most researchers in social cognition, I define stereotyping as the process of making inferences about a target individual based on that person's membership in a social group or category to which the perceiver ascribes particular characteristics.

General Practice Effects

One of the more important facts about stereotypes, which is surprisingly often unacknowledged in the literature on stereotyping, is that every person can be multiply categorized (cf. Rothbart & John, 1985). A "Black person" is never just that, but is also young or old, male or female, a professor or a lab technician, well or poorly dressed, tall or short, friendly or hostile, from the South or the North. Therefore, the first question involving stereotypic perceptions of an individual must be: Which category is used, when? To suggest a partial answer to this question, I draw an analogy between the multiple categorizability of any real individual and the multiple trait implications that can be drawn from any behavior. Earlier in this chapter, I showed that practice making a particular trait inference may bias subjects toward drawing that implication rather than others when they evaluate a behavior in a relatively unconstrained way. Similarly, practice categorizing people in a particular way may influence social perceptions by biasing them toward using the practiced categories (say, Black vs. White) rather than alternatives (say, male vs. female) when they encounter new individuals. This is a general practice effect: Practice in classifying people in general by gender, socioeconomic status (SES), or race should make the perceiver more likely to use that category rather than an alternative as a cue in stereotype trait assignment or overall evaluation of new (unpracticed) people.

I have not yet directly tested this hypothesis, but some related results may be mentioned. Zarate and Smith (1988a) measured the time subjects took to categorize yearbook-style head-and-shoulders photographs in different ways. They pressed "yes" or "no" keys to indicate whether or not the photo was in a target category (*Black, White, man, woman,* and others) which was presented at the beginning of each trial. The results showed that response times for different categorizations differ systematically. They depend in part on the target person's (photo's) characteristics. For instance, photos of Whites were categorized by gender more rapidly than photos of Blacks, and photos of males could be categorized by race more rapidly than those of females. This pattern suggests that a photo's differences from a hypothesized cultural norm (White, male) may be noted and processed automatically, slowing down the detection of other potential category memberships for such a target.

The response times also depended on subjects' own characteristics. For gender in particular, there was an "ingroup advantage": Sex categorizations for same-sex photos were made more rapidly than for opposite-sex photos. This finding nicely illustrates one way in which social judgments intrinsically differ from nonsocial ones: Ingroup–outgroup dynamics may always be a factor when social judgments are being made (cf. Park & Rothbart, 1982).

The Zarate and Smith (1988a) results, then, although they do not show effects of practice on the speed of alternative categorization judgments, do show that the speed and efficiency of those judgments differ systematically in important ways. Results of a second experiment extend those results by linking measures of categorization speed to subjects' attributions of stereotype-related traits to the target individuals. Subjects completed the categorization task as outlined heretofore. They then saw the same set of photos a second time and, under a cover story involving the pickup of nonverbal cues to personal characteristics, rated the extent to which a given trait characterized each photo. The results showed predicted relationships of categorization speed and trait ascriptions. For instance, the faster that subjects characterized photos of Black females as "Black," the more likely they were to assign Black-stereotype traits to the pictured individual (and the less likely they were to use alternatives, such as the female stereotype). Such results support our overall guiding hypothesis regarding stereotyping processes, that social categorization (which should be influenced by practice with categorization tasks) is both necessary and sufficient for stereotyping (as indexed by the assignment of group-stereotypic traits to a target individual).

Specific Practice Effects

The preceding section described general practice effects. A perceiver might categorize many individuals by gender and become efficient at carrying out whatever cognitive processes are involved, even on new (unpracticed) stimulus persons. However, as we know, practice effects also have a highly specific component, raising the possibility that categorizing *this person* as female (rather than in some alternative way) may facilitate doing the same again, even if the perceiver cannot consciously remember encountering the person before. Similarly, as shown before, judging *this behavior* as friendly makes the person able to give the same judgment again more rapidly. A form of implicit memory may therefore have the effect of getting a perceiver "stuck" in one way of perceiving and hence reacting to an individual, even in the absence of any conscious recollection of having met the target person before. Context (e.g., the target person's being the only female in a group of males) and other influences that may shape the perceiver's initial categorization may therefore have long-lasting effects, as the perceiver may persist in categorizing the target in the same way later, even after the context or other momentary influences have changed.

An experiment to test these hypotheses about specific practice effects on stereotyping might be conducted as follows. Subjects go through a group of photos with the same type of categorization task as above; that is, they answer a question like *Black, White, man,* or *woman* about each photo. In a second block, they then follow the same procedure on the photos they have previously categorized mixed with an equal number of new photos, again answering social categorization questions. The prediction is that photos that have been seen once before, for approximately a second, will be judged more quickly than new photos, particularly when the same categorization is queried both times. We (Zarate & Smith, 1988b) have implemented this design, and preliminary results suggest that (a) old photos are indeed judged significantly more quickly than new ones; however, (b) facilitation is greater when the same question is repeated only for the questions *White* and *male*. The second result is qualified by complex interactions, and further empirical work is clearly necessary.

In summary, stereotyping can be seen as involving two different types of procedures: categorizing the target individual in a particular way, and using the group membership, once accessed, to identify particular stereotype traits to assign to the target person. This discussion has focused on the first of these as potentially subject to practice effects. General practice (e.g., categorizing everyone one encounters along gender as opposed to racial lines) and specific practice (having previously categorized this particular person as female rather than as Black) should both influence the relative efficiency of alternative categorization procedures. They will thus shape the likelihood that the practiced category will be accessed instead of an alternative. This conceptualization leads to several testable hypotheses about effects of perceivers' past experiences on their patterns of social categorization and stereotyping; only a few of these hypotheses were mentioned in this section. Of course, the second process involved in stereotyping, the inference from group membership to stereotypic traits or other characteristics, may also be mediated by cognitive processes that are subject to practice effects, with predictable results for social judgment outcomes.

CONCLUSIONS

Something as obvious as the fact that people get better at doing things when they practice can have non-obvious implications for social judgments. Conceiving of social judgments as procedurally mediated—represented theoretically as productions in Anderson's formalism—gives rise to a number of novel hypotheses in such areas as category accessibility effects, judgments about multiple-implication behaviors, and stereotyping when a target individual falls into multiple social categories. As I argued earlier, these effects may be particularly evident in situations where judgments are made on-line, because the absence of externally set processing goals and the limited time available for processing may make procedural efficiency a particularly potent determinant of the actual processes that are carried out. As outlined in this chapter, I have already tested some of these hypotheses, and work is currently under way on others. The procedural component of social knowledge and judgment skills should not be neglected as a result of social cognition researchers' typical focus on the static contents of social knowledge.

ACKNOWLEDGMENT

This research was supported by the National Science Foundation under grant BNS-8613584.

REFERENCES

Anderson, J. R. (1982). Acquisition of cognitive skill. *Psychological Review, 89,* 369–406.
Anderson, J. R. (1983). *The architecture of cognition.* Cambridge, MA: Harvard University Press.
Anderson, J. R. (1987). Skill acquisition: Compilation of weak-method problem solutions. *Psychological Review, 94,* 192–210.
Brooks, L. R. (1987). Decentralized control of categorization: The role of prior processing episodes. In U. Neisser (Ed.), *Concepts and conceptual development* (pp. 141–174). Cambridge, England: Cambridge University Press.
Carlston, D. E. (1980). Events, inferences, and impression formation. In R. Hastie, T. M. Ostrom, E. B. Ebbesen, R. S. Wyer, D. L. Hamilton, & D. E. Carlston (Eds.), *Person memory* (pp. 89–120). Hillsdale, NJ: Lawrence Erlbaum Associates.
Fazio, R. H. (1986). How do attitudes guide behavior? In R. M. Sorrentino & E. T. Higgins (Eds.), *Handbook of motivation and cognition* (pp. 204–243). New York: Guilford.
Fazio, R. H., Chen, J., McDonel, E. C., & Sherman, S. J. (1982). Attitude accessibility, attitude-behavior consistency, and the strength of the object-evaluation association. *Journal of Experimental Social Psychology, 18,* 339–357.
Fazio, R. H., Sanbonmatsu, D. M., Powell, M. C., & Kardes, F. R. (1986). On the automatic activation of attitudes. *Journal of Personality and Social Psychology, 50,* 229–238.
Fazio, R. H., & Williams, C. J. (1986). Attitude accessibility as a moderator of the attitude-perception and attitude-behavior relations: An investigation of the 1984 presidential election. *Journal of Personality and Social Psychology, 51,* 505–514.
Higgins, E. T., & King, G. (1981). Accessibility of social constructs: Information-processing consequences of individual and contextual variability. In N. Cantor & J. F. Kihlstrom (Eds.), *Personality, cognition, and social interaction* (pp. 69–121). Hillsdale, NJ: Lawrence Erlbaum Associates.
Higgins, E. T., Rholes, W. S., & Jones, C. R. (1977). Category accessibility and impression

formation. *Journal of Experimental Social Psychology, 13,* 141–154.
Kolers, P. A. (1976). Reading a year later. *Journal of Experimental Psychology: Human Learning and Memory, 2,* 554–565.
Mitchell, D. B., & Brown, A. S. (1988). Persistent repetition priming in picture naming and its dissociation from recognition memory. *Journal of Experimental Psychology: Learning, Memory, and Cognition, 14,* 213–222.
Newell, A., & Rosenbloom, P. S. (1981). Mechanisms of skill acquisition and the law of practice. In J. R. Anderson (Ed.), *Cognitive skills and their acquisition* (pp. 1–56). Hillsdale, NJ: Lawrence Erlbaum Associates.
Ostrom, T. M. (1984). The sovereignty of social cognition. In R. S. Wyer & T. K. Srull (Eds.), *Handbook of social cognition* (vol. 1, pp. 1–38). Hillsdale, NJ: Lawrence Erlbaum Associates.
Park, B., & Rothbart, M. (1982). Perception of out-group homogeneity and levels of social categorization: Memory for the subordinate attributes of in-group and out-group members. *Journal of Personality and Social Psychology, 42,* 1051–1068.
Rothbart, M., & John, O. P. (1985). Social categorization and behavioral episodes: A cognitive analysis of the effects of intergroup contact. *Journal of Social Issues, 41*(3), 81–104.
Schacter, D. (1987). Implicit memory: History and current status. *Journal of Experimental Psychology: Learning, Memory, and Cognition, 13,* 501–518.
Smith, E. R. (1984). Model of social inference processes. *Psychological Review, 91,* 392–413.
Smith, E. R. (in press). Content and process specificity in the effects of prior experiences. In R. S. Wyer & T. K. Srull (Eds.), *Advances in social cognition* (vol. 3). Hillsdale, NJ: Lawrence Erlbaum Associates.
Smith, E. R. (1988). *Procedural efficiency: Generality and effects on social judgment.* Unpublished manuscript, Purdue University, West Lafayette, IN.
Smith, E. R., & Branscombe, N. R. (1987). Procedurally mediated social inferences: The case of category accessibility effects. *Journal of Experimental Social Psychology, 23,* 361–382.
Smith, E. R., & Branscombe, N. R. (1988). Category accessibility as implicit memory. *Journal of Experimental Social Psychology, 24,* 490–504.
Smith, E. R., Branscombe, N. R., & Bormann, C. (1988). Generality of the effects of practice on social judgment tasks. *Journal of Personality and Social Psychology, 54,* 385–395.
Smith, E. R., & Lerner, M. (1986). Development of automatism of social judgments. *Journal of Personality and Social Psychology, 50,* 246–259.
Sorrentino, R. M., & Higgins, E. T. (1986). Motivation and cognition: Warming up to synergism. In R. Sorrentino & E. T. Higgins (Eds.), *Handbook of motivation and cognition: Foundations of social behavior* (pp. 3–20). New York: Guilford.
Srull, T. K., & Wyer, R. S. (1979). The role of category accessibility in the interpretation of information about other people: Some determinants and implications. *Journal of Personality and Social Psychology, 37,* 1660–1672.
Wyer, R. S., & Srull, T. K. (1986). Human cognition in its social context. *Psychological Review, 93,* 322–359.
Zarate, M. A., & Smith, E. R. (1988a). *Person categorization and stereotyping.* Unpublished manuscript, Purdue University, West Lafayette, IN.
Zarate, M. A., & Smith, E. R. (1988b). *Specificity of practice effects: Social categorization processes.* Unpublished manuscript, Purdue University, West Lafayette, IN.

3
Trait Attributes as On-Line Organizers in Person Impressions

Bernadette Park
University of Colorado

When we consider social inference processes that are likely to occur on-line as opposed to being memory-based, one of the most likely candidates is a personality impression of an acquaintance. Impression formation refers to the process of going from observable behaviors performed by a target to an inference about an underlying personality trait that is responsible in part for producing such behaviors. At issue is the process by which such inferences proceed. Interestingly, Asch (1946, p. 289), in his seminal work on impression formation, outlined two possible processes by which such social inferences are made. These two alternative hypotheses mirror to a large extent the on-line versus memory-based distinction. One possibility suggested by Asch is that characterization by a trait proceeds as a process of statistical generalization, such that the behaviors performed by a target are noted and remembered and after a critical number of such behaviors has been observed, the trait inference is made. Such a process is memory-based in that no judgment is made at the time the behaviors are seen, but rather the behaviors are stored in memory, and only after some critical number have been observed does the perceiver infer or decide that the trait applies. Any encoding, retention, or retrieval biases that influence memory for the behaviors will therefore have an influence on the inference process of deciding whether the trait applies or not. So, for example, such a model might explain the tendency to infer negative traits more quickly than positive traits (Kanouse & Hansen, 1971; Rothbart & Park, 1986), using the following logic. Negative behaviors, because of their relative infrequency, are likely to be highly memorable. As a result, the critical number for making the trait inference will be reached sooner than in the case of positive behaviors, not so much because the two types of traits have different critical thresholds, but because the negative behaviors accumulate faster, given their greater memorability.

Alternatively, Asch suggested that the process might proceed as one of hypothesis testing. Following just one or two behaviors related to a particular trait dimension, the perceiver forms the hypothesis that the trait characterizes the target. Subsequent behaviors are used to either strengthen or disprove the hypothesis. This process is basically one of on-line impression formation. As each new bit of information is received the perceiver uses it to modify the existing judgment about the person. According to this model, inferences from negative behaviors to negative traits occur more quickly than inferences from positive behaviors both because negative behaviors are particularly salient and likely to be noticed, and perhaps because the criterion for inferring negative traits may be lower. Most importantly, because information is used to update the impression as it is received, rather than depending on what is stored in memory, the particular behaviors recalled need bear little or no resemblance to an inference based on these.

Based on my own research, I argue that the process of deciding that a trait characterizes a target is of an on-line nature (Park, 1986; Park & Flink, in press; Park & Judd, in press). In the earliest of these studies (Park, 1986), I observed a group of seven individuals over the course of 7 weeks as they became acquainted with one another. The subjects wrote open-ended descriptions of each other once a week, and these descriptions were analyzed for the type of attributes mentioned. The five categories used were (from Ostrom, 1975): trait attributes, behaviors performed by the target, physical attributes, attitudes ascribed to the target, and demographic information.

Two effects are of direct relevance to the on-line versus memory-based debate in impression formation. First, by far the most prevalent type of information in the descriptions was trait attributes. Moreover, these outnumbered the other four types of information even in the descriptions written the very first week. This finding argues against a memory-based process of impression formation. If subjects were making trait inferences in a memory-based manner, they should initially observe and remember the behaviors exhibited by the targets and primarily describe these, and only at some future point when a critical number of trait relevant behaviors had been accumulated, make the trait inference. Yet traits were the most prevalent type of attribute used to describe the targets, and they occurred more frequently than descriptions of behaviors even in the very first week of acquaintance. Clearly, trait attributes were at least being considered after this very short period of acquaintance, in contrast to a primary focus on behaviors. In addition, although trait attributes were always used with greater frequency than behaviors, this difference increased over the 7-week period such that trait attributes became even more prevalent in the descriptions, and reports of behaviors became even less frequent. This result suggests that although subjects were not forming trait inferences in a memory-based fashion, neither were they simply forming a complete set of trait inferences during the initial acquaintance that was then left untouched. Rather, the subjects appeared to engage in a process of constructing a knowledge structure that contained information about the target. The structure included both observed attributes (behaviors, physical information) and trait inferences generated from these. The structure was modified and updated in response to new information, so that the process was much like the construction of a "model" or a "story" to describe the particular person. Such a characterization is very much one of an on-line process of impression formation.

In addition, subjects' descriptions often suggested a process of hypothesis testing in the course of forming their impressions. For example, after several weeks of describing one particular target as quiet and shy, a subject noted that the target did not seem as reserved as before, perhaps because he or she was becoming more comfortable with the group. Subjects appeared to form initial hypotheses about the traits that characterized one another, and then to use subsequent information on the following weeks to either confirm these hypotheses, or to disconfirm them. I looked at primacy effects, measured as repetitions on subsequent weeks of attributes previously mentioned. I found that it was true that attributes mentioned early were disproportionately more likely to be repeated in later weeks than attributes first mentioned in the later time periods, taking into account differences in the possible number of times that each attribute could be repeated. Interestingly, however, this effect was primarily due to the fact that most of the unique attributes ever used to describe a target appeared in the first 2 weeks. If a new attribute was mentioned on week 4 or 5, it was as likely as early attributes to be repeated. However, most of the attributes appeared at the first two time periods, and so the later descriptions consisted primarily of these. This suggests that early in the acquaintance, behavior is observed that indicates a particular trait dimension, and the hypothesis is established that the trait is present. In subsequent meetings, further information relevant to the hypothesis is monitored, and the strength of the hypothesis is either increased or decreased. In addition, if behavior relevant to a new trait is exhibited, a new hypothesis is entertained and tested with subsequent information. However, most of the trait hypotheses appear to be formed very early in the acquaintance.

This description of the process suggessts that trait attributes are used to organize incoming behavioral information that is subsequently stored in memory. When the target performs a behavior that is consistent with a trait attribute, the subject forms the hypothesis that the trait characterizes the person. The behavior and the trait hypothesis are stored together in memory. As each new behavior occurs, the subject comprehends its relevance to a particular trait dimension. If the trait has previously been considered, the subject retrieves that hypothesis, in addition to an index of the strength or certainty of the hypothesis. Along with the trait concept are stored the related behaviors that were previously observed. The new behavior is thought about with respect to the hypothesis and these other behaviors, is used to update the strength of the hypothesis, and is stored in memory along with this other information. As a result, the memory representation contains the trait hypothesis and a judgment of its plausibility or likelihood (adjusted on-line in response to new information), relevant behaviors that have been thought about in relation to one another and to the trait concept, and interconnections among all this information. The process is a very constructive one, well described by the analogy of model building. At any point in time, the strength of the existing hypothesis serves as an anchor, and new information is used to adjust the certainty in the hypothesis (Lopes, 1982). This adjusted judgment is then stored as the new strength of the existing hypothesis and is used on subsequent occasions as the anchor from which adjustments are made in response to newly presented behaviors.

Implicit in this formulation is the argument that, although the process by which trait inferences are made is not memory-based, neither is it an automatic process. Rather, I have argued that the process is constructive in that it entails more than simply accumulating behaviors and later judging their implications for a trait attribute, and yet it is not so constructive as to infer with certainty the existence of the trait from a single behavior. With the presentation of several relevant behaviors, the hypothesis that the trait characterizes the target is formed, and the strength of the hypothesis is modified in response to future information. But this is not the same as claiming that from a single behavior the trait inference is made.

Winter and Uleman (1984) have argued that trait inferences are spontaneous, and to some extent automatic (Winter, Uleman, & Cunniff, 1985). In these studies, subjects read about behaviors performed by a variety of characters. They were then asked to recall these behaviors, and they were given either no cue for recall, a cue that was semantically related to the actor, or a trait cue that was related to the behavior. Recall was higher when a trait cue was presented than when either the highly related semantic cue or no cue was provided. Based on the principle of encoding specificity (Tulving & Thomson, 1973), Winter and Uleman argued that the trait concept must have been spontaneously inferred and stored with the behavior at encoding. These studies are well designed and interesting. It is possible, however, that in comprehending each behavior, subjects understood the semantic relevance to a trait concept (e.g., this is a friendly behavior), without necessarily inferring that the trait characterized the target, (e.g., without deciding that this is a friendly person). Understanding and encoding the relevance of the behavior to a trait could result in high levels of recall when the trait was presented as the cue. This does not, however, necessitate that an inference was made that the target could, in general, be characterized by the trait in question. I suspect that the semantic relation of a behavior to a trait dimension occurs spontaneously in the process of comprehending a behavior, but this is not the same as spontaneously or automatically inferring that the trait characterizes the target. Instead, I argue that the inference process begins when several such behaviors are observed, and is at that point regarded as a hypothesis rather than as a certainty. Bassili and Smith (1986) have shown that the effectiveness of the trait as a retrieval cue can be increased by instructing subjects to form impressions of the characters. This further supports the argument that trait inferences are not made in a full-blown fashion following a single relevant behavior. That the trait implications of a behavior are readily processed is supported by findings from Smith and Miller (1983), who found that judgments about the trait implications of a behavior were made very quickly, as quickly as a factual judgment such as the gender of the actor.

I was interested in trying to demonstrate in a more rigorous and controlled fashion than was present in the studies of impressions of real people that trait inferences proceed as a process of hypothesis testing. In particular, I wished to demonstrate that trait concepts are used to organize behavioral information about a target, and that the strength of the hypothesis that the trait characterizes the target increases with subsequent consistent behaviors. The following two studies were conducted to look at whether trait inferences appear to occur on-line in a manner that is consistent with the hypothesis-testing formulation put forward by Asch, or whether they appear to operate in a manner more consistent with a memory-based process. The rationale and paradigm for the studies come from fact-retrieval research investigating the "fan effect" in cognitive psychology. Before discussing the studies, a brief digression to present an overview of this literature is necessary.

THE FAN EFFECT PARADIGM AND INTEGRATED KNOWLEDGE STRUCTURES

The fan effect refers to the finding that when a subject is asked to memorize a set of facts about several targets, and the number of facts learned for each target varies, the response time (RT) to verify studied facts or to reject nonstudied facts increases linearly with the number of facts learned about the character (Anderson, 1974, 1976; Anderson & Bower, 1973). It takes longer to respond to items paired with a character of a larger set size than to items from a smaller set size. Anderson interpreted this finding in a spreading activation framework. Each act is connected to the character node by a pathway. When a probe is presented, activation spreads out from the character node and probe node along the pathways. Although the activation spreads instantaneously (Ratcliff & McKoon, 1981), the time it takes activation to accumulate to a given level at a node determines the time it takes to execute the production rule to generate a response. For larger set sizes, the activation spreading from the character node to the acts is distributed over a larger number of pathways, and it will therefore take longer for activation to rise to a given level. this means that it will take slightly longer to generate the response for items from larger sets relative to those from a smaller set size.

A number of researchers have shown that the fan effect can be attenuated and even eliminated under certain conditions (Hayes-Roth, 1977; Moeser, 1977, 1979; Myers, O'Brien, Balota, & Toyofuka, 1984; Reder & Anderson, 1980; Reder & Ross, 1983; Smith, Adams, & Schorr, 1978). For example, in a study by Smith et al. (1978; Smith, 1981), subjects first learned two facts, such as, "Marty broke the bottle," and, "Marty did not delay the trip." Then the subject either did not learn a third fact, learned a third fact that served to integrate these two (such as, "Marty was chosen to christen the ship."), or learned a third fact that did not integrate the two (such as, "Marty was asked to address the crowd."). When the third act conceptually integrated the previous two, RT to any of the three facts was the same as when the third fact had not been learned. When the third fact did not integrate the previous two, a positive fan was obtained. Myers et al. (1984) actually found a negative fan effect in their study, such that RTs were faster to items from sets of larger sizes than to those of smaller sizes. This was true when the sets of items used were causally related to one another. For example, for facts studied with a baseball theme, "Found the first few innings boring" can be causally related to "Went home early."

These researchers argued that fan effects can be eliminated as a result of new links established among the studied items when the items can be conceptually integrated. When facts are studied that are related to a theme, the items can be linked to each other in memory. The additional links provide alternative pathways to reach the probe fact. Thus, during retrieval, activation spreads from the character node and fact nodes to other fact nodes via these additional links. This process can act as one of reverberation so that, depending on the strength and number of links, activation can actually accumulate faster than if the links were not present.

TRAIT ATTRIBUTES AS ORGANIZING ELEMENTS

One way to characterize the role of trait attributes in person impressions is that they act to organize or integrate related behaviors. Just as a theme ties together the individual acts in a story, so too might a trait concept, such as dishonest, tie together the behaviors performed by a person. Drawing on research conclusions from the fan effect literature, the following study was designed. Subjects read about the behavior of several targets, and the number of behaviors learned about each was varied. All behaviors performed by a given target were related to a single trait concept, such as dishonest. If subjects use trait concepts as themes to organize behaviors performed by a target, then this should eliminate fan effects, as when a theme organizes actions in a story. If the process of trait inference does occur on-line, then as subjects learn about each new behavior performed by a target, they should think about it in relation to past actions, and in relation to the trait concept, and use the behavior to strengthen their belief in the hypothesis that the trait characterizes the target. This should result in a highly unified and interconnected structure with links between the behaviors and the trait concept, and between the behaviors themselves. Moreover, the amount of interconnectedness should increase with greater numbers of related behaviors, because these increase the likelihood that the hypothesis will be entertained, and further increase the strength of the hypothesis. Therefore, the time to verify studied behaviors should actually decrease as set size increases, resulting in a negative fan effect.

When an item that was not studied is presented at test, the subject must respond that the item is false. If the item is consistent with the other items studied with that character (e.g., it is another friendly behavior), this similarity will slow responses to reject the item. That is, to the extent that the subject comprehends that this target performed many friendly behaviors, when a new friendly behavior is presented at test, there will be a conflict in response outputs because the behavior itself is new, but its relation to the trait concept suggests that it is old. Thus, the time to reject as false new items consistent with the behaviors studied for a given character should be relatively long. Moreover, the responses should be even longer for large set sizes, because the trait concept is stronger here. If a test item is presented that is inconsistent with the trait concept studied with that character (e.g., an unfriendly item), rejections should be facilitated, because the trait concept information in this item is in direct opposition to all of that studied with the other behaviors. Both the item information and the trait information indicate that the item is false. Again, this facilitation should be greater for larger set sizes, because the trait concept information is stronger here. In summary, if trait concepts are used to organize the behaviors performed by a target as the behaviors are presented, response times to test items should show a negative fan for both studied acts (true items), and for nonstudied acts that are inconsistent with the trait concept (false inconsistent items). RTs should show a positive fan for nonstudied acts that are consistent with the trait concept (false consistent items). Alternatively, according to a memory-based process, each act should simply be encoded as it is presented, and although the subject may think about the trait implication of the act at the time of encoding, he or she should not think about the relation of the trait implication of this particular act to that of previously studied acts. In no sense should the subject at the time of encoding entertain the hypothesis that the trait characterizes the target, nor should he or she use the trait concept to organize the behaviors. Such a process clearly predicts a positive fan effect for true items, because there is no well-established set of interconnections among these.

In this first experiment, subjects learned a set of 15 behaviors that described the acts of three different men. The number of acts learned for each man was either 3, 5, or 7. These behaviors were generated from four trait concepts (although only three concepts were presented to a given subject). These were: friendly, responsible, dishonest, and stupid. All of the behaviors paired with a given character were related to a single trait concept (e.g., dishonest), and the three characters were presented with different traits for a given subject. Each character was assigned an occupation (e.g., electrician), and the behaviors were studied with these occupations (e.g., the electrician visited his friend in the hospital). Across subjects, the pairings of the occupations and traits with the various set sizes were counterbalanced.

To encourage subjects to think of each character as a real person, the photographs of three men were attached to one side of a 3" × 5" index card with the first and last name and occupation of each character typed on the other side. The subject was asked to study the names and occupations of the three men until they could be accurately recited for each photo. The subject was then asked to learn the 15 behaviors performed by the three men. The instructions were to learn which behavior was performed by which character, and no mention was made of forming an impression of the men. Each of the 15 behaviors was typed on a 3" × 5" index card, and these were randomly ordered for presentation (i.e., they were not blocked by character). To learn the behaviors, the subject was instructed to generate a continuation of any sort of each act and to write this down. For example, if the presented behavior was, "The reporter stole from his friend's wallet," the subject might write, "and got caught." This procedure was repeated a second time with the behaviors arranged in a different random order. To test learning for the behaviors, a cued recall task was performed. The experimenter read each behavior stem to the subject, and the subject generated the occupation of the character who had performed it. If an error occurred, it was corrected, and after all 15 behaviors were tested, items on which an error had been made were retested until the subject got all behaviors correct. In addition, the subject was required to make one complete error-free pass through the 15 behaviors before going on. If an error was made, the item was tested until correctly learned, and a subsequent pass testing all 15 behaviors was performed until all 15 were correct. Typically, one complete pass was sufficient to achieve perfect performance.

At this point, the subject performed a speeded recognition task. Test items were presented one at a time on a CRT screen. Each test item included the name of one of the three characters and a behavior. The subject was to indicate whether that character had ("true") or had not ("false") performed that particular behavior in the set of behaviors learned earlier. The subject was told to read each item, and to decide as quickly as possible while also remaining accurate whether the item was true or false. Response times and responses were recorded. A total of 33 test items were presented. These included the 15 studied (true) items, and 18 false items. The false items were of three types. Six of these (two per character) were behaviors pretested as consistent with the other behaviors performed by that same character (e.g., two additional friendly items), six were pretested as inconsistent with the other behaviors performed by the character (e.g., two unfriendly items), and six were repairings of studied acts with different characters. These last six items were included so that responses could not be accurately made solely on the basis of whether the act was old or new. Subjects were forced to attend to the character performing the act as well. Although these types of items are important to prevent such a strategy, they are not of theoretical interest, and responses to these items were not analyzed. Following the recognition test, the subject was asked to write a short description of each character based on his or her impression. The subject also rated how strong and clear the impression of each character was, and how confident he or she was in each impression. A total of 24 subjects participated in the study.

Mean RTs as a function of set size and type of item are graphed in Fig. 3.1. The error rates in each cell appear in parentheses. The pattern of responses is consistent with the hypothesis that behaviors are organized by trait concepts, and that the likelihood of such organization increases the greater the number of trait relevant acts presented. Responses to true items were predicted to be faster for larger set sizes because there is a greater amount of integration among the items. The linear trend for true items was significant, and, as Fig. 3.1 shows, negative, $F(1, 23) = 4.32, p < .05$. False items inconsistent with the acts performed by a character were predicted to be relatively easy to reject, and increasingly easier for larger set sizes because the trait concept is clearer here. Of the three types of items, inconsistent falses were responded to most quickly, $F(2, 46) = 4.26, p < .025$

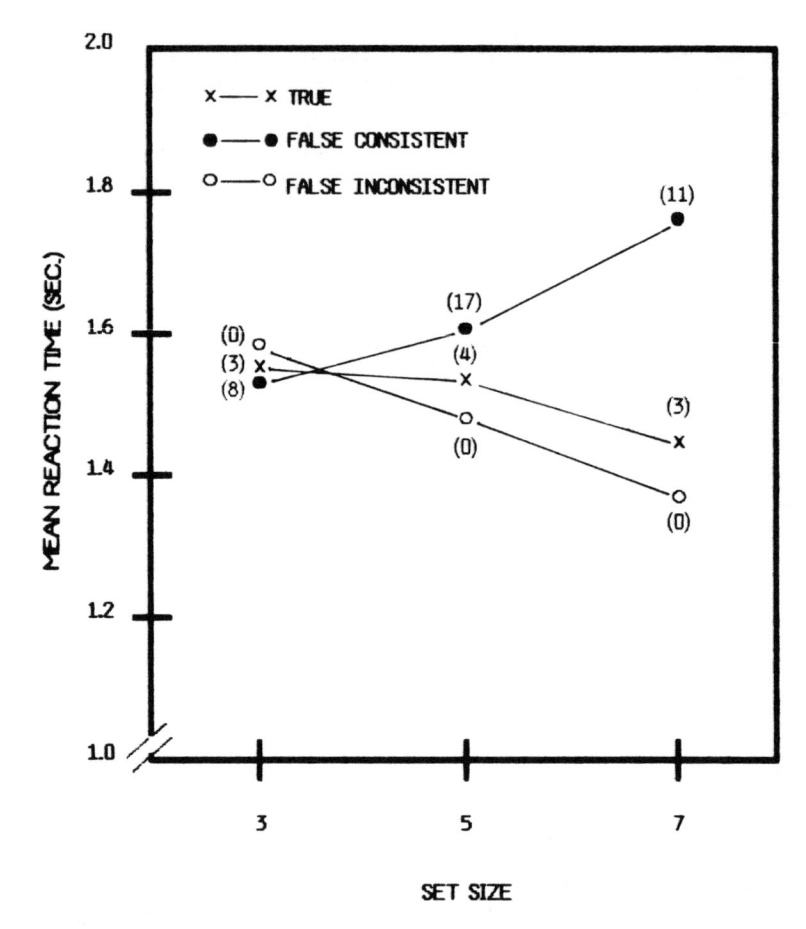

FIG. 3.1. Mean response times and error percentages (in parentheses) as a function of set size and type of item (Experiment 1).

for the main effect of item type, and the responses showed a significant linear decrease with increasing set size, $F(1, 23) = 5.65$, $p < .03$. Finally, false items consistent with the acts performed by a character were predicted to be relatively difficult to reject, and this effect was expected to be even more true for larger set sizes because of the stronger trait information. There was a significant linear increase in RTs to consistent falses, $F(1, 23) = 6.69$, $p < .02$, and of the three types of items, these were responded to most slowly.

The results of this experiment are consistent with an on-line process of trait inference. Response times to true items were actually faster for items from larger than from smaller set sizes. This negative fan effect can only be explained by assuming that items in the larger sets were more highly interconnected than those in the smaller sets. This is exactly the prediction from an on-line process of trait inferences. According to this process, as each new behavior was presented, the subject thought about the trait implications of this act in relation to those of previous acts and, in the process, developed a tightly interconnected network of knowledge. These interconnections allowed for reverberation of activation within the system (Myers et al., 1984), resulting in fast response times. In addition, response times to reject false items that were consistent with the trait concept paired with that character increased with larger set sizes. According to the present argument, this is because the trait concept is stronger for the larger set sizes and therefore produces more interference. The stronger trait concept also produces greater facilitation when rejecting false items that are inconsistent with the trait, resulting in a negative fan effect for false inconsistent items.

ELIMINATING ON-LINE ORGANIZATION OF PERSON IMPRESSIONS

I was interested in the conditions under which the strong integration obtained in the first experiment might be eliminated. I have argued that because the acts studied with a given character were all related to a given trait concept, subjects were able to use that trait concept to organize and integrate the behaviors. If the behaviors were heterogeneous with respect to their trait information, such that they could not be organized by a single trait concept, this should eliminate the effects found in the first experiment. I performed several studies to see whether the apparent organization in the impression of a character found in the first experiment could be eliminated.

In the second experiment, subjects studied the same 15 behaviors as those in the first experiment. However, the behaviors were scrambled so that no single trait dimension could be used to organize the behaviors studied with a given character. For example, the character of set size 7 performed three stupid, two responsible, one dishonest, and one friendly behavior. The character of set size 5 performed two stupid, two responsible, and one dishonest behavior, and the character of set size 3 performed one stupid, one responsible, and one dishonest behavior. As in the first experiment, the number of behaviors relevant to each trait was counterbalanced across subjects, as were the particular behaviors presented with the characters of various set sizes. The false consistent items were always consistent with at least one behavior performed by that character, and the false inconsistent were always inconsistent with at least one behavior performed by that character. They were irrelevant to the remaining acts performed by that character. The false items were not, however, consistent and inconsistent with the entire set of behaviors performed by the character, as they had been in the first experiment.

The procedures for learning and testing in this experiment were identical to those in the first experiment. The only change was that the behaviors studied with a particular character came from a variety of trait dimensions, and no single trait could be used as a theme to organize all behaviors performed by a character. Accordingly, this should result in less integration and organization in the knowledge structures. At a minimum, the negative fan for true and inconsistent falses observed in the first experiment should disappear because the additional behaviors at the larger set sizes do not provided further interconnections to a single trait concept. Similarly, the positive fan for consistent falses should be eliminated because the trait concept is no longer particularly strong for the larger set sizes. In addition, the mean difference in response times to consistent and inconsistent falses should be minimized. In summary, if the results from the first experiment were obtained because the knowledge structures were organized by the trait concept, and this was more true for the larger set sizes, then in this experiment, because the trait concept should be relatively weak for all set sizes, the results due to type of item and set size should not replicate. A total of 36 subjects participated in this experiment.

Response times as a function of set size were flat for all three types of items, and the tests of all three of the corresponding linear trends were nonsignificant. In addition. whereas in the first experiment RTs to reject consistent falses were slower than those to verify trues, the reverse pattern was present in this experiment. Thus subjects were fastest at rejecting false inconsistent items ($M = 1.32$), somewhat slower at rejecting false consistent items ($M = 1.39$), and slowest at verifying studied facts as true ($M = 1.50$). Scrambling the behaviors appears to have reduced the amount of organization in the structures given that the negative fan for true items was eliminated. Moreover, the large amount of interference for false consistent items was not found in the present experiment, nor was the pattern of greater interference for larger set sizes for false consistent items.

The pattern of results clearly suggests that the information stored for each character in this study was less organized that that in the previous study, and that the role that trait information played in responding to false items was greatly minimized. Note, however, that there was still no positive fan effect in this study. That is, it took the same amount of time to respond to an item paired with a character for whom a larger number of behaviors had been studied as to one paired with a character for whom just a few behaviors were learned. This pattern indicates that there was some degree of interconnectedness among the studied facts, or else a positive fan effect would have been obtained. What these results suggest is that, even in the absence of a clear trait concept along which an impression can be organized, subjects still attempt to construct a coherent knowledge structure from a set of acts performed by a target. Flat fan effects have been obtained in studies in the cognitive literature when the researcher provides a theme that organizes the studied facts (Smith et al., 1978). The present results suggest that providing a photo and occupation for each target causes the subject to try to form a coherent impression of the target, and this process in and of itself results in some degree of organization of the behaviors in a manner that is similar to the linkage provided by a theme in a story. Subjects' responses during the learning phase clearly indicated that they were trying to form ideas about what each target was like. When trying to recall who, "stole money from his friend's wallet," a subject might respond that, "It was the janitor. He wasn't very good at math (a stupid behavior), and probably found himself short of cash." Obviously, this experimental situation is far removed from the manner in which one encounters new acquaintances in daily life. The striking aspect of the results comes, however, from the comparison to the previously cited studies in the cognitive literature. Just as a theme provided coherence to a list of sentences in a text, so too does the knowledge that a set of behavioral acts was performed by a person provide or impose a coherence on these.

Still, I was interested in what conditions would produce a positive fan effect using the materials studied thus far. What procedural changes would be necessary to produce a pattern of results that would suggest that there was basically no integration among the acts studied with a particular character? After a number of unsuccessful attempts, the following paradigm was developed. The behaviors were scrambled, as in the last experiment, so that no single trait could be used to organize all the behaviors studied with a given character. However, the procedures for the learning phase of the experiment were changed. First, subjects were not shown photos of the three men. They were told simply that they would be asked to learn information about several characters and then to make some judgments based on what was learned. In addition, rather than generating continuations to each behavior, which tended to promote the formation of impressions, the 15 behaviors were presented one at a time on a CRT screen, and the subject was instructed simply to memorize the behaviors that each character had performed. As in the previous experiments, the behaviors were learned with the characters' occupations. Each behavior stayed on the screen for 6 sec, and the entire set of behaviors was presented two times. The test for learning of the behaviors was the same as in the previous two studies. The experimenter read each behavior stem, and the subject generated the occupation of the character who had performed it. If an error was made, it was corrected, and these items were retested at the end of the set of 15. One complete error-free pass through the 15 behaviors was required before going on. Typically, two passes through the behaviors were sufficient to achieve perfect performance. Following the recognition test, the subject was asked to write a short description of each character, as in the

52 PARK

previous two experiments, and to rate how strong, clear, and confident he or she was in each impression. A total of 24 subjects participated in the experiment.

Mean RTs as a function of set size and type of test item are graphed in Fig. 3.2. Mean error rates appear in parentheses. The analyses revealed a significant linear component, $F(2, 46) = 5.57, p < .03$, such that response times increased as a function of set size. The linear trend did not depend on item type, $F < 1$. In addition, consistent false and inconsistent false items were rejected about equally fast, and faster than the true items were verified, $F(2, 46) = 24.74, p < .001$, for the main effect due to type of item.

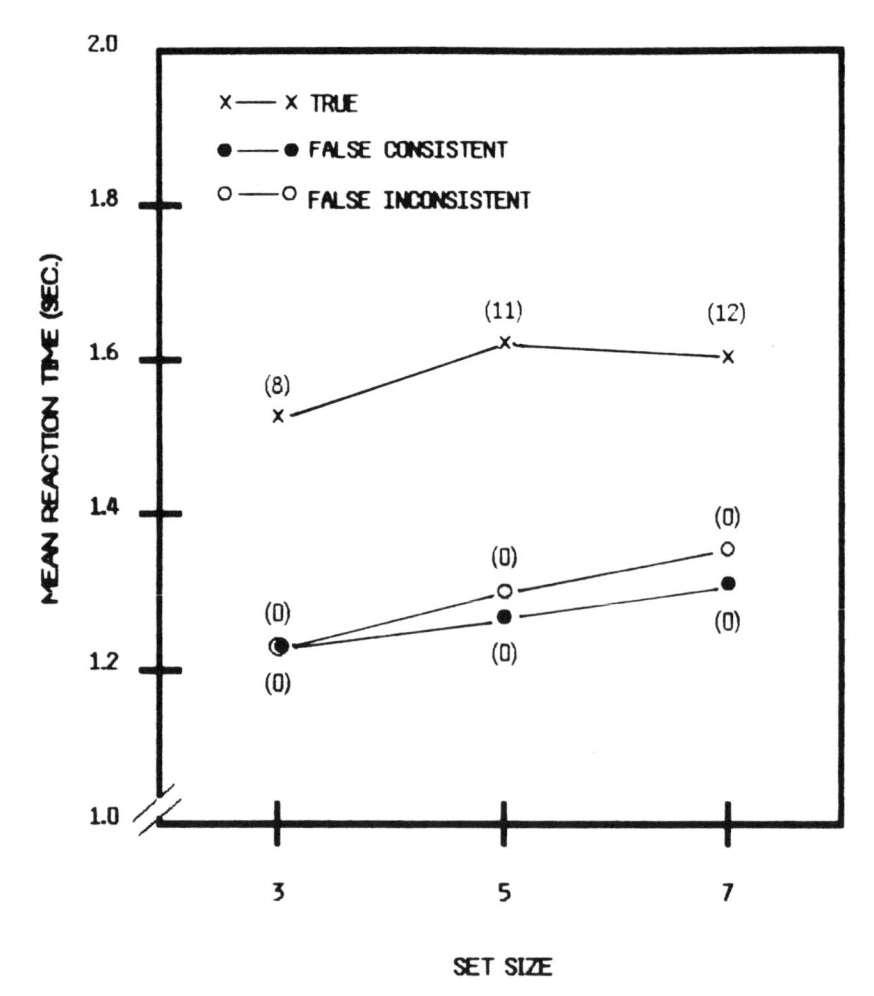

FIG. 3.2. Mean response times and error percentages (in parenthese) as function of set size and type of test item (Experiment 3).

The procedural changes implemented in this experiment appear to have minimized the tendency for subjects to form coherent impressions of the characters. First, a positive fan effect was obtained across all item types, consistent with previous research when the knowledge structure was unintegrated (Anderson, 1974, 1976; Anderson & Bower, 1973). This suggests that the behaviors were not interconnected, but rather were simply linked to the character node, independently of each other. In addition, the false consistent and inconsistent items were both rejected more quickly than the studied items were verified, and they were rejected equally fast. The magnitude of the speedup in rejection times for the false consistent items relative to the first experiment is quite remarkable. It was still the case that the false consistent items shared trait concept information with the studied behaviors, even though this was not organized by character. That is, a particular subject may have learned seven friendly behaviors and no unfriendly behaviors. At test, one might expect that there would still be some interference from a friendly but nonpresented item, relative to an unfriendly, nonpresented item. The response times suggest that this was not the case. There is no evidence whatever that under these experimental conditions the subject is using trait information to organize the studied behaviors.

I was also interested in the rated strength, clarity, and confidence of subjects impressions for each character in the first experiment and in this third experiment. The average of these three ratings are graphed in Fig. 3.3. It is clear from the figure that stronger impressions were formed in the first experiment than in the third, and this was true for all three set sizes, all ts > 2.35, $p < .03$. In addition, subjects reported stronger impressions for characters paired with larger numbers of behaviors.

CONCLUSION

In this chapter, I have discussed two processes by which trait inferences might be made. These were initially suggested by Asch (1946), and they parallel the on-line versus memory-based distinction that is the basis for this book. According to a memory-based approach, the behaviors performed by a target are stored in memory, and only after some critical number have accumulated is a trait inference made. Alternatively, according to an on-line process, following just one or two behaviors, the hypothesis that the trait characterizes the target is entertained. Subsequent behaviors are used either to strengthen the hypothesis or to disconfirm it. The plausibility of the hypothesis is updated in an on-line manner so that a summary judgment of the likelihood of the trait inference is always available.

The studies reported were based on theory and research from cognitive

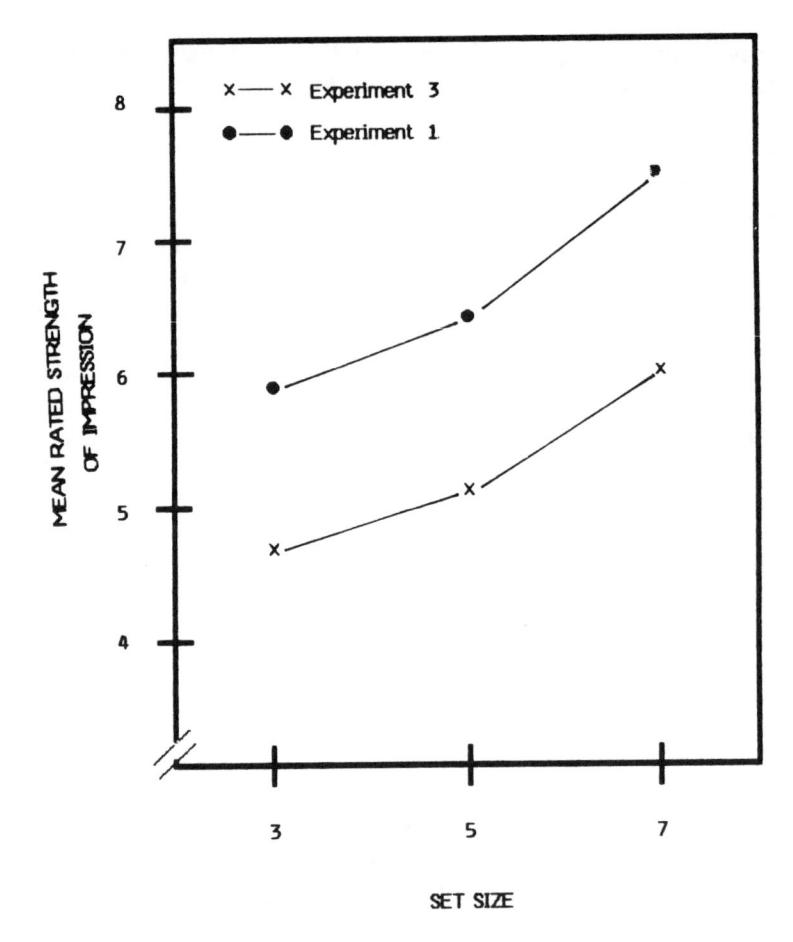

FIG. 3.3 Mean of rated strength, clarity, and confidence of impressions as a function of set and experiment.

psychology on the fan effect. This research has shown that as the number of facts studied with a particular character increases, so too does the time to retrieve these facts, or to reject as false nonstudied facts. However, if there is some mechanism by which the studied facts can be integrated, such as providing a theme or a causal relation among the facts, fan effects can be eliminated and sometimes even reversed. Presumably, this is because the theme provides a way to interconnect the facts themselves. At test, activation is not simply divided among the facts linked to the character node, but it can continue to reverberate among the links between items as well, resulting in faster identification of the test item.

In the first study, items studied with a given character were all related to a single trait concept. If, as the behaviors were studied, subjects thought about the relation of each behavior to the trait, and the relation to other studied behaviors, this should result in a highly interconnected network. The interconnectedness of the network should increase, the greater the number of trait relevant behaviors. Such a process is consistent with an on-line argument of trait inference. In fact, a negative fan was obtained for responses to true items. In addition, subjects were very slow at rejecting false items that were consistent with the trait concept paired with that character, and this was even more true as set size increased. And subjects were very fast at rejecting false items that were inconsistent with the trait concept, and this was even more true as set size increased.

On the whole, these findings support an on-line process of trait inference such that the trait is hypothesized to characterize the target after just a few relevant behaviors, and subsequent behaviors strengthen the belief in the hypothesis. Subjects' written descriptions of the characters were coded as to whether the trait paired with that character (or a synonym) appeared in the description. For the characters of set size 3, 5, and 7, the percentage of subjects correctly mentioning the trait was 96%, 89%, and 96%, respectively. Interestingly, then, subjects were highly likely, and equally likely, to mention the trait for all three set sizes. I suggest that this corresponds to the hypothesis, and it is equally likely to be entertained at all three set sizes. However, when asked to rate the strength, clarity, and confidence in the impressions (Fig. 3.3), differences in the plausibility of the hypothesis appear. So although the hypothesis appears to be well formulated following just a few relevant acts, the strength of the belief in the hypothesis increases with subsequent behaviors.

In the second experiment, the behaviors were scrambled so that no single trait could be used to organize all of the acts studied with a given character. Under these conditions, the negative fan for true items was eliminated. In fact, response times as a function of set size to all item types showed a flat slope. In addition, the time to reject consistent falses was not longer than that to verify trues. Eliminating trait concepts as organizing tools prevented the magnitude of organization observed in the first experiment. Clearly, however, there was still some degree of organization, most likely as a function of forming an impression of each character. It was only in the third experiment, in which the behaviors were scrambled, the photos eliminated, and the learning task was changed to one of memorization, that organization appeared to be completely eliminated. Then positive fans were obtained across all three item types, and consistent and inconsistent falses were rejected fast, and equally fast.

Clearly, such an active, constructive process of trait inferences as that described herein will not be undertaken for every acquaintance encountered (Gordon & Wyer, 1987; Wyer & Gordon, 1984). We would spend our entire lives caught up in the process of forming impressions of others if we were to engage in such elaborate and detailed analysis of behavior for every person we encounter in day-to-day activities. Several factors make the proposed process more reasonable to manage. First, we are likely to engage in the construction of such a network of knowledge only for those with whom we have repeated interactions over a period of time. The bizarre laughing behavior of a fellow bus passenger might catch our attention and cause us to generate hypotheses to explain the behavior, but, in general, we will not bother to scrutinize the actions of every person on the bus and formulate hypotheses regarding his or her behavior. Impressions are likely to be better developed for those with whom we have frequent contact, and for those who have consequences for our lives (Neuberg & Fiske, 1987). The task is also made easier by the fact that individuals remain relatively stable over time. Once a well-formed impression is developed, new information will still be used to check on the accuracy of the knowledge stored, but, in general, little adjustment will be necessary. Finally, this inference process and the construction of impressions appears to be one at which humans are impressively adept. Simply knowing that a series of behaviors were all performed by a single person allows us to understand the behaviors in relation to one another, to see connections and patterns, and thereby to organize the bits of information into a coherent structure.

It is true, however, that the current theoretical push in cognitive psychology regarding the formation of similar knowledge structures is very much in a direction that is opposite to that proposed here. The development of exemplar-based models of category representation (Hintzman, 1986; Medin & Schaffer, 1978) were in large part a reaction against such constructive, abstraction-oriented prototype models of categories (Posner & Keele, 1968, 1970; Reed, 1972). The current emphasis on distributed memory models (McClelland & Rumelhart, 1985) similarly runs counter to top-down processes in the organization and representation of knowledge, and instead emphasize just how well a bottom-up system can function. Kintsch (1988) has argued that even in a domain such as text comprehension, the processes certainly need not be as theory-driven as has typically been assumed. In fact, many of the results of the reported studies can be accounted for without claiming that the trait concept, per se, is explicitly represented. One could argue that in comprehending each behavior, the subject understands the relation of the behavior to a trait concept, and in encoding the behavior, part of what is stored is this semantic analysis of the relation of the behavior to a trait dimension. With such an assumption, a model such as Hintzman's (1986) could account in large part for the obtained pattern of responses. The important distinction between this characterization and that of a constructive process is that it is only in the latter that the subject actively makes an inference about the trait attributes of the target. The former suggests a much more passive process of simply accumulating behaviors without deciding that the trait applies to the target, as in a memory-based process. It is extremely difficult to empirically distinguish between these two models. I have argued in favor of the constructive process, in particular given the difficulty with which subjects were prevented from forming impressions. The results of the present experiments, along with findings such as those of Anderson and Hubert (1963) and Dreben, Fiske, and Hastie (1979), in which a dissociation is found between a judgment and recall for information on which the judgment was presumably based, support the conclusion that trait inferences in impression formation result from on-line processes.

In sum, the present experiments suggest that behaviors performed by a target are organized with respect to trait concepts. The trait characterization is hypothesized after a few such behaviors are observed, and subsequent behaviors serve to strengthen, or to disconfirm, the hypothesis. This process of on-line formation of trait impressions results in a well-integrated structure of knowledge for each target. The process seems to operate relatively spontaneously, and it is difficult to prevent subjects from organizing the behaviors performed by a target. Although it is difficult to conclusively demonstrate on-line versus memory-based processes, the culmination of research on trait inferences suggests that this is an area in which on-line processes dominate.

ACKNOWLEDGMENTS

I would like to thank Reid Hastie for many hours of help with the studies and theortical argument presented in this chapter. Support for this work was partially provided by National Science Foundation Grant Number BNS-8606595 to the author.

REFERENCES

Anderson, J. R. (1974). Retrieval of propositional information from long-term memory. *Cognitive Psychology, 5,* 451–474.

Anderson, J. R. (1976). *Language, memory, and thought.* Hillsdale, NJ: Lawrence Erlbaum Associates.

Anderson, J. R., & Bower, G. H. (1973). *Human associative memory.* Washington, DC: Winston & Sons.

Anderson, N.H., & Hubert, S. (1963). Effects of concomitant verbal recall on order effects in personality impression formation. *Journal of Verbal Learning and Verbal Behavior, 2,* 379–391.

Asch, S. E. (1946). Forming impressions of personality. *Journal of Abnormal and Social Psychology, 41,* 258–290.

Bassili, J. N., & Smith, M. C. (1986). On the spontaneity of trait attribution: Converging evidence for the role of cognitive strategy. *Journal of Personality and Social Psychology,*

50, 239-245.
Dreben, E. K., Fiske, S. T., & Hastie, R. (1979). The independence of item and evaluative information: Impression and recall order effects in behavior-based impression formation. *Journal of Personality and Social Psychology, 37,* 1758-1768.
Gordon, S. E., & Wyer, R. S. (1987). Person memory: Category-set-size effects on the recall of a person's behavior. *Journal of Personality and Social Psychology, 53,* 648-662.
Hayes-Roth, B. (1977). Evolution of cognitive structures and processes. *Psychology Review, 84,* 260-278.
Hintzman, D. L. (1986). "Schema abstraction" in a multiple-trace memory model. *Psychological Review, 93,* 411-428.
Kanouse, D. E., & Hansen, L. R. (1971). Negativity in evaluations. In E. E. Jones, H. H. Kelley, R. E. Nisbett, S. Valins, & B. Weiner (Eds.), *Attribution: Perceiving the causes of behavior* (pp. 47-62). Morristown, NJ: General Learning Press.
Kintsch, W. (1988). The role of knowledge in discourse comprehension: A construction-integration model. *Psychological Review, 95,* 163-182.
Lopes, L. L. (1982). *Toward a procedural theory of judgment.* (Tech. Rep. No. 17). Madison: Wisconsin Human Information Processing Program.
McClelland, J. L., & Rumelhart, D. E. (1985). Distributed memory and the representation of general and specific information. *Journal of Experimental Psychology: General, 114,* 159-188.
Medin, D. L., & Schaffer, M. M. (1978). Context theory of classification learning. *Psychological Review, 85,* 207-238.
Moeser, S. D. (1977). Recognition processes in episodic memory. *Canadian Journal of Psychology, 31,* 41-70.
Moeser, S. D. (1979). The role of experimental design in investigations of the fan effect. *Journal of Experimental Psychology: Human Learning and Memory, 5,* 125-134.
Myers, J. L., O'Brien, E. J., Balota, D. A., & Toyofuka, M. L. (1984). Memory search without interference: The role of integration. *Cognitive Psychology, 16,* 214-242.
Neuberg, S. L., & Fiske, S. T. (1987). Motivational influences on impression formation: Outcome dependency, accuracy-driven attention, and individuating processes. *Journal of Personality and Social Psychology, 53,* 431-444.
Ostrom, T. M. (1975, August). *Cognitive representation of impressions.* Paper presented at the meeting of The American Psychological Association, Chicago.
Park, B. (1986). A method for studying the development of impressions of real people. *Journal of Personality and Social Psychology, 51,* 907-917.
Park, B., & Flink, C. (in press). A social relations analysis of agreement in liking judgments. *Journal of Personality and Social Psychology.*
Park, B., & Judd, C. M. (in press). Agreement on initial impressions: Differences due to perceivers, trait dimensions, and target behaviors. *Journal of Personality and Social Psychology.*
Posner, M. I., & Keele, S. W. (1968). On the genesis of abstract ideas. *Journal of Experimental Psychology, 77,* 353-363.
Posner, M. I., & Keele, S. W. (1970). Retention of abstract ideas. *Journal of Experimental Psychology, 83,* 304-308.
Ratcliff, R., & McKoon, G. (1981). Does activation really spread? *Psychological Review, 88,* 454-457.
Reder, L. M., & Anderson, J. R. (1980). A partial resolution of the paradox of interference: the role of integrating knowledge. *Cognitive Psychology, 12,* 447-472.
Reder, L. M., & Ross, B. H. (1983). Integrated knowledge in different tasks: The role of retrieval strategy on fan effects. *Journal of Experimental Psychology: Learning, Memory, and Cognition, 9,* 55-72.
Reed, S. K. (1972). Pattern recognition and categorization. *Cognitive Psychology, 3,* 383-407.

Rothbart, M., & Park, B. (1986). On the confirmability and disconfirmability of trait concepts. *Journal of Personality and Social Psychology, 50,* 131-142.

Smith, E. E. (1981). Organization of factual knowledge. In H. E. Howe, Jr. & J. H. Flowers (Eds.), *Nebraska symposium on motivation* (Vol. 28, pp. 161-209). Lincoln: University of Nebraska Press.

Smith, E. E., Adams, N., & Schorr, D. (1978). Fact retrieval and the paradox of interference. *Cognitive Psychology, 10,* 438-464.

Smith, E. R., & Miller, F. D. (1983). Mediation among attributional inferences and comprehension processes: Initial findings and a general method. *Journal of Personality and Social Psychology, 44,* 492-505.

Tulving, E., & Thomson, D. M. (1973). Encoding specificity and retrieval processes in episodic memory. *Psychological Review, 80,* 352-373.

Winter, L., & Uleman, J. S. (1984). When are social judgments made? Evidence for the spontaneousness of trait inferences. *Journal of Personality and Social Psychology, 47,* 237-252.

Winter, L., Uleman, J. S., & Cunniff, C. (1985). How automatic are social judgments? *Journal of Personality and Social Psychology, 49,* 904-917.

Wyer, R. S., & Gordon, S. E. (1984). The cognitive representation of social information. In R. S. Wyer, Jr. & T. K. Srull (Eds.), *Handbook of social cognition* (Vol. 2, pp. 73-150). Hillsdale, NJ: Lawrence Erlbaum Associates.

4

Traits as Action Categories Versus Traits as Person Attributes in Social Cognition

John N. Bassili
Scarborough Campus, University of Toronto

Traits are conspicuous elements of social description. In a recent study, for example, members of a college seminar were asked to describe each other at various times during the course (Park, 1986). Fully 65% of their descriptions involved trait concepts. Other studies that have examined open-ended descriptions of others have also supported the importance of traits, although the prevalence of trait references has not always been as striking as in Park's study (Fiske & Cox, 1979; Peevers & Secord, 1973).

The prominence of traits in interpersonal description has not been lost on theorists who have addressed phenomena of person perception. Traits, in fact, have been focal in every major theoretical approach to person perception. In his seminal paper on impression formation, Asch (1946) endeavored to explain how the perceiver integrates diverse characteristics of a person into a unified and coherent impression. Both the set of characteristics and the unified impression in Asch's account were conceptualized in terms of traits. Similarly, the attribution paradigm initiated by Heider (1958) concerned itself to an important degree with determining how people attribute stable dispositions, or traits, to others. In these cases, as well as others (e.g., Anderson, 1965; Rosenberg & Sedlak, 1972), the theoretical assumption has been that traits play a central role in mental representations of others.

Along with the importance granted traits in theoretical accounts of person perception processes, there has been a pervasive assumption among social psychologists that traits are essentially descriptors of people (e.g., Anderson, 1966; Asch, 1946; Jones & Davis, 1965). According to this view, traits are abstract conceptual categories that are used to describe others and to organize information about them (e.g., Cantor & Mischel, 1979; Hastie, 1980).

In this chapter, I refer to the approach that views traits as properties associated with actors as the "traits-as-person-attributes" approach. My aim is not to undermine this familiar and plausible notion. Instead, my thesis is that traits often enjoy a different status in social cognition. I argue that this other status, that I refer to as the "traits-as-event-categories" position, derives from the presence of trait concepts in action schemas that are essential to the interpretation of behavior. Specifically, I attempt to demonstrate that trait concepts can play a central role in capturing the meaning of an action without necessarily serving to describe enduring characteristics of actors.

TRAITS AS ACTION CATEGORIES VERSUS TRAITS AS PERSON ATTRIBUTES

Although the traits-as-person-attributes approach has had a long history in person perception research, it is illustrated most clearly by recent models of how information about persons is represented in memory (e.g., Hastie 1980; Srull, 1981; Wyer, Bodenhausen, & Srull, 1984). One of the first and most influential accounts of such representations was offered by Hastie and Kumar (1979) in the form of hierarchical network structures that were inspired by John Anderson's human associative memory (HAM) theory (Anderson, 1976; Anderson & Bower, 1973).

Figure 4.1 illustrates such a network. The mental structure it represents is composed of idea *nodes* and of associative *links*. At the top level of the structure is a node containing identifying features of the person, such as his

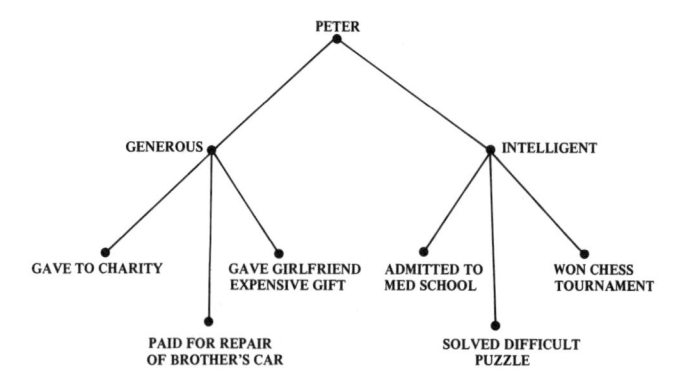

FIG. 4.1. A network structure representing trait information and specific behaviors. (After Hastie & Kumar, 1979).

or her proper name. This is the entry point of the structure from which a search for further information about the person originates. At the second level of the structure are concepts that describe the target and that organize more specific information about him or her. This is where trait concepts have been assumed to play a dominant role in describing others and in organizing information about them. At the bottom level of the hierarchy are examples of specific facts about the target. The facts most commonly represented at this level are behavior descriptions, although other specific facts, such as demographic features of the target, could also be represented here.

The basic assumption behind this approach is that behavioral information about a person is classified into trait categories and that these trait categories serve as efficient descriptors of a person's stable disposition. Suppose, for example, that the following facts were known about Peter: That he gave $1,000 to a charity, that he paid for the repair of his brother's car, and that he gave his girlfriend an expensive camera for Christmas. The perceiver may infer from these facts that Peter is a generous person. As a consequence, the trait "generous" will be linked to the node standing for Peter in the perceiver's mind, and the trait will in turn be linked to the specific behaviors that led to the inference of the traits. Other traits, stemming from other behaviors, may also be associated with Peter, so that upon being asked, "what is Peter like?," the perceiver could look up and report all the traits that are linked with the node representing Peter in memory.

This account of how facts about others are organized in memory has been supported by a number of studies (e.g., Srull, 1981; Srull, Lichtenstein, & Rothbart, 1985; Wyer, Bodenhausen, & Srull, 1984). It is very likely, therefore, that traits do indeed serve as organizing concepts when several pieces of information that are relevant to a person are encountered by a perceiver. This situation, however, is rare in real-world settings. Social encounters seldom afford the multitudes of behavior descriptions that have been given to subjects in experiments that have investigated and provided support for the traits-as-person-attributes notion. Instead, behavioral information in such real-time situations tends to arrive in small pieces and is often not processed in the context of a prior expectation. In such situations, traits may not so readily assume their role of descriptors of actors. This is not to say that traits are irrelevant to situations where little information is available about a target. Instead, I believe that, in such situations, traits can assist in the interpretation and categorization of behavior, without necessarily being attributed to actors. This is when traits serve to capture the meaning of behavior rather than to describe people.

The traits-as-person-attributes approach focuses on the associations that link behaviors to traits and traits to actors. As a consequence, little emphasis is placed in this approach on the preliminary information processing that invokes the appropriate trait concept in response to a particular behavioral episode. This stage of behavior comprehension, however, is far from trivial because it sets the foundations for subsequent processes of person perception (Heider, 1958; Jones & Davis, 1965; Trope, 1986; Wyer & Srull, 1986). This is particularly true in on-line processing conditions where the organization and interpretation of the incoming behavior flow constitute a dominant preoccupation for the perceiver.

To illustrate the richness of the processes involved in the comprehension of a sentence such as the one about Peter, I borrow from recent cognitive theories of the representation of meaning-based knowledge (e.g., Anderson, 1976; Kintsch, 1974; Norman & Rumelhart, 1975). My first assumption is that the information conveyed by this sentence can be represented in terms of propositions (cf. Hastie, 1980). Propositions are the smallest units of knowledge that can stand autonomously. The top panel of Fig. 4.2 illustrates a way of representing the meaning of the sentence, "Peter gave $1,000 to a charity," in propositional terms. For simplicity, I have adopted the representational convention used by Anderson (1985).

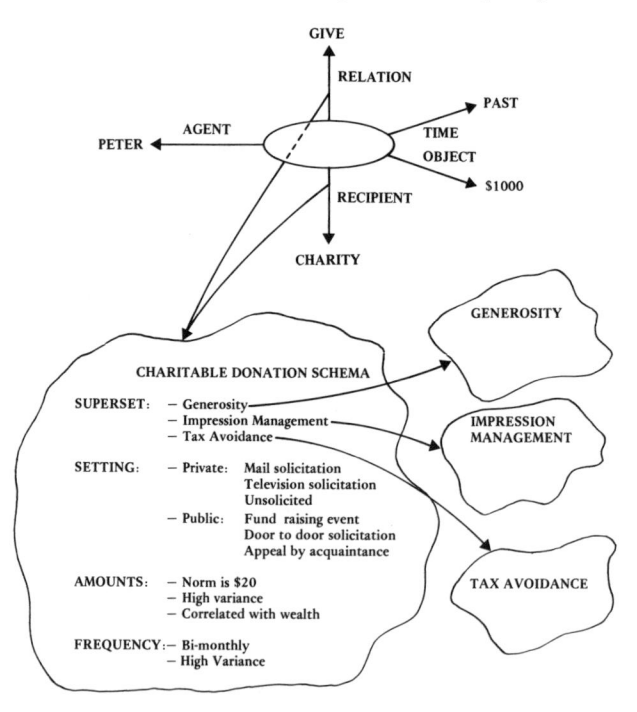

FIG. 4.2. Example of a propositional representation of the sentence "Peter gave $1,000 to a charity" (top panel), an action schema for the interpretation of the sentence (left bottom), and superset concepts linked to the schema (right bottom).

The ellipse in Fig. 4.2 represents the proposition that is linked to its relation and arguments by means of labeled arrows. As it stands, this proposition does a fine job of capturing the information that is stated explicitly in the stimulus sentence. The sentence, however, is likely to conjure up much more meaning than it explicitly states. For example, the perceiver is likely to "know" that the giving in this situation does not imply that anything will be received in return (as, for example, if Peter had *paid* $1,000 to the *store*). The perceiver is also likely to know that $1,000 is a relatively large amount to give to a charity, and finally, the perceiver is likely to assume that Peter has derived personal satisfaction from his act. But if this additional knowledge is not part of the propositional representation of the explicit sentence information, then where does it come from?

The second assumption I make is that the perceiver brings more to the comprehension of stimulus information than a simple capacity to analyze its explicit propositional structure. In addition, the perceiver has generic knowledge that can contribute more information to the representation of the stimulus meaning than is explicitly there at the outset. This preexisting knowledge has, in various circumstances, been described in terms of "frames" (Minsky, 1975), "scripts" (Schank & Abelson, 1977), and "prototypes" (Rosch, 1975). More generally, the label used to describe preexisting abstract knowledge structures is "schema" (Bartlett, 1932, Neisser, 1976). For our purposes it will suffice to assume that *action* schemas are particularly pertinent to the perception of social behavior.

The application of an action schema to our example is illustrated in the lower part of Fig. 4.2. The propositional information that is explicitly stated in the stimulus sentence contains arguments that have the power to elicit relevant action schemas from the perceiver's general knowledge base. In our example, the relation "giving" and the recipient "charity" provide a strong basis for the activation of a "charitable donation" schema. The bottom panel of Fig. 4.1 illustrates the type of knowledge that may be contained in such a schema.

One useful way of capturing the abstract interrelational quality of the schema is to represent its content in terms of a number of slots that specify values that are relevant to the action in question (cf. Anderson, 1985). For example. Fig. 4.2 contains slots for "setting," and "frequency." One or more values is associated with each of these slots, and these values provide the information against which specific events can be evaluated. The $1,000 that Peter gave to the charity would, for example, appear high *in comparison* to the normative value of $20 specified in the schema. By the same token, the perceiver may make some schema-based assumptions about the setting for the donation despite the fact that the stimulus sentence provided no information about it.

In addition to slots having to do with values for specific features of an event, I assume that schemas contain a slot that plays a particularly important role in capturing the gist of the stimulus information. This slot consists of the superset of the action described by the schema. In our example, charitable donations are construed as potential subsets of "generous" behaviors, of "impression management" behaviors, and of "tax avoidance" behaviors. It is not trivial in the domain of person perception that a particular action schema may allow for the categorization of behavior into more than a single category. The fact that social behavior can potentially be explained in a variety of ways is *the* central tenet of attribution theory, and the multiple values associated with the superset slot of an action schema provide a useful means of capturing inherent ambiguities in social behavior.

Of more direct relevance to our present purposes is the fact that each value of the superset slot provides a way of categorizing the action in question. This is because values of the superset slot represent more abstract schemas than does the action schema itself and carry with them all the properties of these superordinate schemas. As an illustration, one of the superset values in the charitable donation schema has to do with generous behavior and is therefore linked to a schema having to do with generosity. Similarly, the value having to do with impression management will give access to all features of the schema that defines this concept. In each of these cases, the invocation of a superordinate schema supplies internally coherent and abstract elements of meaning to the stimulus information or, put another way, provides a gist interpretation of that information.

Given the diversity of meanings that can be derived from an action schema, the question arises as to which meaning will actually get selected in a particular situation. I believe that there are two ways to arrive at the meaning. First, under conditions where sufficient information is available, features of the action schema will determine the value of the superset slot that is given precedence over the others. For example, if the perceiver learned that Peter gave the $1,000 secretly in response to a mail solicitation, and that his income is such that he would benefit little from a tax deduction, then the slot value having to do with generosity would most likely be invoked, and the other two values would be rejected. The dynamics of this process should be familiar to anyone acquainted with attribution theory, because it has receive direct attention from theorists such as Heider (1958), Jones and Davis (1965), and, most particularly with respect to its schematic properties, by Kelley (1972).

In many situations, however, the perceiver does not have the type of additional information that would permit the rejection of potential explanations for the event. Under such circumstances, it is likely that the selection of values from the superset slot will be based on default likelihoods. For a particular individual, the default schematic likelihood that a charitable donation has to do with generosity, for example, may be 70%, whereas those having to do with impression management or tax avoidance may be 20% and 10%, respectively. All else being equal, therefore, that individual will assume that a charitable donation is a generous act.

The fundamental distinction between the traits-as-action-categories and traits-as-person-attributes notions is that, in the former case, a trait concept is invoked in the description of behavior, whereas in the latter case, it is also invoked in the description of the actor. As such, the distinction will be familiar to students of attribution theory because it played a central role in Jones and Davis's (1965) theory of correspondent inference. Correspondent inference was defined by Jones and Davis as "the extent that the act and the underlying characteristic or attribute are similarly described by the inference" (p. 223). Thus, according to this definition, it is possible for a perceiver to "describe" (categorize cognitively) a behavior in a certain way without necessarily inferring that the description applies to the actor. This, of course, is analogous to categorizing Peter's charitable donation as generous behavior without attributing generosity to Peter.

In the section that follows, I review evidence from three experimental paradigms that is consistent with the distinction between the traits-as-attributes and the traits-as-action-categories notions. These lines of evidence do not each make an irrevocable case for the importance of the traits-as-action-categories element of behavior perception. Collectively, however, they present a picture of on-line person perception processes where trait concepts play a pervasive role both in the identification of behavior and in the description of others.

EVIDENCE SUPPORTING THE TRAITS-AS-ACTION-CATEGORIES NOTION

Major advances in social cognition were made recently with the introduction of indirect cognitive indices of trait encoding during behavior comprehension. By avoiding problems of demand characteristics and response bias, these methods have opened promising windows on the on-line cognitive processes that underlie person perception phenomena. Each of the three lines of evidence that I review here relies on one such methodology. Together, their results provide interesting insights into the role of traits both in behavior perception and in person attribution.

EVIDENCE BASED ON REACTION TIMES

In an important study, Smith and Miller (1983) measured how long it took subjects to answer questions about sentences that suggested traits. Their aim was to explore relations among a number of social judgments by testing their relative speed. Subjects read sentences such as "Edward has his neighbors over for dinner" and had to answer one of several questions about the actor. Smith and Miller reasoned that answering times should be reduced to the extent that the answers had been inferred during the reading and comprehension of the sentences. One question in particular, which asked about the gender of the actor, served as a control to establish how long it would take to answer a question that required no inference.

Each trial of this experiment, which was conducted by computer, began with the presentation of a sentence such as the one about Edward. Subjects pressed a key to indicate comprehension of the sentence and were then presented with a one-word probe question, the meaning of which had been learned prior to the experimental procedure. "FRIENDLY?," for example, asked subjects to answer by "yes" or "no" whether they thought Edward was friendly, and "MALE?" asked them whether Edward was male.

Subjects in this experiment were as fast at verifying that a trait applied to the actor (e.g., Edward is friendly) as at verifying the gender of the actor (e.g., Edward is male). By contrast, questions about traits not suggested by the sentences (e.g., Edward is clever) and about whether it was something about the actor or the situation that caused the action described in the sentence took substantially longer to answer. Starting with the assumption that answering the gender question required no inference, Smith and Miller reasoned that trait inferences occurred as the stimulus sentences were comprehended and thus necessitated no inference during responding.

The speed of trait judgments in Smith and Miller's experiment is provocative, especially in juxtaposition with the relatively long times taken for attributional judgments. Still, the conclusion that trait inferences about actors occurred during comprehension suffers from an interpretive problem. The problem is that the alacrity of both the gender and the trait judgments may derive from the relatively simple and direct inferences they require rather than from the lack of such inferences during the question-answering phase.

Despite this problem, Smith and Miller's results contain a noteworthy finding, namely that the verification that a trait is implied by a sentence can be done *very* quickly. It is interesting that in these results, the disqualification of a trait that is *not* implied by a sentence takes considerably longer than the affirmation of a trait that *is* implied by it. It is not that trait judgments are generally fast, therefore, but that questions about implied traits can be answered particularly readily.

One interpretation of this result, as we have seen, is that implied traits are attributed to the actor during the comprehension process. In answering a subsequent question about the trait, therefore, the perceiver needs only verify that an association exists between the trait and the actor. Because no inference is required at this point, the answer can be arrived at very quickly. This interpretation stems directly from the trait-as-attribute view.

However, there is another possibility based on the traits-as-action-categories notion that is also consistent with the finding of rapid verification of implied traits. According to this view, the comprehension process may involve the activation of an action schema having to do with behavior toward neighbors. Here, friendliness may feature prominently in the superset slot of this schema. Upon being asked if "friendly" describes the person in the sentence (Edward), the subject may simply check the trait against the gist interpretation of the sentence and answer yes the moment a match is found. It is instructive that all sentences in this study were specifically selected to imply a high likelihood trait. It is natural, therefore, that such traits would enjoy high status in the superset slots of the relevant action schemas.

There is a feature of the traits-as-action-categories hypothesis that may appear perplexing, especially in light of the fact that the trait question is phrased in such a way as to inquire about the *actor* in the stimulus sentence. Why would subjects answer whether traits apply to actors on the basis of the gist of behavior if they have not attributed the traits to the actors? The answer, I believe, is that they have no choice. Smith and Miller's procedure involves single sentences that provide little basis for a judgment other than the actions they describe. From the point of view of the subject, therefore, answering questions about the actor and answering questions about the gist of their actions may be functionally equivalent.

Recently, Smith and his colleagues (Smith, 1984; Smith & Branscombe, 1987; Smith, Branscombe, & Bormann, 1988; see chap. 2 in this volume for a review) have developed an account of behavior-to-trait inferences based on the efficiency of "if-then" productions. Although traits are still considered inferences about people in this approach, I believe that Smith's notion of procedural efficiency is equally applicable to traits in their role of behavior descriptors.

To summarize, Smith and Miller's reaction-time study demonstrates that trait judgments are made very quickly when the stimulus information is highly suggestive of the trait. I have argued that the rapidity of these judgments may be attributable as much to the presence of the suggested trait in the action schema that served to interpret the stimulus sentence as to the attribution of the trait to the actor during the comprehension process. This finding, therefore, is as consistent with the traits-as-action categories notion as it is with the traits-as-person-attributes notion.

Cued-Recall Studies

An exciting cued-recall methodology was recently introduced by Uleman and his colleagues to investigate the spontaneity of trait inferences in on-line social judgments (Winter & Uleman, 1984; Winter, Uleman, & Cunniff, 1985). The methodology is based on Tulving's encoding specificity hypothesis (Tulving & Thomson, 1973), which holds that contextual events at input determine the structure of a memory representation and hence its retrievability. In particular, the effectiveness of a cue at retrieving information from memory has been shown to depend on whether the cue was encoded with the information at the time of presentation. For example, Thomson and Tulving (1970) have demonstrated that recall is best when an input cue is present during retrieval. When recall is cued by unstudied semantic associates of the stimulus, performance is no better than noncued recall.

Winter and Uleman (1984) and Winter et al. (1985) applied the encoding specificity paradigm to the study of trait attributions. Their study material consisted of sentences similar to those developed by Smith and Miller (1983) — for example, "The secretary solves the mystery half-way through the book." They reasoned that if a trait inference (e.g., clever) is made spontaneously as the sentence is comprehended, then the inference will be stored with the sentence and should act as a good retrieval cue for the sentence.

Uleman and his colleagues (Winter & Uleman, 1984; Winter et al., 1985) reported two experiments where the effectiveness of dispositional cues at retrieving the actor, verb, object, and prepositional phrase of each sentence was compared to the effectivness of semantic asssociates of the actor as cues (e.g., typewriter). In both cases, dispositional cues proved more effective than semantic cues at retrieving most sentence parts, leading the investigators to conclude that trait attributions were encoded with the memory representation of the sentences and must, therefore, have been inferred during comprehension.

Some conditions of the preceding experiments also led Uleman and his colleagues to suggest that trait inferences actually occur automatically during the comprehension process. Specifically, they noted that the superiority of dispositional cues over semantic cues in their experiments manifested itself under conditions where (a) subjects had no awareness of having inferred traits, (b) subjects had little reason to intend to infer traits, and (c) concurrent cognitive activities did not interfere with the effectiveness of trait cues. Because lack of awareness, intentionality, and interference have all been invoked as criteria for automatic processing in the cognitive literature (Schneider & Shiffrin, 1977; Shiffrin & Schneider, 1977), Uleman and his colleagues reasoned that trait inferences in their experiments may have occurred not only spontaneously (i.e., without solicitation from the experimenter) but automatically as part and parcel of the comprehension process.

The preceding account of trait encoding clearly falls in the tradition that views traits as attributes. The notion is that, upon reading a sentence such as the one with the secretary, the subject may infer the trait "clever" automatically, and thus form a cognitive representation of the secretary that includes a link with the trait. I believe that this view suffers from two problems, one associated with the claim of automatism in trait encoding, and the other with the assumption that trait concepts in this paradigm are necessarily linked to actors.

With respect to autonomatism, the problem is that although lack of awareness, intentionality, and inference are indeed criteria for automatic processes, these criteria are also consistent with processes that do not occur at all. To demonstrate automatism, it is necessary to demonstrate that a process occurs consistently and that its occurrence is characterized by the criteria. The consistent, unsolicited occurrence of trait encoding during sentence comprehension, however, has not been established unambiguously.

For example, Marilyn Smith and I (Bassili & Smith, 1986) replicated Winter and Uleman's (1984) research with the addition of a variable manipulating the orienting task given to subjects. Following Winter and Uleman, half of the subjects were asked to study the stimulus sentences for later recall. The other half of the subjects, however, were asked to think about the kind of person the subject of the sentence was. We reasoned that if subjects consistently make trait attributions automatically or spontaneously, then their performance in recalling sentences cued by dispositional traits should be similar under the two orienting tasks. This, however, was not the case: The retrieval effectiveness of dispositional cues was sharply superior following attribution instructions than following memory instructions.

In a related study (Bassili, 1987), I extended the range of orienting tasks to five. Subjects in this study were asked for each sentence either: (a) to think of a trait to describe the actor in the sentence; (b) to rate the likeability of the actor; (c) to form an image of the action described in the sentence; (d) to memorize the sentence; or (e) simply to understand the sentence. Again, my results revealed that the cue effectiveness of dispositional traits depend in an important way on the cognitive strategy adopted by subjects while reading the stimulus sentences. Specifically, when trait cues were provided, sentences learned under instructions to think of traits were recalled better than sentences learned under either imagery or impression instructions. Recall performance following impression formation instruction was, in turn, significantly superior to that following comprehension and memory instructions. These results, along with similar ones on the effect of orienting tasks reported by Moskowitz and Uleman (1987), further raise doubts about the consistent automatism or spontaneity of trait encoding during comprehension (see also Uleman, Newman, & Winter, 1988).

We turn now to the assumption that traits in this paradigm represent inferences about actors. This assumption is related to the logic of the encoding specificity notion, which states that the effectiveness of a cue for retrieving information from memory depends on whether the cue was encoded with the information during encoding. In applying this logic to trait encoding, Uleman and his colleagues have suggested that the cue effectiveness of a trait reflects its presence in the memory representation of the initial information by virtue of having been inferred about the actor. There is a problem with this logic, however, because although the cue effectiveness of a trait may well reflect its presence in the cognitive representation of the initial information, it does not necessarily indicate that the trait is there because it was inferred about the actor. According to the traits-as-action-categories notion, the trait concept may be part of the action schema that was initially used to interpret the stimulus sentence. Cleverness, for example, may be an important entry in the action schema that is invoked to interpret situations where mysteries are solved prematurely. The recall cue "clever," therefore, may derive its effectiveness from the access it provides to the stimulus information via the relevant interpretive schema rather than via an association with the subject of the sentence.

This possibility is demonstrated nicely in research on a similar problem involving instrument inferences rather than trait inferences. Paris and Lindauer (1976) constructed sentences describing actions that made it very likely that particular instruments were used. In half of the sentences, the high-probability instrument was explicitly mentioned (e.g., The lawyer cooked dinner on a stove), whereas in the rest of the sentences, the instrument was only implicit (e.g., The lawyer cooked dinner). In a subsequent recall task, the instrument cue was as effective in aiding recall of the sentences when the instrument had been implicit as when it had been presented explicitly. From this, and in accordance with the encoding specificity hypothesis, Paris and Lindauer argued that the instruments must have been inferred as the sentences were read. This reasoning, of course, is identical to that used in the application of the encoding specificity hypothesis to investigate the spontaneity of trait inferences.

The reasoning, however, suffers from a problem that was demonstrated by Corbett and Dosher (1978), who replicated the Paris and Lindauer study with the addition of a condition where the high likelihood instrument was replaced in the sentence by another less probable intrument. For example, the high likelihood instrument "scissors" in the sentence "The athlete cut out an article with scissors for his friend" was replaced by the less likely instrument "razorblade." Corbett and Dosher reasoned that because the latter sentence mentions an instrument, it gives no opportunity for subjects to infer that scissors were involved in the action. Yet, their results demonstrated that the high-likelihood instruments were just as effective at cuing recall of sentences that mentioned another instrument as they were at cuing recall of sentences that mentioned the high likelihood instrument or that made no mention of an instrument.

This result raises serious questions about the use of cue effectiveness as an index of inferences that occur at encoding. Instead, it suggests that cue effectiveness may have to do with an interaction between processes that occur at encoding and processes that occur at retrieval. In fact, Corbett and Dosher (1978) explained their finding by suggesting a mechanism that is analogous to that described here in relation to the traits-as-action-categories notion. Specifically, they stated that "Cue effectiveness apparently may be mediated by abstract preexperimental relations linking the object to the instrument role" (p. 489). These relations were further conceived as originating in schemata that were activated in the course of sentence comprehension. Thus, for example, the action of "cutting something out of a newspaper" may trigger a schema that contains "scissors" as an important entry. The presence of scissors in the action described in the sentence may be negated by an explicit reference to another instrument, but the object "scissors" will still be an effective retrieval cue for the stimulus material by virtue of being part of the relevant interpretive schema.

The implications of Corbett and Dosher's result for the traits-as-action-categories notion are important. By analogy, one may imagine a situation where an actor who is known to have a certain trait engages in behavior that is inconsistent with that trait. For example, consider the information that Peter, the known scrooge, gave $1,000 to a charity. If we made the unwarranted assumption that the information that Peter is a scrooge does not interact with the information about his charitable donation, then Corbett and Dosher's result would suggest that the cue "generous" would still be effective in retrieving the sentence even though it could not have been inferred about Peter. The reason for the effectiveness of the cue in this imaginary situation would derive directly from the traits-as-action-categories notion. Specifically, the link between the stimulus information and the trait "generous" would exist by virtue of the presence of the trait in the action schema used in the interpretation of the charitable donation and not from its association with the actor.

It is unfortunate that people's propensity for "resolving" inconsistent information about others (Asch & Zukier, 1984) vitiates the possibility of conducting an experiment analogous to Corbett and Dosher's with traits. Be that as it may, Corbett and Dosher's results raise serious questions about the interpretation of cued-recall studies that aim to test whether inferences are made spontaneously at encoding. More importantly, their results provide a clear indication of the power of interpretive schemas in supplying information that gets linked with the cognitive representation of the stimulus event.

Before leaving cued-recall studies, I would like to discuss another result that I believe is also consistent with the traits-as-action-categories notion.

The result stems from two studies by Uleman and his colleagues (Uleman, Newman, & Winter, 1988; Winter, Uleman, & Cunniff, 1985), where subjects read sentences such as "The child tells his mother that he ate the chocolates" and then tried to recall them in the presence of a cue consisting of a semantic associate of the actor (toys), a trait suggested by the sentence (honest), or a word capturing the gist of the sentence (confessing). Gist cues proved at least as effective in aiding recall of the sentences as trait cues, and both were significantly more effective than semantic cues in doing so.

Although this result has received little attention in the past, I believe that it demonstrates one of the most important phenomena to sprout from the application of the encoding specificity paradigm to the study of trait inferences. Specifically, it demonstrates that the effectiveness of a cue may depend on whether it conveys gist information about the to-be-recalled stimulus rather than on whether it was inferred about the actor during the comprehension of that stimulus.

Together, therefore, this result and that reported by Corbett and Dosher in the context of instrument inferences raise some doubts about the trait-as-attribute interpretation of cued-recall studies. The action-schema and traits-as-action-categories notions, in contrast, provide an attractive alternative explanation for these results.

Word-Fragment Completion Research

So far, the argument I have presented for the traits-as-action-categories view has been based on retrospective interpretation of existing data. To be convincing, the distinction between the traits-as-action-categories and traits-as-person-attributes views ought to lead to predictions that can be tested in new research. Recently, I have completed a study that provides such a test (Bassili, in press). The study relied on a word-fragment completion task where the object is to complete words from which letters have been deleted (e.g., g-n−o-s or c-r-le-s). Recent research (e.g., Schacter, 1987; Tulving, Schacter, & Stark, 1982; Watkins & Peynircioglu, 1984) has demonstrated that this task is very sensitive to prior exposure to a word. In fact, if the reader attempts to solve these two word-fragments, he or she may find the first one easier than the second (generous and careless, respectively) even though normative data show them to be of about equal difficulty. In the past, I have conducted research with Marilyn Smith and Colin MacLeod (Bassili & Smith, 1986; Bassili, Smith, & MacLeod, in press) that demonstrates that the technique is sensitive to the activation of inferred words as well as actually seen ones.

The purpose of the study was to distinguish between two conditions, one where a trait is specifically linked to the actor in a sentence and one where a trait is activated without necessarily being linked to the actor. The logic behind the approach is that when traits act as attributes of actors, links should exist between traits and the actors that they describe. When traits serve to categorize action, however, they may show general activation without being specifically linked to actors.

Subjects in the relevant conditions of the study were instructed to form an impression of the target people. The stimulus information they received consisted of vignettes describing events involving a number of people. A third of the vignettes contained distinctiveness and consensus information that suggested a person attribution, a third contained distinctiveness and consensus information that suggested a situation attribution, and the rest contained irrelevant attributional information. For example, the sentence "The secretary solved the mystery halfway through the book" was followed by one of the following continuations: "The secretary often solves mysteries before the end of books. Few other people who read this mystery solved it before the end of the book" (low distinctiveness and low consensus); "The secretary seldom solves mysteries before the end of books. Many other people who read this mystery solved it before the end of the book (high distinctiveness and high consensus); or "The secretary is 38 years old. She lives in a high-rise and commutes to work" (irrelevant information).

Stimulus vignettes were presented to subjects in a counterbalanced manner so that each appeared an equal number of times with each type of information across subjects. In addition, a portion of the vignettes was withheld from each subject in order to provide baserates for word-fragment completion performance under "unprimed" conditions.

Following the presentation of the stimulus vignettes, subjects were presented with word-fragments of the traits suggested by the opening sentences (e.g., "clever" in the case of the sentence involving the secretary). To differentiate between the activation of a trait concept that occurred independently from association with an actor and the activation that occurred in conjunction with such an association, half of the word-fragments were accompanied by a cue, whereas the other half were presented alone. The cue always consisted of the actor of the relevant sentence ("secretary" in the preceding example).

The purpose of the cue was to assess specifically the relation between traits and actors. According to the traits-as-person-attributes view, the completion of recently activated trait-fragments should be facilitated by a simultaneous cue representing the actor with whom the trait has been associated. This is because an associative link should exist between attributes and actors about whom the attributes have been inferred. The traits-as-action-categories view, however, posits that a trait concept can be activated without necessarily being associated with an actor. The activation in this case is assumed to result from the presence of the trait in a schema that served in the comprehension of the stimulus information. When this is the case, trait-completion may indicate prior activation without benefiting from the presence of an actor cue.

Table 4.2 shows the increases in trait-fragment completion performance over baseline in the various presentation conditions of this experiment. The first question of interest is whether there is any evidence in these data for the association of traits with actors. According to Kelley's (1967) covariation model, trait attributions should occur particularly when covariation information suggests a person attribution. This, therefore, is the condition where the actor cue should prove particularly effective in aiding the completion of fragmented trait words. This expectation is clearly confirmed by the results: Cued trait-completion performance was superior in the person-information condition to that in either the situation or the irrelevant-information condition.

According to the trait-as-action-categories notion, trait concepts can be activated independently from associations with actors. To test for this kind of activation, the following test was performed. Trait completion performance was compared to baseline performance in the five cells where no trait–actor association was predicted or indicated in the preceding results (see Table 4.1). Overall, performance in these conditions was significantly better than baseline performance, indicating that trait concepts were activated even without being associated with actors.

The picture that emerges from these results is one where trait concepts are activated alone and, in an incremental fashion, in association with actors. It appears, therefore, that by the time the initial behavioral information is comprehended and categorized, a trait has already emerged as a salient entity in the representation of the stimulus input. Whether or not the trait is associated with the actor, however, depends on the presence of relevant contextual information.

This picture bears strong similarities to that presented by attribution theorists such as Jones and Davis (1965) in their account of trait attribution processes. It is ironic, however, that Kelley's (1967) covariation model has been construed in terms that are relatively free of trait concepts. For example, Jones and McGillis (1976) have suggested that Kelley's (1967) model is more attuned to determining whether causality is to be attributed

TABLE 4.1
Percentage Increase in Word-Fragment Completion Performance from Baseline

	Covariation Information		
	Person	*Situation*	*Irrelevant*
Cue	14.0	6.2	5.5
No cue	6.2	6.2	3.2

to the person or to the situation than to determining whether specific traits apply to actors. The traits-as-action-categories notion, along with the present results, suggests that trait concepts become cognitively relevant very early in the comprehension of behavior. Whether or not covariation information suggests that something about the person caused an event, the "something" is likely to be conceptualized in terms of traits. Moreover, when covariation information suggests a person attribution, the trait is likely to be linked to the actor.

DISCUSSION

In this chapter, I have argued that traits play two roles in social cognition, one that has been explicitly recognized in past theorizing and another that has been implicit. The first role relates to the function that traits serve in cognitive representations of *people*, whereas the second relates to their function in cognitive representations of *behavior*. Although these two roles stand in a complementary rather than a contradictory relation, recent discussions of social judgment processes have focused exclusively on the former role while neglecting the latter.

Three lines of enquiry have formed the basis of my review. The first, which was reported by Smith and Miller (1983), relied on a reaction-time methodology. The finding of greatest interest in this research is that question about whether implied traits are true can be answered very quickly. In fact, because such judgments can be made as fast as the verification of gender from a person's first name, they seem to require no inference-making. I have argued that this finding is also consistent with the trait-as-action-categories view. Specifically, I have attributed the rapidity of the judgment to the presence of the trait-concept in the action schema that served in the initial interpretation of the actor's behavior. In other words, trait verification is rapid because it only requires that a match exist between the trait and elements of the cognitive representation of the stimulus information.

The second line of enquiry was based on the encoding specificity hypothesis and on the power of trait cues to aid recall. The main finding deriving from this research is that, when behavioral information clearly implies a trait, that trait can be quite effective in cueing the recall of that information. When interpreted in the context of the trait-as-attribute notion, this result suggests that the trait must have been linked to the actor during the initial encoding of the information.

I have argued, however, that two ancillary findings make the trait-as-action-categories interpretation of this results particularly attractive. The first of these was reported by Corbett and Dosher (1978) in research on instrument inferences. Cues consisting of instruments normally associated with particular actions proved just as effective in retrieving sentences describing such actions when *other* instruments were mentioned in the sentences as when the high likelihood instruments were mentioned explicitly or remained implicit. Because the mention of alternate instruments makes it unlikely that the common ones were inferred at encoding, this result undermines the utility of cue-effectiveness as an index of spontaneous inferences. Instead, it suggests that the cue-effectiveness of high-likelihood instruments derives from their links with the schemas that serve to interpret the stimulus information. This, of course, is exactly the point that I have been promoting in the realm of traits.

The second result within the cued-recall paradigm that supports the traits-as-action-categories notion has to do specifically with gist cues. In two studies, Uleman and his colleagues (Uleman, Newman, & Winter, 1988; Winter, Uleman, & Cunniff, 1985) found that a cue that captured the gist of a sentence was at least as effective in cueing the recall of the sentence as traits that were implied by it. The very fact that gist cues are so effective at aiding recall demonstrates that features associated with *sentence meaning* rather than with *actors*, can mediate the effects observed in cued-recall studies. Although the mechanisms responsible for the effect of gist cues in these studies may differ from those responsible for the effect of trait cues, this finding raises the possibility that the effectiveness of trait cues derives from their function as action categories rather than their function as actor attribute.

The most direct evidence for the distinction between the trait-as-attribute and the traits-as-action-categories notions stems from research that used a trait-fragment completion task. Because this task is sensitive to the prior activation of a concept, it provides a good measure of the extent to which a trait has been invoked during the processing of behavioral information. By adding to this task a manipulation of the presence of an actor cue, it is further possible to assess if trait activation has occurred in association with an actor or independently.

I have reported an experiment that used this methodology to demonstrate that behavioral information can result in trait activation both in association with actors and in the absence of such associations. This finding provides positive evidence for the dual role that traits can play in the cognitive representation of behavioral information. Moreover, it provides, along with the previous results, a good basis for the distinction between situations where traits act as attributes of actors and situations where they serve as categories of actions.

The Distinction in a Broader Theoretical Context

The distinction drawn in this chapter has parallels in the person-perception literature. In his seminal book, Heider (1958) described the complexities of behavior perception by demonstrating the equivocal relation that exists between acts and their potential meanings. The doing of a favor, for example, is ambiguous in that it can "mean" any number of things, such as friendliness, grateful reciprocity, expectant self-interest, or grudging obligation. Fortunately, contextual information often allows the perceiver to choose one from among several potential meanings of behavior.

Even when this is done, however, an attributional problem remains before a dispositional inference can be made. For example, even the unambiguously friendly behavior of a person can be caused by situational forces. According to Heider, this additional inferential step also requires disambiguating information that relates to concepts such as "intend," "try," and "can."

Subsequent attribution theorists made it even clearer that dispositional attributions consist of two stages, one having to do with the interpretation of behavior and the other with the mapping of the interpretation into properties of the actor and of the environment. As we saw earlier, Jones and Davis (1965) suggested that trait attribution consists, to an important degree, of the description of actors and their behavior in corresponding terms. In other words, the mere perception and identification of behavior involves concepts that are also relevant to the description of actor characteristics.

Recently, Trope (1986; chap. 6 in this volume) has argued that attribution processes can be decomposed into a behavioral identification component and a dispositional inference component. Like other attribution theorists before him, Trope assumes that identification processes initially represent behavioral information in terms of categories that are relevant to dispositional attributions. The output of the identification process in Trope's model serves as input to inferential processes that are responsible for dispositional attributions.

Although Trope did not elaborate on the role of trait concepts in the two components of his model, the analysis I have presented here is compatible with his identification-inference decomposition. The distinctive and innovative aspect of Trope's model consists of its predictions regarding how behavioral and situational cues interact at the two stages of the model to produce final attributions.

There is another line of investigation in social cognition that is generally compatible with the notion that social behavior is analyzed in trait terms early during the comprehension process. There is now an extensive literature demonstrating that trait constructs can be "primed" by exposure to relevant behavior descriptions and that such priming influences the subsequent interpretation of behavior (e.g., Higgins, Rholes, & Jones, 1977; Smith & Branscombe, 1988; Srull & Wyer, 1979, 1980). In a series of studies for example, Srull and Wyer presented subjects with a number of priming items consisting of scrambled words such as "leg break arm his" from which subjects could form sentences relevant to a trait construct (hostility in this case). Subsequently, subjects read about a target person in a paragraph that described behaviors ambiguous with respect to the primed construct. The interpretation of ambiguous behaviors as well as ratings of the target person were affected significantly by the priming sentences, suggesting that the initial priming sentences as well as the ambiguous behaviors were categorized in terms of a trait concept.

Although the correspondence between behavior description and actor description has been implicit in most of attribution theory, this correspondence has not previously been related to the dual role of trait concepts that I have discussed here. This omission, I believe, derives from two factors that have little to do with a conceptual enmity for the description of behavior in trait terms.

The first factor has to do with the fact that very little attention has been given in person perception research to processes of behavior perception. With the exception of isolated efforts (e.g., Bassili, 1976; Heider & Simmel, 1944; Heider, 1958; Newtson, 1976; McArthur & Baron, 1983) and the investigations on the perception of emotions (e.g., Bassili, 1978, 1979; Ekman & Friezen, 1975), little attention has been directed at the mechanisms responsible for the perception and identification of social behavior. Instead, most person perception research has focused on phenomena that start from the point where behavior, or even traits, have already been identified. It is not surprising, therefore, that few accounts of the concepts that are relevant to behavior perception have surfaced in the literature.

The second factor that has mitigated against the use of trait concepts to explain behavior perception may have to do with the dictionary definition of the term. By definition, traits are distinguishing features of people. The point I stress in this chapter is that the very cognitive structure that gives a trait its meaning and its ability to describe a person also allows it to give meaning to and to describe behavior.

Schemas Once Again

There is another important element of the present approach that has parallels in the social psychological literature. One of the most influential examples of such an application was proposed by Cantor and Mischel (1977, 1979), who focused on the categorical properties of traits. In this approach, trait concepts are organized in terms of ideal or "prototypical" instances such as "extrovert" or "intellectual." On answering a question such as "What is Peter like?", the perceiver is thought to assess the family resemblance between features of Peter and features of relevant prototypes. Once Peter is placed into a category, the perceiver is likely to think of him in terms of the full set of features of the cognitive prototype.

This approach, which is only one of several "schematic" treatments of trait concepts (e.g., Fiske & Taylor, 1984; Hastie, 1981) has received good empirical support, notably from research on person memory (Cantor & Mischel, 1977; Tsujimoto, 1978). There is an important distinction, however, between the schematic properties of traits suggested by this approach and, alternatively, those suggested by the traits-as-action-categories approach. In the traditional approach, trait concepts are, themselves, thought to constitute schemas. The concept "extrovert," for example, constitutes a mental structure that defines the schema or prototype.

In developing the traits-as-action-categories notion, I have placed the emphasis on *action schemas* rather than on *trait schemas*. I have argued, for example, that a trait concept such as "extrovert" may constitute a value in the superset slot of an action schema. The presence of this value in the action schema would, of course, provide a link to the full trait schema. The two schematic notions are, therefore, complementary. Moreover, many of the issues that have received attention in the context of trait schema research, such as the hierarchical structure of trait categories (Cantor & Mischel, 1979), or the role of schemas in triggering affect (Fiske, 1982) are also relevant to the action-category function of traits. Much stands to be gained, therefore, from considering the schematic properties of trait concepts both independently and in their relation with action categories.

Automatism in the Context of the Distinction

Earlier in this chapter, I argued against past claims for the automatism of dispositional inferences (Winter, Uleman, & Cunniff, 1985). Furthermore, Uleman and his colleagues have recently gathered evidence that suggests that making trait inferences uses some cognitive capacity at encoding (Uleman, Newman, & Winter, 1988). All-in-all, therefore, there presently appears to be little evidence that perceivers infer characteristics of others automatically. The possibility remains, however, that trait concepts are activated automatically when action schemas with which they are linked serve to interpret behavior.

Available evidence suggests that this is not the case. Consider first evidence on the automatism of inferences during text comprehension. A substantial body of research suggests that readers only make inferences when the inferences are necessary to integrate information that is stated explicitly in the text (McKoon & Ratcliff, 1986). A popular example of such inferences involves anaphoric references where a pronoun or other "anaphor" and its antecedent refer to the same concept. For instance, to understand the sentences "A burglar surveyed the garage set back from the street. The criminal slipped away from the street lamp.", it is necessary to relate the anaphor "criminal" to the prior referent "burglar." Without such inferences, text would be disjointed and incoherent, and available evidence suggests that anaphoric inferences do indeed occur automatically (McKoon & Ratcliff, 1980).

By contrast, there is little evidence to support the automatism of schema-based inferences that are not essential for the integration of explicitly stated information (Alba & Hasher, 1983). In situations such as those discussed in this chapter, basic comprehension does not require trait-related inferences. For example, the fact that the secretary solved the mystery half-way through the book is perfectly comprehensible without the inference that her action was clever. Although the concept "clever" can add layers of meaning to the secretary's action, the concept is not necessary to integrate the information stated explicitly in the sentence.

More direct evidence for the lack of automatism in trait categorizations derives from cued-recall studies (Bassili & Smith, 1986; Winter & Uleman, 1984). As we have seen, these studies demonstrate that the effectiveness of trait cues depend on the subjects' processing goal at encoding (Bassili & Smith, 1985; Moskowitz & Uleman, 1987). Because the effectiveness of trait cues can derive from their activation either in the context of a dispositional inference or in the context of behavior categorization, it appears that neither of these processes is impervious to task demands, a fact that argues against their automatism.

The importance of processing goals for trait activation is further demonstrated in a result from my study using word-fragment completions (Bassili, in press). The results that I presented earlier in this chapter (see Table 4.1) were all from a condition where subjects were instructed to form impressions of the stimulus persons. In another condition, subjects had to allocate causality for the stimulus actions either to the actor or to the situation. Word-fragment completion performance did not differ from baseline performance in any of the information or cue conditions for these subjects, suggesting that the causal allocation task mitigated against both schema-based activation and trait concepts and dispositional inferences about actors.

In summary, trait inferences do not seem to be automatic, and this conclusion applies equally to dispositional attributions and to action categorizations. Instead, it appears that subjects' processing goals determine the extent to which trait-relevant action schemas are invoked for the interpretation of behavior.

Implications of a Traits-as-Action-Categories View for Person Perception

The distinction between the role of traits in describing people and their role in describing behavior is subtle to the point where one may question its

4. TRAITS IN SOCIAL COGNITION 83

utility for person perception research. I believe, however, that the distinction has both theoretical and practical implications. At the level of theory, the distinction suggests a demarcation between the cognitive operations that are responsible for the initial activation of trait concepts, and those ultimately responsible for dispositional inferences. Although this demarcation has been suspected by other theorists, little evidence has been produced for it in the past, nor has it been given much heed.

At a practical level, the distinction suggests that great care must be taken in interpreting subjects' use of trait concepts in social psychological research. In particular, it should not be assumed that trait judgments necessarily reflect judgments about the characteristics of people. Nor should it be assumed that the difference between the description of people's behaviors and the description of their distinguishing features is salient to subjects. In on-line processing situations, the person perceiver is primarily concerned with making sense of the behavior flow. As we have seen, trait concepts can play an important role in this process. From the point of view of the subject, however, this role is probably undifferentiated so that references to trait concepts can relate either to characteristics of actors, or to characteristic of their behavior.

Both of these points are demonstrated nicely in a phenomenon that has received a lot of attention in attribution research. It is now commonly accepted among social psychologists that people have a strong tendency to perceive other people's behavior as being caused by their internal dispositions. This tendency, which has been called a "fundamental attribution error" (Ross, 1977), has proven pervasive and robust in person perception research (e.g., Jones, 1979; Ross, 1977). The most common explanation of this tendency has been based on Heider's (1958) notion that "behavior . . . tends to engulf the total field" (p. 54), the assumption being that because behavior is vivid and salient, the perceiver devotes more attention to it and to the actor than to situational forces.

Recently, other factors that may contribute to the phenomenon have been identified. For example, Quattrone (1982) has proposed an account of the bias based on Kahneman and Tversky's notion of anchor/adjust processes. According to Quattrone, perceivers may first draw dispositional inferences about actors, and then adjust these inferences (insufficiently) to take into account situational factors. Gilbert and his colleagues (e.g., Gilbert, Pelham, & Krull, 1988) have suggested a related explanation of the fundamental attribution error. These authors have extended Trope's distinction between identification and inferential processes by suggesting that person perception includes three stages: categorization (what is the actor doing?), characterization (what trait does the action imply?), and correction (what situational constraints may have caused the action?). The fundamental attribution error, according to these authors, derives from the fact that correction is less "automatic" and more susceptible to disruption than either categorization or characterization.

Although each of these notions has demonstrable merit, I believe that the trait-as-action-categories concept offers an intriguingly simple account of the cognitive dynamics that may promote the phenomenon. The central idea is that because of their prominence in both the identification and dispositional inference stages of person perception, trait concepts may come to dominate the cognitive representation of information about actors. Recent discussions of the role of category accessibility in social judgment processes provide an interesting way to conceptualize this process (e.g., Higgins, King, & Mavin, 1982; Higgins, Rholes, & Jones, 1977). To put it simply, the activation of a trait concept during the identification of a behavioral episode may raise the accessibility of this concept and the likelihood of its application in subsequent stages of information processing. The end result of this "auto-priming" effect may be that dispositional concepts end up playing a much more dominant role in the cognitive representations of others than situational concepts that are not normally the object of concern in the comprehension process.

It should be noted in passing that Eliot Smith (Smith & Branscombe, 1987, 1988; chap. 2 in this volume) has proposed a new interpretation of the category accessibility notion that is also applicable here. According to Smith, the priming effects that have been attributed to increases in the accessibility of categories can also be explained in terms of procedural efficiency. For our purposes, it is possible to conceptualize the activation of an action schema and of a trait concept in terms of "if-then" productions. Accordingly, the initial activation of the production in the early stages of behavior identification may raise the probability that the production will "fire" subsequently during the dispositional inference phase of attribution. The fundamental attribution error, therefore, may be conceived in terms of increases in the procedural efficiency of trait-relevant productions.

The present discussion is, by necessity, speculative. Moreover, it does not deal with the reasons for what is a fundamental difference in the salience of trait concepts as compared to situation concepts in social cognition. Be that as it may, my schema-based account of the role of trait concepts illustrates *how* traits can exercise their dominant status in perception. By focusing on the dynamics of the cognitive operations that are responsible not only for dispositional inferences but also for the comprehension of behavior, this account provides a more integrated picture of the mechanisms responsible for person perception that has been available.

CONCLUSION

The data relied on in this chapter benefit from an important virtue and suffer from an equally important limitation. Their virtue is that they all stem from techniques that provide indirect and unobtrusive indices of on-line cognitive processes in person perception. Without such techniques, it would have been very difficult to track the vicissitudes of trait concepts as they apply either to the identification of behavior or to the description of people. Moreover, the freedom of these techniques from demand characteristics and from response biases lend further credibility to the results they have yielded.

The limitation of the data stems from their reliance, in all cases, on sentences that are highly suggestive of traits. This dependence on simple and unambiguous verbal information poses two threats. First, it raises the obvious possibility that trait concepts lose much of their power, either to categorize action or to describe people, when the stimulus information grows in complexity. Second, it fosters concerns about ecological validity, especially in relation to the salience of verbal categories in situations where the behavior flow is observed directly rather than read about.

These concerns will have to be addressed. On balance, however, the cognitive techniques reviewed here have opened important new windows on the on-line cognitive processes that underlie person perception. Trait concepts seem to play a prominent role in these processes, and this role extends to capturing the gist qualities of behavior and well as those of people. Moreover, the distinction presented here provides new insights into the organization of action schemas that are used to interpret social behavior. Although there presently exists little direct evidence for the operation of these schemas in the social domain, their theoretical potential is clear and should lead to a new understanding of person perception phenomena.

ACKNOWLEDGMENTS

Support for this work was provided by Social Sciences and Humanities Research Council of Canada Grant Number 410-85-1115. I would like to thank Colin MacLeod and Bernadette Park for their helpful comments on this chapter.

REFERENCES

Alba, J. W., & Hasher, L. (1983). Is memory schematic? *Psychological Bulletin, 93,* 203–231.
Anderson, J. R. (1976). *Language, memory, and thought.* Hillsdale, NJ: Lawrence Erlbaum Associates.
Anderson, J. R. (1985). *Cognitive psychology and its implications.* New York: Freeman.
Anderson, J. R., & Bower, G. H. (1973). *Human associative memory.* Washington, DC: Winston.
Anderson, N.H. (1965). Primacy effects in personality impression formation using a generalized order effect paradigm. *Journal of Personality and Social Psychology, 2,* 1–9.

Anderson, N. H. (1966). Component ratings in impression formation. *Psychonomic Science, 6,* 179-180.
Asch, S. E. (1946). Forming impressions of personality. *Journal of Abnormal and Social Psychology, 41,* 258-290.
Asch, S. E., & Zukier, H. (1984). Thinking about persons. *Journal of Personality and Social Psychology, 46,* 1230-1240.
Bartlett, F. C. (1932). *Remembering: A study in experimental social psychology.* London: Cambridge Press.
Bassili, J. N. (1976). Temporal and spatial contingencies in the perception of social events. *Journal of Personality and Social Psychology, 33,* 680-685.
Bassili, J. N. (1978). Facial motion in the perception of faces and of emotional expression. *Journal of Experimental Psychology: Human Perception and Performance, 4,* 373-379.
Bassili, J. N. (1979). Emotion recognition: The role of facial movement and the relative importance of upper and lower areas of the face. *Journal of Personality and Social Psychology, 37,* 2049-2058.
Bassili, J. N. (1987). *Actor focus as an instigator of attribution.* Unpublished manuscript.
Bassili, J. N. (in press). Trait encoding in behavior identification and dispositional inference. *Personality and Social Psychology Bulletin.*
Bassili, J. N., & Smith, M. C. (1986). On the spontaneity of trait attributions: Converging evidence for the role of cognitive strategy. *Journal of Personality and Social Psychology, 50,* 239-245.
Bassili, J. N., Smith, M. C., & MacLeod, C. M. (in press). Auditory and visual word-stem completion: Separating data-driven and conceptually driven processes. *Quarterly Journal of Experimental Psychology: Human Experimental Psychology.*
Cantor, N., & Mischel, W. (1977). Traits as prototypes: Effects on recognition memory. *Journal of Personality and Social Psychology, 35,* 38-48.
Cantor, N., & Mischel, W. (1979). Prototypes in person perception. In L. Berkowitz (Ed.), *Advances in experimental social psychology* (vol. 12, pp. 3-52). New York: Academic Press.
Corbett, A. T., & Dosher, B. A. (1978). Instrument inferences in sentence encoding. *Journal of Verbal Learning and Verbal Behavior, 17,* 479-491.
Ekman, P., & Friezen, W. V. (1975). *Unmasking the face.* Englewood Cliffs, NJ: Prentice-Hall.
Fiske, S. T. (1982). Schema-triggered affect: Applications to social perception. In M. S. Clark & S. T. Fiske (Eds.), *Affect and cognition: The 17th annual Carnegie Symposium on Cognition* (pp. 55-78). Hillsdale, NJ: Lawrence Erlbaum Associates.
Fiske, S. T., & Cox, M. G. (1979). Person concepts: The effects of target familiarity and descriptive purpose on the process of describing others. *Journal of Personality, 37,* 25-38.
Fiske, S. T., & Taylor, S. E. (1984). *Social cognition,* Reading, MA: Addison-Wesley.
Gilbert, D. T., Pelham, B. W., & Krull, D. S. (1988). On cognitive busyness: When person perceivers meet persons perceived. *Journal of Personality and Social Psychology, 54,* 733-740.
Hastie, R. (1980). Memory for behavioral information that confirms or contradicts a personality impression. In R. Hastie, T. M. Ostrom, E. B. Ebbesen, R. S. Wyer, D. Hamilton, & D. E. Carlston (Eds.), *Person memory: The cognitive basis of social perception* (pp. 155-177). Hillsdale, NJ: Lawrence Erlbaum Associates.
Hastie, R. (1981). Schematic principles in human memory. In E. T. Higgins, C. P. Herman, & M. P. Zanna (Eds.), *Social cognition: The Ontario Symposium* (vol. 1, pp. 39-88). Hillsdale, NJ: Lawrence Erlbaum Associates.
Hastie, R., & Kumar, P. A. (1979). Person memory: Personality traits as organizing principles in memory for behaviors. *Journal of Personality and Social Psychology, 37* 25-38.
Heider, F. (1958). *The psychology of interpersonal relations.* New York: Wiley.

Heider, F., & Simmel, M. (1944). An experimental study of apparent behavior. *American Journal of Psychology, 57,* 243-259.
Higgins, E. T., King, G. A., & Mavin, G. H. (1982). Individual construct accessibility and subjective impressions and recall. *Journal of Personality and Social Psychology, 43,* 35-47.
Higgins, E. T., Rholes, W. S., & Jones, C. R. (1977). Category accessibility and impression formation. *Journal of Experimental Social Psychology, 13,* 141-154.
Jones, E. E. (1979). The rocky road from acts to dispositions. *American Psychologist, 34,* 107-117.
Jones, E. E., & Davis, K. E. (1965). From acts to dispositions: The attribution process in person perception. In L. Berkowitz (Ed.), *Advances in experimental social psychology* (vol. 2, pp. 219-266). New York: Academic Press.
Jones, E. E., & McGillis, D. (1976). Correspondent inferences and the attribution cube: A comparative reappraisal. In J. H. Harvey, W. J. Ickes, & R. F. Kidd (Eds.), *New directions in attribution research* (vol. 1, pp. 389-420). Hillsdale, NJ: Lawrence Erlbaum Associates.
Kelley, H. H. (1967). Attribution theory in social psychology. In D. Levine (Ed.), *Nebraska symposium on motivation* (pp. 192-238). Lincoln: University of Nebraska Press.
Kelley, H. H. (1972). *Causal schemata and the attribution process.* Morristown, NJ: General Learning Press.
Kintsch, W. (1974). *The representation of meaning in memory.* Hillsdale, NJ: Lawrence Erlbaum Associates.
McArthur, L. Z., & Baron, R. (1983). Toward an ecological theory of social perception. *Psychological Review, 90,* 215-238.
McKoon, G., & Ratcliff, R. (1980). The comprehension process and memory structures involved in anaphoric reference. *Journal of Verbal Learning and Verbal Behavior, 19,* 668-682.
McKoon, G., & Ratcliff, R. (1986). Inferences about predictable events. *Journal of Experimental Psychology: Learning, Memory, and Cognition, 12,* 82-91.
Minsky, M. (1975). A framework for representing knowledge. In P. H. Winston (Ed.), *The psychology of computer vision* (pp. 211-277). New York: McGraw-Hill.
Moskowitz, G., & Uleman, J. S. (1987). *The facilitation and inhibition of spontaneous trait inferences.* Unpublished manuscript.
Neisser, U. (1976). *Cognition and reality: Principles and implications of cognitive psychology.* New York: Freeman.
Newtson, D. (1976). Foundations of attribution: the perception of ongoing behavior. In J. H. Harvey, W. J. Ickes, & R. F. Kidd (Eds.), *New directions in attribution research* (vol. 1, pp. 223-247). Hillsdale, NJ: Lawrence Erlbaum Associates.
Norman, D. A., & Rumelhart, D. E. (1975). *Explorations in cognition.* New York: Freeman.
Paris, S. C., & Lindauer, B. K. (1976). The role of inference in children's comprehension and memory for sentences. *Cognitive Psychology, 8,* 217-227.
Park, B. (1986). A method for studying the development of impressions of real people. *Journal of Personality and Social Psychology, 41,* 907-917.
Peevers, B. H., & Secord, P. F. (1973). Developmental changes in attribution of descriptive concepts to persons. *Journal of Personality and Social Psychology, 27,* 120-128.
Quattrone, G. A. (1982). Overattribution and unit formation: When behavior engulfs the person. *Journal of Personality and Social Psychology, 42,* 593-607.
Rosch, E. (1975). Cognitive representations of semantic categories. *Journal of Experimental Psychology: General, 104,* 192-223.
Rosenberg, S., & Sedlak, A. (1972). Structural representations of implicit personality theories. In L. Berkowitz (Ed.), *Advances in experimental social psychology* (vol. 6, pp. 235-297). New York: Academic Press.
Ross, L. (1977). The intuitive psychologist and his shortcomings: Distortions in the attribution process. In L. Berkowitz (Ed.), *Advances in experimental social psychology* (vol. 10,

pp. 173-220). New York: Academic Press.

Schacter, D. L. (1987). Implicit memory: History and current status. *Journal of Experimental Psychology: Learning, Memory, and Cognition. 13,* 501-518.

Schank, R. C., & Abelson, R. (1977). *Scripts, plans, goals, and understanding.* Hillsdale, NJ: Lawrence Erlbaum Associates.

Schneider, W., & Shiffrin, R. M. (1977). Controlled and automatic human information processing: I. Detection, search, and attention. *Psychological Review, 84,* 1-66.

Shiffrin, R. M., & Schneider, W. (1977). Controlled and automatic human information processing: II. Perceptual learning, automatic attending, and a general theory. *Psychological Review, 84,* 127-190.

Smith, E. R. (1984). Model of social inference processes. *Psychological Review, 91,* 291-413.

Smith, E. R., & Branscombe, N. R. (1987). Procedurally mediated social inferences: The case of category accessibility effect. *Journal of Experimental Social Psychology. 23,* 361-382.

Smith, E. R., & Branscombe, N. R. (1988). Category accessibility as implicit memory. *Journal of Experimental Social Psychology. 24,* 490-504.

Smith, E. R., Branscombe, N. R., & Borman, C. (1988). Generality of the effects of practice on social judgment tasks. *Journal of Personality and Social Psychology, 54,* 385-395.

Smith, E. R., & Miller, F. D. (1983). Mediation among the attributional inferences and comprehension processes: Initial findings and a general method. *Journal of Personality and Social Psychology, 44,* 492-505.

Srull, T. K. (1981). Person memory: Some tests of associative storage and retrieval models. *Journal of Experimental Psychology, 7,* 440-462.

Srull, T. K., Lichtenstein, M., & Rothbart, M. (1985). Associative storage and retrieval processes in person perception. *Journal of Experimental Psychology: Learning, Memory, and Cognition, 11,* 316-345.

Srull, T. K., & Wyer, R. S., Jr. (1979). The role of category accessibility in the interpretation of information about persons: Some determinants and implications. *Journal of Personality and Social Psychology, 37,* 1660-1672.

Srull, T. K., & Wyer, R. S., Jr. (1980). Category accessibility and social perception: Some implications for the study of person memory and interpersonal judgments. *Journal of Personality and Social Psychology, 38,* 841-856.

Thomson, D. M., & Tulving, E. (1970). Associative encoding and retrieval: Weak and strong cues. *Journal of Experimental Psychology, 86,* 255-262.

Trope, Y. (1986). Identification and inferential processes in dispositional attribution. *Psychological Review, 93,* 239-257.

Tsujimoto, R. N. (1978). Memory bias toward normative and novel trait prototypes. *Journal of Personality and Social Psychology, 36,* 1391-1401.

Tulving, E., Schacter, D. L., & Stark, H. A. (1982). Priming effects in word-fragment completion are independent of recognition memory. *Journal of Experimental Psychology: Learning, Memory, and Cognition, 8,* 336-342.

Tulving, E., & Thomson, D. M. (1973). Encoding specificity and retrieval processes in episodic memory. *Psychological Review, 80,* 352-373.

Uleman, J. S., Newman, L., & Winter, L. (1988). *Making spontaneous trait inferences uses some cognitive capacity at encoding.* Unpublished manuscript.

Watkins, M. J., & Peynircioglu, Z. F. (1984). Determining perceived meaning during impression formation: Another look at the meaning change hypothesis. *Journal of Personality and Social Psychology, 46,* 1005-1016.

Winter, L., & Uleman, J. S. (1984). When are social judgments made? Evidence for the spontaneousness of trait inferences. *Journal of Personality and Social Psychology, 47,* 237-252.

Winter, L., Uleman, J. S., & Cunniff, C. (1985). How automatic are social judgments? *Journal of Personality and Social Psychology, 49,* 904-917.

Wyer, R. S., Bodenhausen, G. W., & Srull, T. K. (1984). The cognitive representation of persons and groups and its effect on recall and recognition memory. *Journal of Experimental Social Psychology, 20,* 445-469.

Wyer, R. S., & Srull, T. K. (1986). Human cognition in its social context. *Psychological Review, 93,* 322-359.

5

The Relation Between Opinion and Memory: Distinguishing Between Associative Density and Structural Centrality

Shinobu Kitayama
Eugene Burnstein
University of Michigan

Since the classic work by Hovland and his colleagues (Hovland, Janis, & Kelley, 1953), persuasion, as well as resistance to persuasion, is commonly explained in terms of strength of learning. In the former case, it is assumed that well-learned arguments in a message exert more influence on opinion than poorly learned ones; and in the latter, that individuals are able to resist persuasion because supportive arguments are learned better than nonsupportive ones (Hass & Grady, 1975; McGuire, 1964). In both cases, the basic idea is that knowledge that is congruent with the opinion is more memorable than knowledge that is incongruent with the opinion.

Not surprisingly, there are difficulties with this explanation. Several well-known phenomena suggest that the relationship between the opinion and the memorability of the arguments is not straightforward and that persuasive effects do not vary in a regular way with memory. For example, learned arguments can "boomerang" so that information that is supposed to weaken the opinion instead ends up actually strengthening it. There are also "sleeper" effects, so that the opinion change observed soon after a message is learned may later be either reduced or augmented even though no additional learning has taken place in between (cf. Cook & Flay, 1978). Obviously, then, it is not solely a matter of memorizing the message that determines its impact (see Greenwald, 1968).

A further problem for the learning approach arises when the relation between opinion and memory is directly examined. Studies typically find that arguments that are congruent with the opinion are recalled *no better* than ones that are incongruent with the opinion. For instance, Anderson and Hubert (1963) had their subjects form an impression of a person described by a series of trait descriptions. They observed that although descriptions that were presented *earlier* in the series had the greatest impact on the impression, those that were presented *later* were recalled best. Similarly, Greenwald (1968) presented subjects with a persuasive message and then later had them recall the contents of the message. He found virtually no correlation between opinion change due to the message and recall of the message contents. In sum, whereas theories of persuasion have postulated a relationship between the opinion and memory for arguments, when we attempt to directly assess it in a recall task, no such relation appears to exist.

Besides learning theory, there is another class of explanations of persuasion that may be called *structural* (e.g., Peak, 1955). Whereas the learning approach focuses on the sheer number of arguments acquired, the structural approach emphasizes their organization. According to this formulation, arguments stored in memory are said to differ in terms of their *associative density* and *structural centrality*. The former refers to the extent to which arguments are connected to each other and the latter, the extent to which arguments are connected to the opinion. The distinction between these two properties of a knowledge structure implies that even though arguments are well learned and, thus, densely interconnected, they may or may not be associated with the representation of the opinion. The structural approach suggests, therefore, that in order to understand the relation between opinion and memory, the centrality of arguments has to be taken into account in addition to the sheer amount of learning as reflected in associative density.

In this chapter, we follow the structural approach and incorporate the concepts of associative density and structural centrality within an information-processing model. Our primary concern is *on-line* opinion formation, namely, cases in which individuals form an opinion in the course of acquiring pertinent information (Hastie & Park, 1986). Predictions regarding the relationship between opinion and memory under on-line conditions are made, and an experiment is reported that tests these predictions. Finally, the model is used to integrate other findings in the literature, including those concerning *memory-based* cases, where individuals form an opinion using arguments they remember.

ASSOCIATIVE DENSITY AND STRUCTURAL CENTRALITY

Opinion formation involves encoding the message and abstracting a gist (Burnstein & Schul, 1982, 1983; Hamilton, Katz, & Leier, 1980; Schul, 1983; Wyer & Srull, 1986). Individuals elaborate on arguments contained in the message and, in so doing, the arguments become interconnected (Greenwald, 1968; Petty & Cacioppo, 1986). *Associative density* refers to the number of connections in this network of arguments. Simultaneously with the encoding of arguments, an opinion is abstracted and given a separate representation. The opinion, therefore, constitutes a summary or gist of the more detailed information contained in the message. It may, for example, be a running tally about a person, perhaps in the form of a hypothesis or a narrative, that summarizes the arguments for and against he or she being likable (e.g., Anderson & Hubert, 1963; Dreben, Fiske, & Hastie, 1979).

Opinion formation as a process, however, does not stop when an opinion is established. Our analysis assumes that the gist is used as a basis for organizing the arguments in memory. That is to say, arguments become associated with the gist to the extent that their meaning is contained in the latter (Dellarosa & Bourne, 1984). This implies that congruent arguments are more likely to be directly connected with the opinion and accessed when the opinion is activated than are incongruent or irrelevant arguments. In other words, the arguments are positioned according to their importance in maintaining the opinion (cf. Lewin, 1951; Peak, 1955; Zajonc, 1960). The location of an argument vis-a-vis the opinion is called its *structural centrality*. According to the present view, therefore, post-decisional organization of arguments results in a knowledge structure in which arguments vary in the degree to which they are associated with each other (i.e., associative density), as well as in the degree to which they are associated with the opinion (i.e., structural centrality).

This formulation is illustrated in Fig. 5.1. The upper half of the figure is a flow chart that describes the mental operations involved in opinion formation. Below the flow chart, the structure of information at each stage of processing is illustrated in simplified memory diagrams. Each circle represents an argument that is either pro-X or pro-Y. The box at the top of each diagram is a gist, which could represent either opinion X or opinion Y. Associative links are indicated by lines that connect these components of knowledge.

The present model has some important implications for the recall of arguments. When individuals attempt to remember what they know about an issue, usually the first thing that comes to mind is the gist (e.g., Fazio, Sanbonmatsu, Powell, & Kardes, 1986). This, we think, is due to the fact that the probes in everyday life are relatively abstract (e.g., "Is Professor Jones' course any good?"), so that in time, whenever the issue is raised, the gist is automatically activated. In any case, once the gist comes to mind, memory-search spreads along the associative paths that were laid down during encoding. As a result, the arguments underlying the gist are accessed according to their structural centrality. It follows then that even under conditions in which all arguments are highly memorable and well learned,

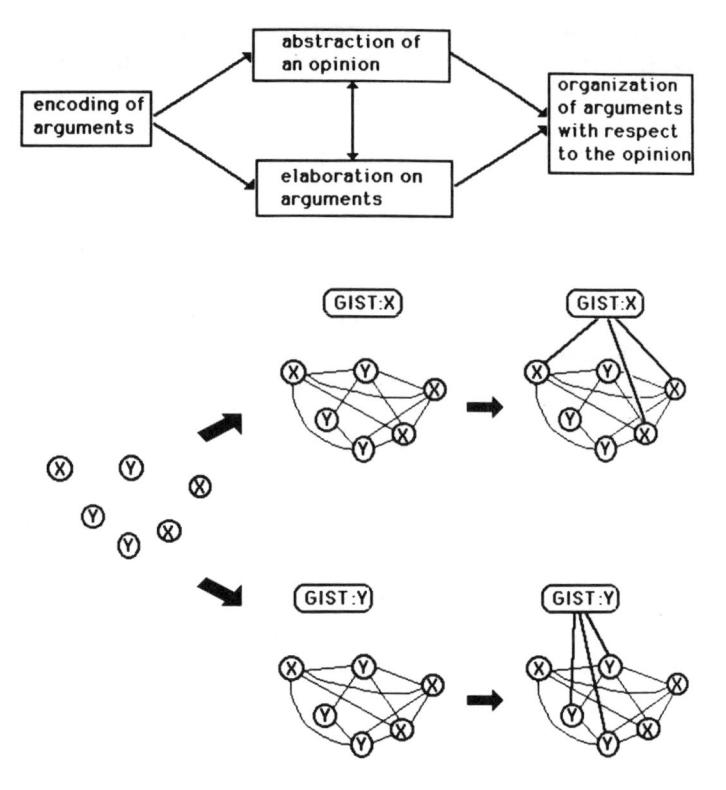

FIG. 5.1. On-line opinion formation: Cognitive operations and opinion structure.

those that are congruent with the opinion have priority of entry into working memory over those that are incongruent with the latter.

Our hypothesis, therefore, specifies the conditions under which there will or will not be a relationship between opinion and *probability* of recall. That is to say, if the message as a whole is well learned, the probability of recalling a particular argument depends on *when* memory-search is terminated. In the typical recall task, individuals try to remember as many arguments as they can. Hence, memory-search is *exhaustive*. Under these conditions, the incongruent arguments are just as likely to be activated as the congruent arguments; the former simply have to wait awhile until the latter have been accessed. On the whole, therefore, the likelihood of recalling the message depends on the number/strength of connections among arguments, that is, their associative density (Bradshaw & Anderson, 1979; Srull & Brand, 1983; Tulving & Pearlston, 1966).

Associative density may be affected by a number of factors (Hastie, 1980). For instance, when an opinion has already been established, say, when it reflects a preexisting stereotype, arguments that are incongruent with the opinion have to be either discounted or reinterpreted, whereas there is no such need with regard to the arguments that are congruent with the opinion. Hence, the incongruent arguments receive a greater amount of elaboration than the congruent arguments (e.g., Hastie & Kumar, 1979; Srull, 1981). As a result, associative density is higher for the former than for the latter. Alternatively, when the person has no firm position on the issue to begin with, the congruence of each argument will not become clear until an opinion is actually developed. Under these conditions, therefore, to-be-congruent and to-be-incongruent arguments should not differ in terms of their associative density. This implies that when an opinion is formed *on-line* and when memory-search is exhaustive, congruent arguments need *not* be recalled better than incongruent arguments.

In ordinary life, however, recall most often is not an end in itself. Individuals do not retrieve arguments simply to show how much they can remember. Usually, we access information because it is instrumental in achieving a goal. Suppose, for example, we want to explain our point of view to another person. Under these conditions, memory-search is rarely exhaustive. Instead, we will discontinue the process once we have retrieved *sufficient* information to communicate our ideas. In short, memory-search is typically *self-terminating*. In these circumstances, because congruent arguments have priority of entry in recall over incongruent arguments, the former gain a distinct recall advantage in that they are more likely to be accessed than the incongruent arguments *before the individuals discontinue searching*. This implies that to the extent that a self-terminating search strategy prevails, the likelihood of recalling an argument *can* be predicted from the opinion. That is to say, we believe that in most natural settings, opinion-congruent arguments have a higher probability of being recalled than do opinion-incongruent arguments, due to the fact that memory-search is usually self-terminating. In experimental situations, however, the recall task demands an exhaustive search. Under these conditions, probability of recall and opinion are unrelated in that opinion-congruent arguments are no more likely to be remembered than are opinion-incongruent arguments.

To summarize, the present model assumes that, whereas elaborative encoding increases associative density between arguments, structural centrality depends on the organization of arguments with respect to the opinion. It follows then that opinion and recall probability are related only if memory-search is self-terminating. When the search is exhaustive, the relationship vanishes. This formulation, thus, resolves the apparent disagreement between (a) theories of persuasion that imply that arguments that are congruent with the opinion have a greater likelihood of being recalled than arguments that are incongruent with the opinion and (b) the absence of such findings in research on the recall of persuasive messages where the standard procedure encourages exhaustive search.

Past studies of opinions formed on-line are generally in accord with our analysis. As noted earlier in this chapter, Greenwald (1968) observed no correlation between an opinion induced by a persuasive message and memory of the message contents. More recently, in one of their experimental conditions, Sherman, Zehner, Johnson, and Hirt (1983, Exp. 2) had subjects read various pieces of information about two football teams in order to predict the outcome of the game played between them. They found that the predictions that the subjects made were unrelated to the kind of information they recalled. Several other studies provide comparable data (e.g., Hastie & Park, 1986; Lichtenstein & Srull, 1987). Hence, our conjecture about the absence of a relationship between the opinion and the *likelihood of recalling* an argument under standard experimental conditions seems fairly well documented. On the other hand, the evidence that there is a relationship between opinion and *priority of entry in recall* is more problematic. So far, there have been only a few studies in the literature that speak to this issue.

Schul and Burnstein (1983) found that arguments that are useful in deciding between alternative opinions (informative arguments) are recalled better than arguments that are not useful in this regard (uninformative arguments). Not only that, the informative arguments were also recalled prior to the uninformative arguments, even when probability of recall was controlled. The latter finding is consistent with our analysis that arguments are associated with the representation of the opinion to the extent that their meaning is contained in the latter. Structurally, this implies that informative arguments are located nearer to the gist and, thus, when the gist is accessed, they are retrieved sooner than uninformative arguments. However, in the Schul and Burnstein study, the informative arguments were always congruent with the opinion. Hence, it was not possible to observe whether congruence determines priority of entry in recall.

A recent experiment by Lichtenstein and Srull (1987) provides a suggestive finding. In one of the conditions of this study, subjects read a number of behaviors attributed to a person in order to form an impression of the person. Consistent with prior work, no relation was found between the impression and the kind of behaviors that were remembered. More importantly, however, Lichtenstein and Srull also examined the order in which this information was recalled. In their study, each of the behaviors had been rated for likability. Hence, it was possible to correlate the final impression both with the average likability of behaviors that were recalled early and with the average likability of behaviors that were recalled later. When this was done, the correlation for the "early" behaviors tended to be positive, whereas the one for the "later" behaviors tended to be negative. Although this effect was rather weak, it nonetheless suggests that the impression *can* influence priority of entry in recall, such that behaviors that are congruent with the impression are retrieved before behaviors that are incongruent.

AN EXPERIMENT ON THE EFFECTS OF OPINION FORMATION ON THE PROBABILITY OF RECALL AND PRIORITY OF ENTRY IN RECALL

The primary purpose of our experiment is to test predictions regarding the relationship between an opinion that is formed *on-line* and memory for the arguments underlying the opinion. Our model implies that there will be no relation between opinion and probability of recall — that is, congruent arguments will be recalled no better than incongruent arguments. However, even in the absence of any advantage for congruent over incongruent arguments in terms of probability of recall, the former will have priority of entry in recall over the latter.

The stimulus materials used in this experiment involve not only informative arguments, either congruent or incongruent, but also uninformative arguments. This design allows us to test some additional implications of our model. Most straightforward would be, firstly, that informative arguments receive a greater amount of elaboration and thus have higher associative density than uninformative arguments; and, secondly, that the former are likely to be represented in the opinion and thus are located more centrally than the latter. Hence, informative arguments are not only more likely to be recalled than uninformative arguments, but also more likely to be recalled earlier (Schul & Burnstein, 1983).

In addition, we manipulate the extent to which individuals elaborate on informative arguments. Evidence indicates that the amount of elaboration increases to the extent that the arguments in a message imply different positions so that forming an opinion is difficult (e.g., Brewer, Dull, & Lui, 1981; Burnstein & Schul, 1983; Hastie & Kumar, 1979; Srull, 1981; Srull, Lichtenstein, & Rothbart, 1985; Stern, Marrs, Millar, & Cole, 1984; Wyer, Bodenhausen, & Srull, 1984; Wyer & Gordon, 1982). We also assume that the amount of elaboration depends on the processing goal. Specifically, elaboration increases if the outcome of processing involves explaining the opinion to others (the *communication* goal; see Tetlock, 1983); conversely, it is reduced when the person anticipates additional information later and suspends forming an opinion (the *reception* goal; see Cohen, 1961; Leventhal, 1962; Zajonc, 1960). Regardless of how it is manipulated, as elaboration increases, so will associative density. And as associative density increases, so will the probability of recall for the informative arguments (cf. Hamilton et al., 1980). Amount of elaboration, however, need have no effect on organization of the arguments with respect to the opinion. This implies that structural centrality is functionally independent of associative density. In principle, therefore, priority of entry in recalls is invariant with amount of elaboration.

METHOD

Subjects

Forty-seven male and 46 female undergraduates participated as subjects in partial fulfillment of their introductory psychology course requirements.

Materials

Four sets of 12 arguments were used. Each set described a different person who engaged in a certain activity (i.e., graduate student, TV producer, swimmer, baseball player). They all began with an introductory remark that specified the context (e.g., John is a second-year graduate student in a PhD program in chemistry at a midwestern university). When the processing goal involved forming an opinion (see the *Procedure* section that follows), the context sentence was followed by a question about the person's future success in the specified activity (e.g., Do you think John is likely to succeed or fail in getting a PhD?). The question was not given when the goal did not require forming an opinion. Twelve separate arguments were then presented. Half of them were informative with regard to the decision (e.g., John earned nearly perfect scores on the quantitative and verbal parts of the GRE), and half were uninformative (e.g., Next summer, John hopes to go to Madrid where his sister lives with her husband and three children). A separate group of 85 undergraduates rated the informativeness of each argument, that is, how useful it was in judging each preson's future success. This was done on six point scales (1 = not useful at all, 6 = extremely useful). The informative arguments were indeed rated to be useful (M = 5.2) and uninformative arguments, not useful (M = 1.5).

Three of the informative arguments in each set described the person's ability in the designated activity and the remaining three described his or her motivation. Each set described the person in one of four ways, namely, as high in both ability and motivation (HH), low in both (LL), high in ability but low in motivation (HL), and low in ability but high in motivation (LH). The informative arguments in the first two sets, therefore, are *consistent* with respect to an opinion, and the those in the latter are *inconsistent*.[1]

---

[1] We use the term *consistency* to refer to the extent to which the set of informative arguments clearly implies a single position, and we reserve the term *congruence* to refer to the relationship

Pairs of arguments were written so that one argument implying high ability or high motivation had its low-ability or low-motivation counterpart. For instance, the high-ability argument about John that was given earlier had as its low ability counterpart, "John earned very low scores on the quantitative and verbal parts of the GRE." One of the arguments in each pair was used depending on the congruence condition to which a given set was assigned. Congruence of the arguments (i.e., HH, LL, HL, LH), order of presentation of sets (i.e., 1st, 2nd, 34d, 4th), and the stimulus set (i.e., graduate student, TV producer, swimmer, and baseball player) were counterbalanced within a 4 × 4 greco-latin square design. Further examples of arguments used are given in the Appendix.

Procedure

Subjects were run in groups of two to six individuals. Those in a given session were all assigned one of the three processing goals. Two of the goals explicitly solicited opinions about each person's future success. In one of them, the subjects were asked to form an opinion and to be prepared to communicate it to other participants who were alleged to be waiting in a separate room (*communication* goal). In the other, they were simply asked to form an opinion without any mention of future communication (*opinion* goal). In the third condition, however, *reception* was activated as a goal. Here, the subjects expected to receive additional information. Specifically, they were told that they would first hear 12 of 24 arguments for each of the four sets and that the remaining 12 arguments would be given to them later. They were asked to familiarize themselves with the arguments and prepare to receive additional arguments.

The subjects then listened to the four tape-recorded sets of arguments. The arguments were presented at a fixed pace with a 2-second interval between them. Six informative arguments and six uninformative arguments appear in turn, with the exact order of the arguments being randomly determined for each combination of the counterbalanced factors, namely, congruence, the four stimulus sets, and their presentation order. Therefore, any findings regarding priority of entry in recall cannot be attributed to the order in which arguments were presented. Immediately after the presentation of each set, subjects under the communication and the opinion goal indicated their position with respect to the future success of the person on

---

of each argument to the opinion. Congruence, therefore, can be defined only after an opinion has been formed. To illustrate, once an opinion exists, all the arguments in a *consistent* set will turn out to be *congruent* with the opinion. However, when the set of arguments is inconsistent, some of them will turn out to be *congruent* with the opinion, whereas the others will turn out to be *incongruent* with the latter.

a scale ranging from "He or she will definitely fail" (1) to "He or she will definitely succeed" (7).

When all four sets of arguments were completed, the subjects worked for 3 minutes on a distraction task made up of analogy problems, after which a surprise recall task was given. In the recall task, a four page booklet was distributed. At the top of each page there appeared the context sentence for one of the sets of arguments (e.g., John is a second-year graduate student in a PhD program in chemistry at a midwestern university) followed by 12 lines drawn the width of the page. The subjects were asked to recall as many of the arguments associated with the sentence as possible and to write them down, one per line in any order, with the first one that came to mind on the first line, the second one that came to mind on the second line, and so on. The subjects recalled a particular set of arguments for 4 minutes, turned the page, recalled the next set, and so on, until all four sets were completed. The order of the sets was randomized over subjects.

RESULTS

Five subjects who reported that they anticipated a recall test and prepared for it while the arguments were being presented, were discarded. The data from the remaining 88 subjects were analyzed. A recalled argument was coded as correct if (a) it could be uniquely identified with one of the arguments given in the set, and (b) it was recalled in connection with the appropriate target person. All protocols were coded by one judge who was blind to the experimental condition. Half of them were also coded by another blind judge. The two judges agreed on 93% of the cases. In cases of disagreement, the decision of the first judge ruled.

In the following subsection, we first compare the memory for informative arguments as a whole with that for uninformative arguments. Then, we compare the memory for informative arguments as a function of their congruence with the stated opinion. There we draw upon data from only those conditions in which the processing goal involved opinion formation and the arguments were inconsistent (see footnote 1). Finally, we examine the relationship between recall probability and priority of entry in recall.

Memory for Informative Versus Uninformative Arguments

Our analysis implies that when an opinion is formed, both associative density and structural centrality increase to the extent that arguments are informative. Hence, informative arguments will be recalled not only better but also earlier than uninformative arguments. We have also assumed that associative density and structural centrality reflect distinct mental operations, namely, connecting arguments to each other and connecting them to the gist, respectively. Because the informativeness of arguments is assumed to have a positive impact on both these operations, this variable by itself may not speak to their functional independence. Nevertheless, certain interactive effects of informativeness with other variables may do so. To this end, we manipulated the processing goal and information congruence. If associative density and structural centrality are distinct operations, variables that influence one should not necessarily affect the other.

Recall Probability. Although our manipulation of congruence yielded four levels (i.e., HH, LL, HL, and LH), the theoretically important comparisons are between the former two cells, the consistent condition, and the latter two, the inconsistent condition. Percent recall of informative and uninformative arguments was averaged across the two cells in each consistency condition and then submitted to an ANOVA.

Percent recall is shown in Fig. 5.2. We expected that associative density would increase when individuals elaborated on the arguments more thoroughly, and that the thoroughness with which they did so would increase when they expected to communicate their opinion (say, as compared to when they expected to receive still more information). In support of this hypothesis, recall of informative arguments was best under the communication goal (.70), moderate under the opinion goal (.66), and worst under the reception goal (.60). A significant difference was found between the former two goals, where opinion formation was involved, and the latter one, where opinion formation was suspended ($t(192) = 4.29$, $p < .001$). The difference between the former two goals, however, failed to achieve significance ($p > .10$). Interestingly, recall of uninformative arguments

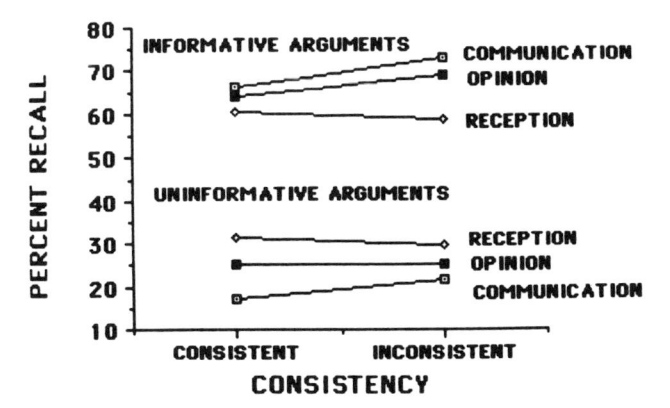

FIG. 5.2. Recall probability for informative and uninformative arguments as a function of consistency and processing goals.

showed the reverse pattern, namely, it was worst under the communication goal (.21), moderate under the decision goal (.25), and best under the reception goal (.31). Again, the former two goals were significantly different from the latter ($t(192) = 4.30$, $p < .001$); but the difference between the former two did not reach significance ($p > .10$). As implied by this pattern, the interaction between Informativeness and Processing Goal proved significant ($F(2,192) = 16.7$, $p < .0001$). Total recall, however, was invariant across the processing goals ($F < 1$). The latter finding suggests that the elaboration performed on informative arguments and that performed on uninformative arguments compete for a common and limited pool of processing resources (Kahneman, 1973). As a result, when the processing goal requires that there be greater elaboration performed on informative arguments, elaboration on uninformative arguments inevitably decreases, even though the total amount of processing effort, as indicated by total recall, is the same over the different goals.

Elaborative encoding in opinion formation was also expected to increase when the informative arguments are inconsistent. This prediction was supported. Informative arguments in the inconsistent sets had a higher recall probability (.71) than those in the consistent sets (.65) under the communication and the opinion goals combined ($t(192) = 2.67, p < .01$). By contrast, the comparable difference under the reception goal was negligible (.59 vs. .60, $t < 1$). The planned contrast representing this interactive pattern was significant ($t(192) = 1.98, p = .05$). Consistency of the informative arguments did not have any effects on memory for uninformative arguments under any processing goal ($ts < 1$).

Finally, informative arguments were recalled far better than uninformative arguments, even under the reception goal ($t(192) = 18.2, p < .0001$), where no demand was imposed to selectively elaborate on informative over uninformative arguments. In all likelihood, this is due to an inadvertent feature of the present material: All of the informative arguments described in a single domain of activity, whereas each of uninformative arguments described a different domain. Evidence suggests that arguments are already connected with each other in memory to the extent that they pertain to a single event, activity, or a theme, that is, when they are *thematically related* (e.g., Bransford, Barclay, & Franks, 1972; Cantor & Mischel, 1977; Smith, Adams, & Schorr, 1978; for a review see Taylor & Crocker, 1981).

Priority of Entry in Recall. We also predicted that when an opinion is formed, informative arguments will have priority of entry in recall over uninformative arguments. To test this prediction, we used the *Pr* index devised by Schul and Burnstein (1983). The *Pr* index, in effect, is the observed probability of informative items being recalled prior to uninformative items, relative to the observed probability of uniformative items being recalled prior to informative items. To obtain a *Pr*, for each recall protocol, all possible pairs of recalled informative and uninformative arguments are constructed. The number of pairs in which the informative argument was recalled prior to the uninformative argument and the number of those in which the uninformative argument preceded the informative argument are calculated. The latter value is then subtracted from the former. This difference is positive if informative arguments have priority of entry in recall over uninformative arguments, and negative if the tendency is opposite. To make adjustment for the fact that the absolute value of the difference is inflated as the number of recalled informative arguments and the number of recalled uninformative arguments increase, this difference is divided by both the number of recalled informative arguments and the number of recalled uninformative arguments. The resulting value defines a priority index (*Pr*). Notice that this index takes a positive score, up to +1, if informative arguments are recalled prior to uninformative arguments; a negative score, up to −1, if the reverse happens; and zero if neither tendency is apparent.

There are two important features of the *Pr* measure that should be mentioned. First, it is a measure of the *overall* trend in recall order. This point may be highlighted by comparing our measure with another apparently similar measure in Srull (1981; Srull et al., 1985). Srull used the probability of one type of argument entering recall directly *adjacent* to another type of argument. This measure reflects recall order at a local level. However, it does not capture recall order at a global level. To illustrate, consider the following two recall protocols in which *I* stands for an informative argument and *U* stands for an uninformative argument.

[1] IIIUUUI   [2] IUUUIII

In both protocols there are four informative items recalled, but only one of them is immediately followed by an uninformative item; thus, the conditional probability of an uninformative item being recalled given recall of an informative one in the prior, adjacent position is ¼. Similarly, the conditional probability of an informative item being recalled given recall of an uninformative one in the adjacent, prior position is ¼ in both protocols. Nevertheless, there is an obvious difference between the two in terms of *overall* recall order: Whereas informative items tend to enter recall prior to uninformative ones in the first protocol (*Pr* = +.5), the reverse happens in the second (*Pr* = −.5). For our purpose, therefore, the *Pr* index is more suitable than the one based on conditional probabilities.

Second, the *Pr* index does not have any built-in property that forces a certain relationship between recall priority and recall probability: Even though one set of items is recalled better than another set, there is no reason inherent in the calculation of the measure prescribing that the former appear to be recalled either earlier or later than the latter. The relationship between recall probability and recall priority, therefore, is an empirical issue that can be addressed in terms of substantive psychological theories.

Because the distribution of *Pr* was found to be reasonably normal, an ANOVA was performed, which showed only a significant main effect for Processing Goal ($F(2,51) = 6.09, p < .005$). As can be seen in Fig. 5.3, the *Pr* score was higher in the two conditions in which an opinion was formed (.32) than in the reception condition ($-.002$) ($F(1,51) = 23.6, p < .001$), indicating that informative arguments were recalled earlier in the former than in the latter. More important, the *Pr* means for the communication and the opinion conditions were greater than zero ($ps < .01$), indicating that in each instance informative arguments were recalled significantly earlier than chance. We, thus, replicated Schul and Burnstein's original finding.

Two additional findings are worthy of mention. First, the means in the reception condition were virtually zero ($ts < 1$). Note that this happened despite the fact that, under these conditions, informative (i.e., thematically related) arguments are far better recalled than uninformative (i.e., thematically unrelated) arguments. Elaborative encoding induced by thematic relatedness of arguments, thus, is *not* sufficient for the priority of entry effect to occur; whereas forming an opinion *is*. Second, under the conditions in which an opinion was formed, informative arguments were recalled prior to uninformative arguments, *regardless* of whether the former were consistent or inconsistent ($Fs < 1$ for all pertinent pair wise comparisons). This was the case despite the fact that the informative arguments were better recalled if they were inconsistent than if they were consistent. Together, these findings indicate that making connections among arguments (i.e.,

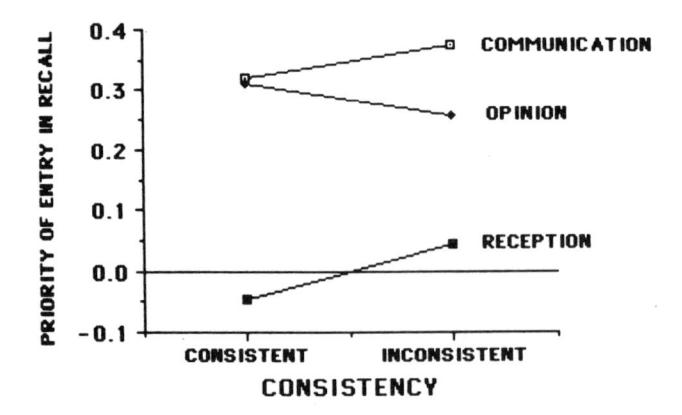

FIG. 5.3. Priority of entry in recall of informative over uninformative arguments as a function of consistency and processing goals.

elaboration) does not necessarily affect the post-decisional organization of the arguments with respect to the opinion. As such, they support our contention that these two mental operations are functionally separate.

Finally, one additional piece of evidence nicely illustrates that uninformative arguments occupy very peripheral positions in the underlying representation. It was found that 39% of the subjects (34 out of 88) recalled at least one uninformative argument in connection with the *wrong* stimulus person. Furthermore, these intrusive errors tended to be recalled at the very end, after the correct uninformative arguments ($Pr = -.29$, $t = 1.98$, $p < .06$). Not surprisingly, there were virtually no intrusive errors involving informative arguments. These findings suggest that uninformative arguments are not connected with other knowledge and, as a result, tend to "float around" in memory.

In sum, we have found that when an opinion is formed, informative arguments are recalled both better and earlier than uninformative arguments. This finding is consistent with our analysis that informativeness increases both associative density and structural centrality. However, a more important assumption of the model is that the two properties of an opinion structure are derived from functionally distinct mental operations, namely, elaboration, or connecting arguments with each other, and organization, or connecting them to the opinion. In support of this distinction, the variables that increased associative density of arguments (i.e., thematic-relatedness and information consistency) did not enhance their structural centrality.

Memory for Congruent Versus Incongruent Arguments

Further implications of the distinction between associative density and structural centrality can be tested by comparing memory for arguments that turn out to be congruent with an opinion and those that turn out to be incongruent with the latter. We have assumed that both congruent and incongruent arguments may be equally interconnected but only the former are directly connected to the opinion. This implies, first, that congruent arguments will be recalled *no better* than incongruent arguments, and, second, than even if no difference is found between congruent and incongruent arguments in terms of their probability of recall, the former will have priority of entry in recall over the latter.

Recall Probability. For each recall protocol from the two incongruent sets (i.e., HL, LH), the probability of recall for arguments favoring failure (i.e., low ability or low motivation) was subtracted from the probability of recall for those favoring success (i.e., high ability or high motivation). This score, of course, takes a positive number if success-arguments are better recalled than failure-arguments and a negative number if the reverse happens. The scores were then classified into three groups according to the opinion the subject stated for the corresponding set, namely, failure (a scale value of 1, 2, or 3), neutral (a scale value of 4), and success (a scale value of 5, 6, or 7). An ANOVA, performed on the mean difference scores, showed that the main effect for Opinion was far from significant ($F < 1$). Also, neither the main effect for Processing Goal nor the interaction between Opinion and Processing Goal attained significance ($Fs = 1.60$, 1.71, respectively). As in past studies (e.g., Hastie & Park, 1986), there is no reliable relation between opinion and recall probability. This finding, thus, supports our notion that in on-line judgments, associative density does not depend on the congruence of the arguments with respect to the opinion.

Priority of Entry in Recall. A major prediction of our model is that even when there is no difference in associative density, congruent arguments will be more centrally represented than incongruent arguments. To the extent that this is the case, there will be an overall effect for recall order such that congruent arguments are remembered *prior* to incongruent arguments. The *Pr* index was used to capture the degree to which arguments favoring success are recalled prior to arguments favoring failure. Note that this index varies from -1 to $+1$. The tendency for arguments that are congruent with success to have priority of entry in recall over those that are congruent with failure is reflected in a positive score, whereas the reverse tendency is reflected in a negative score. An ANOVA showed a highly significant main effect for Opinion ($F(2,108) = 6.21$, $p < .003$). Neither the main effect for Processing Goal nor its interaction with Opinion was significant (*F*s respectively). The mean *Pr* values as well as the mean probabilities of recall for the three opinion groups, divided by the appropriate standard error, are plotted in Fig. 5.4.

In support of our model, *Pr* was significantly lower when the opinion favored failure than when it favored success ($t(108) = 3.45$, $p < .001$), with *Pr* for the neutral opinion lying in between. More important, when the opinion favored failure, *Pr* was significantly negative $t(108) = 3.13$, $p < .005$), indicating that arguments that were congruent with failure were recalled earlier than those that were congruent with success. In contrast, when the opinion implied success, the effect was reversed ($t(108) = 1.89$, $p < .06$), suggesting a tendency for arguments that were congruent with success being recalled earlier than those that were congruent with failure. We may conclude, therefore, that regardless of the position taken, arguments that were congruent with the opinion had priority of entry in recall over those that were incongruent. Finally, as expected, when the opinion was neutral, *Pr* was virtually zero ($t < 1$), indicating that arguments on one

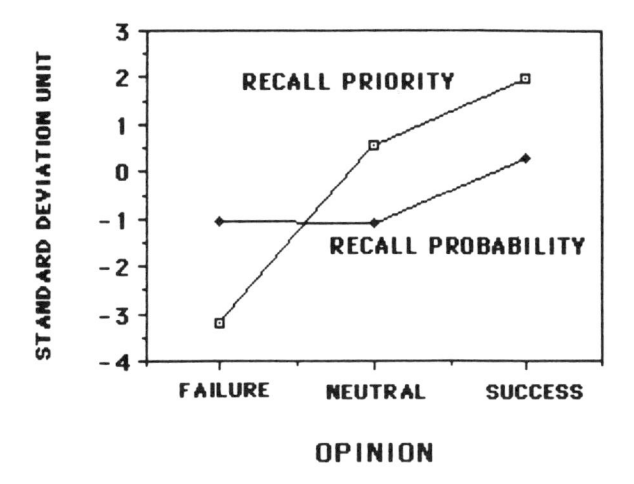

FIG. 5.4. Probability of recall and priority of entry in recall as a function of stated opinions.

side of the issue had no more priority of entry in recall than arguments on the other side. In short, despite the absence of a reliable relationship between opinion and recall probability, there is still a substantial relationship between opinion and recall order. This, of course, is consistent with the hypothesis that associative density and structural centrality reflect distinct mental operations.

Relationship Between Probability of Recall and Priority of Entry in Recall

To estimate more directly the relation between our two indices of memory, the priority of entry in recall of congruent arguments over incongruent ones (Pr) was correlated with the recall probability for the former minus that for the latter. The comparable analysis was also performed for informative versus informative arguments. In both cases, the correlation coefficient in each of our experimental conditions ranged from $-.16$ to $+.36$ and were all nonsignificant ($p < .10$). To enhance statistical power, partial correlations were calculated with the experimental factors being controlled. As expected, the partial correlation was nonsignificant for informative versus uninformative arguments ($r = .15$, $t(113) = 1.59$, $p > .10$). Interestingly, for congruent versus incongruent arguments, the partial correlation, if anything, was *negative* ($r = -.23$, $t(113) = 2.47$, $p < .02$). This might suggest that much elaborative effort is devoted to discounting arguments supporting the to-be-rejected position. Indeed, such elaboration may be required before individuals can unambiguously endorse the alternative position. Under these conditions, therefore, arguments that have received *more* elaboration actually would be *less* centrally represented. In any case, these correlational data rule out the possibility that priority of entry in recall is a positive function of elaboration (or vice versa). Instead, they provide additional support for our contention that recall probability and recall priority reflect functionally separate features of memory organization, namely associative density and structural centrality.

DISCUSSION

In the typical study of recall probability and opinion, the recall task leads to an *exhaustive* memory-search. Under these conditions, arguments that are congruent with the opinion are recalled *no better* than arguments that are incongruent with the opinion. Nevertheless, when we examined overall recall order, a substantial relationship emerged; that is, opinion-congruent arguments were recalled *prior* to opinion-incongruent ones. An important implication of this order effect is that if the person had stopped memory-search earlier, opinion and recall probability would have been closely related. Indeed, in everyday life, memory-search is usually nonexhaustive; and it should not be uncommon for individuals to access more congruent than incongruent arguments. The necessary and sufficient conditions for this to happen is, first, that the individuals have formed an opinion and, second, that in trying to recollect the arguments involved they do not feel compelled to remember all.

The finding that in exhaustive memory-search an opinion predicts priority of entry in recall but not probability of recall supports our contention that associative density, which is assumed to mediate recall probability, and structural centrality, which is assumed to mediate recall priority, reflect functionally distinct mental operations. The present study, however, provides additional support in this regard. To begin with, although informative arguments were recalled both better and earlier than uninformative arguments, the factors that determine probability of recall are not the same as those that determine priority of entry. Overall, recall probability was a function of associative density, that is, the amount of elaboration performed on the arguments. Thus, memory for informative arguments increased when they were used to form an opinion and when they were inconsistent with respect to the opinion—it was under these conditions that elaborative encoding was presumed to increase. Additionally, even when opinion formation was suspended, informative arguments were recalled better than uninformative arguments. This was due to the fact that the former were thematically related and, thus, were automatically connected in memory. In contrast, priority of entry in recall depended mainly on whether the arguments were used to form an opinion. The factors that increased recall probability—that is, consistency and thematic relatedness—had no effect on recall priority. Finally, correlational analysis indicated that there is virtually no correspondence between probability of an argument being recalled and its priority of entry in recall.

Overall, the present experiment suggests that our distinction between associative density and structural centrality is quite useful in understanding the memory structure underlying an opinion. In the following sections, we expand on our analysis and suggest some further implications.

ON-LINE VERSUS MEMORY-BASED OPINION FORMATION

So far, we have examined memory for arguments under conditions in which individuals form an opinion *on-line*. Several theorists have recently pointed out, however, that the relationship between opinion and memory may be quite different when the opinion is *memory-based* (e.g., Hastie & Park, 1986). In the memory-based situation, individuals usually first familiarize themselves with a set of arguments but are not instructed to form an opinion, nor do they expect to. Only later are they asked to make a judgment based on their memory of these arguments. Because the present model was developed to account primarily for on-line opinion formation, it is interesting to see to what extent it can handle memory-based cases.

In the memory-based paradigm, when the arguments are initially presented, subjects are not given any specific processing goal. Usually, they are asked merely to examine or to learn them. Under these conditions, we assume that arguments will be stored in memory without undergoing much elaborative encoding. Thus, they will not be highly connected, that is, associative density is low. Also, at this point there is no opinion and, hence, structural centrality is nonexistent. Later, the individuals are instructed to retrieve these arguments and use them to form an opinion. Because the arguments are only weakly connected in memory, they are most likely to be activated serially. We expect that this is quite effortful. As a result, a considerable portion of the person's processing resources has to be allocated to the retrieval operation and only a small portion is left to elaborate on the arguments actually retrieved.

Furthermore, besides the scarcity of available processing resources, individuals may also believe that if information is in memory, then it must *per force* be coherently organized. In other words, the "feeling of remembering" leads one to infer a "feeling of understanding." It may not be until individuals are asked to explain what they recall that they begin to recognize that this inference is unjustified. In any case, to the extent that a "feeling of remembering" does lead to a "feeling of understanding," individuals will not experience a need to elaborate further on the arguments that they retrieve. All in all, then, we hypothesize that under conditions of memory-based opinion formation, arguments, because they receive minimal elaboration during encoding and retrieval, have low associative density. Nevertheless, these arguments still serve as the basis for the opinion. That is to say, they will be abstracted, and a gist will be constructed. As in the on-line situation, once the opinion is formed, it serves to organize the arguments. Hence, the arguments that are congruent with the gist will be directly connected to the latter, whereas those that are incongruent with the gist will not. In other words, the former are more *centrally* represented than the latter.

The present model suggests, therefore, that when opinion formation is memory-based, arguments are elaborated on less than when opinion formation is on-line. As a result, associative density in the former is less than in the latter; whereas the connections between opinion and arguments, that is, structural centrality, may exist to the same degree in both. The modified flowchart and memory diagrams that describe memory-based opinion formation are shown in Fig. 5.5.

When individuals try to recall what they know about an issue, memory-search starts at the gist and spreads out along previously laid associative paths. Compared to the on-line case, in memory-based opinions the primary associative connections are between the gist and arguments that are congruent with it. Hence, priority of entry effects in memory-based opinions should be similar to those observed in on-line opinions: Arguments that are congruent with the opinion will come to mind before those that are incongruent with it. With regard to recall probability, however, we expect an appreciable difference between these two kinds of opinions. When the opinion is on-line, congruent arguments will have a distinct recall advantage over incongruent arguments, if memory-search is self-terminating (see Fig. 5.1). If, on the other hand, memory-search is exhaustive, the recall advantage of the opinion-congruent over the opinion-incongruent arguments disappears. This line of reasoning does not apply in respect to memory-based opinions, because here, unlike on-line opinions, associative density is low (see Fig. 5.5). In memory-based case, therefore, arguments that are congruent with the opinion have a higher probability of being recalled than arguments that are incongruent with the opinion, *even if memory-search is exhaustive.*

In fact, as far as we can tell, the few studies that have found a reliable relation between opinion and recall probability all involved memory-based opinions. For example, Sherman et al. (1983) had an experimental condition in which subjects memorized several facts. Later, the subjects were asked to make a judgment based on these facts, after which they were given a surprise recall test. The result showed that, to a substantial degree, memory depended on the judgment: Facts that were congruent with

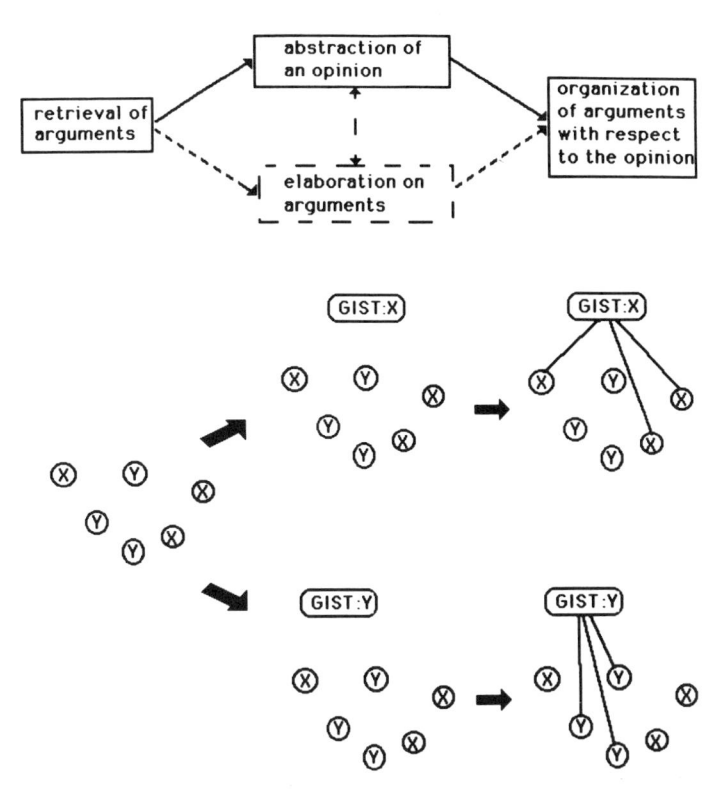

FIG. 5.5. Memory-based opinion formation: Cognitive operations and opinion structure.

judgment were better recalled than facts that were incongruent with it. Several experiments by Hastie and Park (1986) obtained the same effect with a variety of different materials. Moreover, Lichtenstein and Srull (1987) found that, under memory-based conditions, congruent arguments are recalled earlier as well as better the incongruent arguments. Finally, our analysis implies that even when an opinion is formed on-line, a substantial relation will obtain between opinion and probability of recall to the extent that the elaborative encoding normally performed on arguments is inhibited, and, thus, associative density is attenuated. In line with this prediction, Bargh and Thein (1985) examined on-line opinion formation and found that recall probability was related to opinion only when it is quite difficult to elaborate on the arguments, namely, when there is considerable information overload *and* the encoding structure that would allow the person to process the arguments is not readily accessible.

We have assumed that when an opinion is memory-based, associative connections exist primarily between the gist and congruent arguments. As a result, congruent arguments are recalled not only *earlier* but also *better* than incongruent arguments (see Fig. 5.5). One could argue, however, that it is not necessary to assume such associative links. Indeed, Hastie and Park (1986) have suggested that if opinion formation is memory-based, individuals use the availability heuristic (Tversky & Kahneman, 1973) to infer their opinion (cf. Rothbart, Fulero, Jensen, Howard, & Birrell, 1978). Hence, the opinion will correspond to the most available arguments. Moreover, there is no reason to believe that the arguments that are available when an opinion is formed become unavailable later when recall is tested. And, if the same arguments are available during *both* opinion formation *and* recall, there is bound to be a close relation between opinion and recall probability (also see Lichtenstein & Srull, 1987; Sherman et al., 1983, who has made the same assumption).

According to the Hastie and Park formulation, therefore, the relation between opinion and memory is spurious in that it is mediated by a third variable that determines both opinion and recall, namely, the availability of arguments. One would expect, then, that if availability is controlled, there will be no effect of opinion on recall of arguments. By contrast, our model implies that *independent of their initial availability,* arguments that turn out to be congruent with an opinion will be recalled better than those that turn out to be incongruent.

One way to distinguish between the availability hypothesis and the present formulation would be to provide subjects arbitrarily with an opinion, instead of having them form one on their own. It is possible, in that way, to examine the effects of having an opinion on later recall, independent of availability of arguments. Dellarosa and Bourne (1984) conducted exactly this experiment (see also Sherman et al., 1983). Subjects first memorized arguments that suggested either the success or failure of a given enterprise. They were later told the *correct* opinion to form, that is, the actual outcome of the enterprise: Finally, a surprise recall test was given. It was found that the arguments that were congruent with the opinion arbitrarily provided by the experimenter were better recalled than those that were incongruent with this opinion. These data suggest that the positive correlation between opinion and memory, obtained when opinion formation is memory-based, is not spurious. It cannot merely be the result of the same arguments being available both during opinion formation and recall. Instead, the effect seems to follow from the associative link established between an opinion and the arguments that are congruent with it.

OPINION AS A RECALL CUE

So far, we have argued that, when an opinion is formed on-line, a reliable relation is found only between the opinion and priority of entry in recall, whereas, when an opinion is memory-based, the opinion is related *both* to priority of entry in recall *and* to probability of recall. Our formulation also implies, however, that these relationships occur only to the extent that the gist, that is, the representation of the opinion, is activated first and, thus, is available as a recall cue for arguments. Of course, in some situations, there may exist powerful retrieval cues other than the gist. For instance, memory for the most recent arguments (e.g., Anderson & Hubert, 1963; Dreben et al., 1979; see also Bjork & Whitten, 1974) or arguments embedded in a coherent script-like structure (e.g., Cohen & Ebbesen, 1979) may not be predicted by the opinion.

An example of powerful recall cues overwhelming the opinion can be found in one of the conditions of the aforementioned experiment by Lichtenstein and Srull (1987). This experiment had two memory-based conditions. In one, the subjects were instructed to memorize a number of behaviors, whereas in the other, the subjects were instructed merely to comprehend them. Later, they were asked to form an impression of the target individual. In the *comprehension* condition, as predicted by our model, congruent information was recalled better as well as earlier than incongruent information. These effects however, vanished in the *memorize* condition. As Lichtenstein and Srull themselves argued, the reason is that when memorizing, subjects rehearsed the material so as to be able to reproduce it later verbatim. This kind of rehearsal typically leads individuals to assign cue value to graphic or phonetic features of a sentence, to visual images associated with certain words or phrases used in the sentence, and the like, which is not done when the goal is comprehension. To the extent that such cues are used in recall, the relation between opinion and memory is attenuated.

The same consideration may apply to an experiment by Shedler and Manis (1986, Exp. 1). They examined on-line opinion formation and showed that arguments were *both* easier to remember *and* more influential if they were accompanied by vivid details than if they were not (see also Reyes, Thompson, & Bower, 1980). In addition, however, they observed that when vividness was statistically controlled, influential arguments, namely, those that turned out to be congruent with the opinion, were no longer recalled better or earlier than uninfluential arguments, namely, those that turned out to be incongruent. The failure to find any systematic relation between opinion and recall order is probably due to the power of their vividness manipulation. That is to say, when sufficiently vivid, the details of an argument become stronger recall cues than the opinion.

Overall, failures to observe a relationship between opinion and memory seem to occur when there are recall cues that are stronger or more available than the opinion. These effects, therefore, are not incompatible with our contention that arguments that are congruent with the opinion are more likely to be recalled or are likely to be recalled earlier than those that are incongruent with the opinion, *given that* the opinion is activated as a recall cue. Needless to say, however, in order to test these conjectures, we must manipulate the extent to which a gist (versus some other cue) is likely to be activated in a recall task. One way to do this could be to ask individuals different questions immediately before they attempt to recall arguments. We would predict that a reliable relation will be found between opinion and memory if the question is one designed to activate a gist (e.g., "Was Professor Jones' course exciting?") and not if the question is one designed to activate more specific information (e.g., "Did Professor Jones' course cover retroactive inhibition?").

IMPLICATIONS FOR OPINION CHANGE

Although an opinion is only one of many possible recall cues, it is likely to be routinely activated during social interaction. Moreover, in such settings, memory-search is generally self-terminating: The arguments underlying an opinion come to mind only to the degree that the information represented in the opinion is insufficient to convey the intended meaning (cf. Grice, 1975). Typically, therefore, structural centrality, rather than associative density, determines the likelihood that an argument will be recalled. According to this line of reasoning, then, when the proper experiments are done, a variety of phenomena involving opinion and memory, such as perseverance of a prior belief (Ross, Lepper, & Hubbard, 1975), thought-induced polarization (Tesser, 1978), and resistance to persuasion (McGuire, 1964), might well turn out to depend largely on the fact that belief-congruent information is structurally more central than belief-incongruent information.

In this section, we illustrate the preceding point by reviewing a study we have just carried out (Burnstein & Kitayama, 1988). The purpose of the research was to examine effects of activating an opinion: Does thinking about an opinion attenuate or polarize it? Our analysis suggests that effects of thinking depend on how exhaustively memory is searched. To explore this notion, we chose an opinion on an important social issue, namely, the Soviet Union and its relation with the United States. It can be shown that most college students have a fairly clear position regarding the Soviet Union. Not only that, they also have a large number of relevant arguments so that it would take considerable time and effort to exhaust this knowledge. Analyzing opinions of this kind should increase our chances of observing the effects of self-terminating versus exhaustive memory-search.

On the whole, our respondents had a rather negative stereotype of the Soviet Union. Hence, our expectation was that if they consult only this information while considering the questions we posed to them about Soviet behavior, their opinions would be unqualifiedly negative. Some of these individuals, however, may go beyond the stereotype and activate the more specific arguments that underlie it. According to our formulation, if they do, their opinions would not be unqualifiedly negative. That is to say, the notion of structural centrality also implies that as memory-search becomes increasingly exhaustive, eventually arguments come to mind that are incongruent with the stereotype. Therefore, our general hypothesis is that respondents who search exhaustively should give less stereotypic—that is less anti-Soviet—answers than those who search non-exhaustively.

Note that the model assumes that memory-search will have the effect of attenuating opinion only if the stereotype is activated early on and used as a recall cue. Circumstances, however, may prevent this. For instance, if the question raises *concrete* issues, the person is obliged to bypass the stereotype, which ordinarily is too abstract to be useful in this case, and to activate knowledge that is more pertinent, namely, specific arguments associated with the stereotype. Hence, whether individuals are generally predisposed to search memory exhaustively or to search it perfunctorily makes little difference when the question itself requires them to access information underlying the opinion.

On the other hand, suppose the question is relatively *abstract*. An abstract question most readily activates knowledge at the corresponding level in memory, that is, the stereotype, and can be answered effortlessly in terms of the latter information. At the same time, it usually is quite possible for individuals, if they are inclined, to deliberate further so as to activate more concrete knowlege and to base their answer to the question on this information rather than on the stereotype. Under these conditions, therefore, whether the person chooses a self-terminating or exhaustive search strategy does make a difference. This allows us to qualify our general hypothesis: Respondents who search memory non-exhaustively will express opinions that correspond more closely to the stereotype than respondents who search memory exhaustively, *if* the question posed involves abstract rather than concrete issues.

To examine these ideas, we asked 490 undergraduates at the University of Michigan a variety of questions about the Soviet Union. Some of the questions were relatively *abstract* (e.g., Do you agree with the statement, "The Soviet Union is an evil empire"?), whereas others were relatively *concrete* (e.g., Do you agree with the statement, "It is a good idea to prohibit the sale of our advanced computer systems to the Soviet Union"?). To manipulate amount of memory-search, one third of the respondents were asked *not to think* about the issue before answering questions and another one third, *to think considerably* beforehand; no specific instruction was given to the remaining one third. The interaction between the thinking instructions and the type of questions (i.e., abstract vs. concrete) proved to be significant ($p < .05$). As can be seen in Fig. 5.6, if the issue was

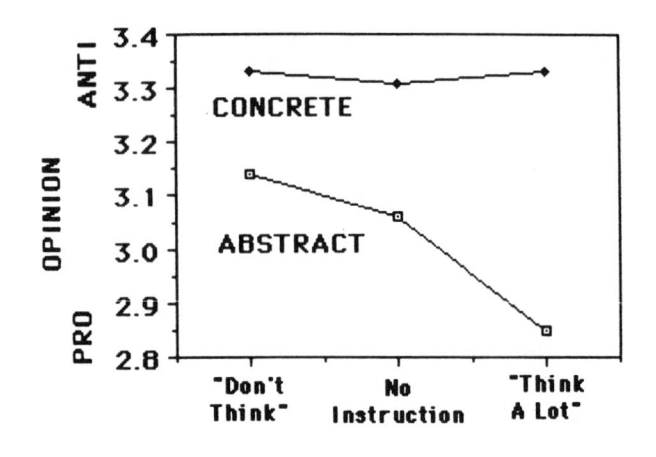

FIG. 5.6. Opinion toward the Soviet Union as a function of memory-search and type of issue.

concrete, the amount of search, as reflected in the thinking instruction, had no impact. However, when the issue was abstract, the stated opinion was most negative when the memory-search was self-terminating, that is, when respondents were asked not to think before answering, moderate when they were given no thinking instruction, and least negative when memory-search was exhaustive, that is, when they were asked to think extensively about the issue before answering.

We also examined effects of individual differences in memory-search on opinion attenuation. Cacioppo and Petty (1982) have proposed that some of us habitually deliberate about an issue at greater length or elaborate upon knowledge more—that is, search memory more exhaustively—than others. This tendency has been called *need for cognition.* Our model suggests the following line of reasoning: Those with a high need for cognition characteristically engage in more exhaustive search before expressing an opinion than do those with a relatively low need for cognition. Hence, if the issue is abstract, the opinion expressed by the former individuals will be less negative than the opinion expressed by the latter. If the question is concrete, however, it demands that the person go beyond the stereotype regardless of his or her inclination. Accordingly, there will be little or no effect of the need for cognition.

As predicted, the interaction between the respondents' level of need for cognition and the types of issue proved highly significant ($p < .001$). As can be seen in Fig. 5.7,, when the question was abstract, the opinions about

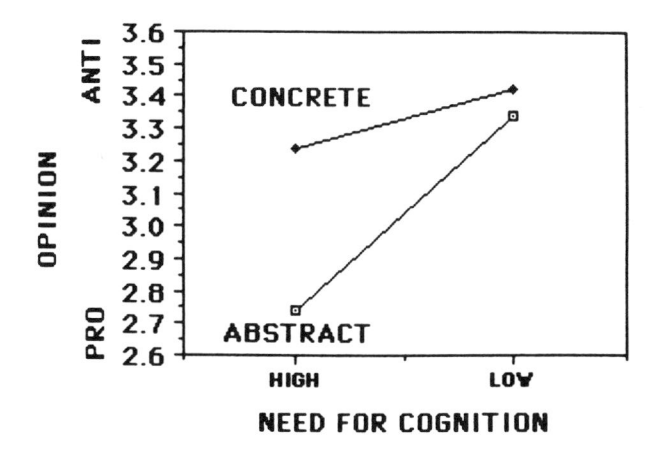

FIG. 5.7. Opinion toward the Soviet Union as a function of need for cognition and type of issue.

the Soviet Union was much less negative for individuals with a high need for cognition than those with a low need for cognition. When the question was concrete, however, the difference in opinion vanished.

SUMMARY AND CONCLUSION

In this chapter, two properties of the knowledge structure underlying an opinion were distinguished, namely, the strength/number of connections among arguments, called *associative density*, and the strength/number of connections between the arguments and the representation of the opinion or gist, called *structural centrality*. Our analysis attempted to clarify the relationship between an opinion that is formed *on-line* and the memory for arguments underlying it. We hypothesized that when memory-search is exhaustive, central arguments are recalled *prior to* peripheral arguments, independent of their associative density. In ordinary life, where memory-search is usually self-terminating, congruent arguments are more likely to be retrieved than are incongruent arguments before search is discontinued. However, when the search is exhaustive, as in the typical recall task, the mnemonic advantage of congruent over incongruent arguments tends to disappear.

An experiment was reported that tested some implications of the present analysis. We found that, to the extent that memory-search is exhaustive, congruent arguments were recalled *no better* than incongruent arguments. Nevertheless, the former were recalled *prior to* the latter. Thus, despite the absence of a reliable relationship between opinion and recall probability, there was a substantial relationship between opinion and recall order. Furthermore, informative arguments, either congruent or incongruent, were recalled better than, as well as prior to, uninformative ones. These effects, however, seemed to be determined by different factors: First, whereas recall probability increased with the amount of elaboration, recall priority depended on the organization of arguments with respect to the opinion. Second, there was no correlation between probability of an argument being recalled and its priority of entry in recall. This supports our contention that associative density and structural centrality reflect distinct mental operations, namely, elaboration and organization.

Next, we used the model to examine relationship between opinion and recall in memory-based (vs. on-line) opinion formation. Specifically, we argued that, in memory-based opinion formation, less elaboration is performed on arguments than in on-line opinion formation. This notion led to several predictions that were found to have received reasonable support in the literature. Finally, we illustrated some implications of the present model for opinion change. That is, evidence was presented that opinions tend to be attenuated when individuals engage in exhaustive memory-search. The present chapter, thus, highlights the importance of distinguishing between associative density and structural centrality not only for research in person memory but also for understanding of a wider range of attitudinal phenomena.

ACKNOWLEDGMENTS

This research was supported by a grant from the National Science Foundation (BNS 85-4286). The work of the first author was facilitated by a Fulbright scholarship. We thank Bob Josephs for his helpful comments on an earlier version.

REFERENCES

Anderson, N.H., & Hubert, S. (1963). Effects of concomitant verbal recall on order effects in personality impression formation. *Journal of Verbal Learning and Verbal Behavior, 2,* 279-391.

Bargh, J. A., & Thein, R. D. (1985). Individuals construct accessibility, person memory, and the recall-judgment link: The case of information overload. *Journal of Personality and Social Psychology, 49,* 1129-1146.

Bjork, R. A., & Whitten, W. B. (1974). Recency-sensitive retrieval processes in long-term memory free recall. *Cognitive Psychology, 6,* 173-189.

Bradshaw, G. L., & Anderson, J. R. (1979). Elaborative encoding as an explanation of levels of processing. *Journal of Verbal Learning and Verbal Behavior, 18,* 309-318.

Bransford, J. D., Barclay, J. R., & Franks, T. J. (1972). Sentence memory: A constructive versus interpretive approach. *Cognitive Psychology, 3,* 193-209.
Brewer, M. B., Dull, V., & Lui, L. (1981). Perception of the elderly: Stereotypes as prototypes. *Journal of Personality and Social Psychology, 41,* 656-670.
Burnstein, E., & Kitayama, S. (1988). *Forming opinions about the Soviet Union: The role of recall strategy.* Unpublished manuscript, University of Michigan, Ann Arbor.
Burnstein, E., & Schul, Y. (1982). The informational basis of social judgment: The operations in forming an impression of another person. *Journal of Experimental Social Psychology, 18,* 217-234.
Burnstein, E., & Schul, Y. (1983). The informational basis for social judgments: Memory for integrated and nonintegrated trait descriptions. *Journal of Experimental Social Psychology, 19,* 49-57.
Cacioppo, P. E., & Petty, R. E. (1982). The need for cognition. *Journal of Personality and Social Psychology, 42,* 116-132.
Cantor, N., & Mischel, W. (1977). Traits as prototypes: Effects on recognition memory. *Journal of Personality and Social Psychology, 35,* 38-48.
Cohen, A. R. (1961).Cognitive tuning as a factor affecting impression formation. *Journal of Personality, 29,* 235-245.
Cohen, C. E., & Ebbesen, E. B. (1979). Observational goals and schema activation: A theoretical framework for behavior perception. *Journal of Experimental Social Psychology, 15,* 305-329.
Cook, T. D., & Flay, B. R. (1978). The persistence of experimentally induced attitude change. In L. Berkowitz (Ed.), *Advances in experimental social psychology* (Vol. 11, pp. 1-57). New York: Academic Press.
Dellarosa, D., & Bourne, L. E. (1984). Decisions and memory: Differential retrievability of consistent and contradictory evidence. *Journal of Verbal Learning and Verbal Behavior, 23,* 669-682.
Dreben, E. K., Fiske, S. T., & Hastie, R. (1979). The independence of item and evaluative information: Impression and recall order effects in behavior-based impression formation. *Journal of Personality and Social Psychology, 37,* 1758-1768.
Fazio, R. H., Sanbonmatsu, D. M., Powell, M. C., & Kardes, F. R. (1986). On the automatic activation of attitudes. *Journal of Personality and Social Psychology, 50,* 229-238.
Greenwald, A. G. (1968). Cognitive learning, cognitive response to persuasion, and attitude change. In A. G. Greenwald, T. C. Brock, & T. M. Ostrom (Eds.), *Psychological foundation of attitudes (pp. 147-170).* New York: Academic Press.
Grice, H. P. (1975). Logic and communication. The William James Lectures, Harvard University, 1967-68. In P. Cole & J. L. Morgan (Eds.), *Syntax and semantics, Vol. 3: Speech acts* (pp. 41-58). New York: Academic Press.
Hamilton, D. L., Katz, L. B., & Leirer, V. O. (1980). Cognitive representation of personality impression: Organizational processes in first impression formation. *Journal of Personality and Social Psychology, 39,* 1050-1063.
Hass, R. G., & Grady, K. (1975). Temporal delay, type of forewarning, and resistance to influence. *Journal of Experimental Social Psychology, 11,* 459-469.
Hastie, R. (1980). Memory for behavioral information that confirms or contradicts a personality impression. In R. Hastie, T. M. Ostrom, E. B. Ebbesen, R. S. Wyer, D. L. Hamilton, & D. E. Carlston (Eds.), *Person memory: The cognitive basis of social perception* (pp. 155-177). Hillsdale, NJ: Lawrence Erlbaum Associates.
Hastie, R., & Kumar, A. P. (1979). Person memory: Personality traits as organizing principles in memory for behaviors. *Journal of Personality and Social Psychology, 37,* 25-38.
Hastie, R., & Park, B. (1986). The relationship between memory and judgment depends on whether the judgment task is memory-based or on-line. *Psychological Review, 93,* 258-268.
Hovland, C. I., Janis, I. L., & Kelley, H. H. (1953). *Communication and persuasion.* New

Haven, CT: Yale University Press.
Kahneman, D. (1973). *Attention and effort.* Englewood Cliffs, NJ: Prentice-Hall.
Leventhal, H. (1962). The effect of set and discrepancy on impression change. *Journal of Personality, 30,* 1-15.
Lewin, K. (1951). *Field theory in social psychology.* New York: Harper.
Lichtenstein, M., & Srull, T. K. (1987). Processing objectives as a determinant of the relationship between recall and judgment. *Journal of Experimental Social Psychology, 23,* 93-118.
McGuire, W. J. (1964). Inducing resistance to persuasion: Some contemporary approaches. In L. Berkowitz (Ed.), *Advances in experimental social psychology* (Vol. 1, pp. 191-229). New York: Academic Press.
Peak, H. (1955). Attitude and motivation. In M. R. Jones (Ed.), *Nebraska symposium on motivation* (pp. 149-188). Lincoln: University of Nebraska Press.
Petty, R. E., & Cacioppo, J. T. (1986). The elaboraton likelihood model of persuasion. In L. Berkowitz (Ed.), *Advances in experimental social psychology* (Vol. 19, pp. 123-205). New York: Academic Press.
Reyes, R. M., Thompson, W. C., & Bower, G. H. (1980). Judgmental biases resulting from differing availability of arguments. *Journal of Personality and Social Psychology, 39,* 2-39.
Ross, L., Lepper, M. R., & Hubbard, M. (1975). Perseverence in self-perception and social perception: Biased attribution processes in the debriefing paradigm. *Journal of Personality and Social Psychology, 32,* 880-892.
Rothbart, M., Fulero, S., Jensen, C., Howard, J., & Birrell, P. (1978). From individual to group impressions: Availability heuristics in stereotype formation. *Journal of Experimental Social Psychology, 15,* 343-355.
Schul, Y. (1983). Integration and abstraction in impression formation. *Journal of Personality and Social Psychology, 44,* 45-54.
Schul, Y., & Burnstein, E. (1983). The informational basis for social judgments: Memory for informative and uninformative arguments. *Journal of Experimental Social Psychology, 19,* 422-433.
Shedler, J., & Manis, M. (1986). Can the availability heuristic explain vividness effects? *Journal of Personality and Social Psychology, 51,* 26-36.
Sherman, S. J., Zehner, K. S., Johnson, J., & Hirt, E. R. (1983). Social explanation: The role of thinking, set, and recall of subjective likelihood estimation. *Journal of Personality and Social Psychology, 44,* 1127-1143.
Smith, E. E., Adams, N., & Schorr, D. (1978). Fact retrieval and the paradox of interference. *Cognitive Psychology, 10,* 438-464.
Srull, T. K. (1981). Person memory: Some tests of associative storage and retrieval models. *Journal of Experimental Psychology: Human Learning and Memory, 7,* 440-463.
Srull, T. K., & Brand, J. F. (1983). Memory for information about persons: The effect of encoding operations on subsequent retrieval. *Journal of Verbal Learning and Verbal Behavior, 22,* 219-230.
Srull, T. K., Lichtenstein, M., & Rothbart, M. (1985). Associative storage and retrieval processes in person memory. *Journal of Experimental Psychology: Learning, Memory, and Cognition, 11,* 316-345.
Stern, L. D., Marrs, S., Millar, M. G., & Cole, E. (1984). Processing time and the recall of inconsistent and consistent behaviors of individuals and groups. *Journal of Personality and Social Psychology, 47,* 253-262.
Taylor, S. E., & Crocker, J. (1981). Schematic bases of social information processing. In E. T. Higgins & M. P. Zanna (Eds.), *Social cognition: The Ontario symposium* (pp. 89-134). Hillsdale, NJ: Lawrence Erlbaum Associates.
Tesser, A. (1978). Self-generated attitude change. In L. Berkowitz (Ed.), *Advances in exper-*

imental social psychology (Vol. 11, pp. 289-338). New York: Academic Press.

Tetlock, P. E. (1983). Accountability and complexity of thought. *Journal of Personality and Social Psychology, 45,* 74-83.

Tulving, E., & Pearlston, Z. (1966). Availability versus accessibility of information in memory for words. *Journal of Verbal Learning and Verbal Behavior, 5,* 381-391.

Tversky, A., & Kahneman, D. (1973). Availability: A heuristic for judging frequency and probability. *Cognitive Psychology, 5,* 207-232.

Wyer, R. S., Bodenhausen, G. W., & Srull, T. K. (1984). The cognitive representation of persons and groups and its effect on recall and recognition memory. *Journal of Experimental Social Psychology, 20,* 445-469.

Wyer, R. S., & Gordon, S. E. (1982). The recall of information about persons and groups. *Journal of Experimental Social Psychology, 18,* 128-164.

Wyer, R. S., & Srull, T. K. (1986). Human cognition in its social context. *Psychological Review, 93,* 322-359.

Zajonc, R. B. (1960). The process of cognitive tuning in communication. *Journal of Abnormal and Social Psychology, 61,* 159-168.

APPENDIX

Following are the arguments used in one of the four sets:

Introductory sentence: Mary is a producer working for a major TV station. She was recently assigned the project of producing a new comedy show.

Question: Do you think she is likely to succeed or fail?

Informative Arguments

Ability

1. High: Mary has an uncanny sense of which scripts and actors are funny and which are not.
2. Low: Mary has a poor sense of which scripts and actors are funny and which are not.
3. High: Mary has received several important awards from TV critics for the creativity of her work.
4. Low: Critics dislike Mary's work because of its lack of creativity.
5. High: Mary coordinates actors, technicians, writers, and others extremely well, and they love to work with her.
6. Low: Mary has much difficulty coordinating actors, technicians, writers, and others, and they don't like to work with her.

Motivation

1. High: Mary will concentrate completely on this project and put aside other projects for several months.

2. Low: Mary does not want to concentrate on this project because another project looks much more promising to her.
3. High: By persistent effort on her part, Mary persuaded a talented and popular actress to star in the show.
4. Low: Although she had a good opportunity to do so, Mary would not even try persuading a talented and popular actress to star in the show.
5. High: Mary very much wants this work to be a new and distinctive approach to TV comedy.
6. Low: Mary does not want to bother with new ideas for this show and will probably settle on some old, trite comedy formulas.

Uninformative Arguments

1. Mary got married ten years ago when she became an assistant producer.
2. Mary lives in a suburb of New York City mainly because she likes gardening.
3. Mary was elected chairman of her college alumni association.
4. Mary enjoys a scotch and soda before dinner but tends to avoid beer and wine.
5. Mary collects 19th century prints as a hobby and is very proud of her collection.
6. Mary wears sunglasses because her eyes often become irritated when she is out in the sun.

6

The Multiple Roles of Context in Dispositional Judgment

Yaacov Trope
New York University

One of the most elementary features of cognition is the distinction between figure and background, stimulus and context. A variety of motivational and informational factors lead us to single out certain objects, events, or properties as focal and others as background. We may intend to—and actually believe we do—react to the inherent properties of the stimulus. However, a large amount of research suggests that our reactions depend on the context as much as they depend on the stimulus itself (see e.g., Higgins & King, 1981; Nisbett & Wilson, 1977; Kahneman & Miller, 1986; Wyer & Srull, 1986).

The influence of context may extend beyond the immediate stimulus. The interpretation of the stimulus may derive from the context. Yet, the contextually derived interpretation may subsequently be used *as if* it was independent evidence for new judgments (see e.g., Higgins & Lurie, 1983; Marcel, 1980; Schvaneveldt & McDonald, 1981). These new judgments may agree or disagree with those implied by the context itself. As a result, stimulus interpretations may strengthen or weaken the implications of the very context from which they were initially derived.

This issue is particularly relevant to dispositional inferences from behavior. Ordinarily, information about a target person's behavior is accompanied by information about the situational context. The amount of situational information may vary, but it is usually available to us. We can see the difficulty of the task that the athlete performs, the group that a speaker addresses, or the reward that is offered for compliance. The situation can, therefore, serve as context that determines the interpretation of behavior. The question, then, is whether perceivers will rely on the derived behavior interpretation *as if* it was independent evidence for subsequent inferences regarding the target's dispositions. If they do, then the implications of the situation may be altered by the behavioral interpretations that the situation itself originally produced.

The present chapter describes a research program on these issues. The research was guided by a two-stage model of dispositional judgments (Trope, 1986). I first present the model. Then I describe a series of studies that test the model's predictions. Finally, I discuss the implication of the results regarding the determinants and consequences of contextual effects in dispositional judgment.

THE TWO-STAGE MODEL OF DISPOSITIONAL JUDGMENTS

The model assumes that dispositional judgments are end products of an identification stage and an inferential stage (see Fig. 6.1). At the identification stage, the stimulus cues are encoded in terms of disposition relevant categories. First, the actor's verbal or nonverbal behavioral cues are encoded in terms of the disposition they overtly express. For example, before making inferences about the speaker's true liberalism or conservatism, perceivers first identify the content of the speech as liberal or conservative. Second, the situational cues to which the target person responds are identified in terms of the disposition they elicit. For example, the audience addressed by the speaker may be identified as expecting a liberal or a conservative speech. Finally, perceivers may have information about the target's past behavior. In our example, this information may consist of statements that the speaker has made in the past on various issues. These statements are retrieved and identified in terms of liberalism--conservatism.

In Fig. 6.1, behavior identification is jointly determined by the behavioral data and by the context. The context in this case consists of prior knowledge about the actor and the situation in which the behavior occurs. It is assumed that situational and prior information act as priming cues or as active expectancies that may shift behavior identification in a context-congruent direction. A speech is more likely to be perceived as taking a liberal stance if this is what the speaker has done in the past and the present audience is liberal. Similarly, a child will be perceived as working harder on a task if he or she is highly rewarded for performing it well and he or she has been industrious in the past.

It is assumed that the magnitude of these contextual effects depends on the ambiguity of the context, the ambiguity of the stimulus, the match between the context and the stimulus, and the temporal order in which they

6. ROLES OF CONTEXT IN DISPOSITIONAL JUDGMENT   125

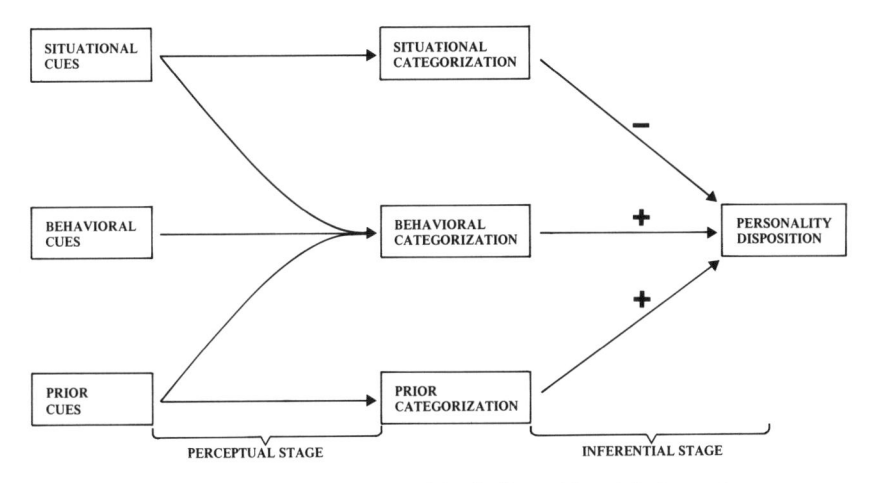

FIG. 6.1. A two-stage model of dispositional judgment.

are presented. An unambiguous context (one that is strongly associated with one and only one category) generates strong expectancies regarding the categorization of the stimulus. These expectancies will actually have an effect to the extent that the stimulus is ambiguous (i.e., strongly associated with different categories), the stimulus follows the context, one of its alternative categorizations matches the contextually invoked category, and the context precedes the stimulus.

Given that prior and situational cues are presented first, they will affect behavioral categorization to the extent that the behavioral cues are associated with more than one category and the prior and situational cues ambiguously invoke one of these categories. A smile is an example of a behavioral cue that can have positive as well as negative meaning. In an unambiguous friendly situation, a smile will be perceived as a sympathetic reaction, whereas in the context of an unambiguously unfriendly situation, it will be perceived as a sarcastic or defensive reaction (Frijda, 1969).

The results of the identification stage serve as input for the inferential stage. As is shown in the right hand side of Fig. 6.1, the perceiver uses the behavioral, situational, and prior categorizations to determine whether the actor truly possesses the disposition he or she overtly expressed. The inferences are presumably guided by people's beliefs regarding the causes of behavior (Kelley, 1972). Specifically, given that both situational inducements and the actor's personal dispositions determine behavior, dispositional inference requires *subtraction* of the contribution of situational inducements from the disposition implied by the behavior itself.

By the subtractive rule, an actor will be attributed any given disposition to the extent that his or her behavior is perceived to display the disposition and the behavior deviates from situational expectancies. For example, a speaker will be attributed liberal attitudes if he or she takes a strong liberal stance and the audience is conservative. Similarly, when congruent with group norms, cooperative behavior provides little information regarding the actor's dispositional cooperativeness, but when incongruent with group norms, the same cooperative behavior allows strong inferences regarding the correspondent disposition. In line with these assumptions, the right hand side of Fig. 6.1 indicates that dispositional attribution is positively related to perception of the corresponding behavior and negatively related to the perceived contribution of situational inducements.

Note that the subtractive rule is used here to refer both to Kelley's (1972) *discounting* and *augmentation* principles. Subtraction of situational inducements that *facilitate* behavior results in discounting of the correspondent disposition; in contrast, the subtraction of situational inducements that *inhibit* behavior results in augmentation of the correspondent disposition.

Finally, the model assumes that the immediate behavioral and situational information is integrated with prior information. Social judgment research suggests that when the immediate evidence is less than perfectly diagnostic, prior knowledge will affect final judgment (Ajzen & Fishbein, 1975; Darley & Fazio, 1980; Ginossar & Trope, 1980, 1987; Miller & Turnbull, 1986; Trope, 1974; Trope & Burnstein, 1975).

THE CONTEXTUAL AND INFERENTIAL EFFECTS OF SITUATIONAL INDUCEMENTS

Given the preceding assumptions about the identification and inferential processes, let us focus now on the effect of situational inducements on dispositional judgment. Figure 6.1 suggests that situational inducements are used both to identify the disposition the actor expresses (behavior identification) and to infer the disposition he or she truly possesses (dispositional inference). At identification, the situation serves as context that biases the identification of behavior as expressing the very disposition from which the situation is subsequently subtracted. The reliance on this context-produced behavior identification *as if* it was independent evidence for the corresponding disposition counteracts subtractive effects of the situation.

The preceding analysis suggests that situational inducements will not necessarily produce subtractive effects on dispositional judgments even when they are fully subtracted at the inferential stage. For example, perceivers may be aware that the child is extrinsically rewarded for performing well and may fully subtract the contribution of the reward when inferring the child's industriousness. However, the reward may bias perceivers to identify high performance levels, even higher than justified by the reward. As a result, the child will be attributed no less and even more industriousness when rewarded than when not rewarded.

RELEVANT RESEARCH

According to the two-stage model, the effect of situational inducements on dispositional judgments should depend on the magnitude of the situation's contextual effect on behavior identification. Large contextual effects may attenuate or reverse subtractive effects. As suggested earlier, the magnitude of these contextual effects depends on the ambiguity of the behavior, the ambiguity of the situation, the temporal order of the two kinds of information, and on the match between the two. To test the model, we conducted a series of studies that varied one determinant of the situation's context effect, namely, the ambiguity of the behavior. The situation was always presented first, it was always unambiguous, and its meaning could match the meaning of the behavior. The predictions of the model are straightforward: Behavior ambiguity should increase the contextual effect of the situation which, in turn, should offset its subtractive effect on dispositional judgment.

The initial studies presented subjects with either ambiguous or unambiguous facial reactions to unambiguous positive or negative emotional situations. The unambiguous reactions (as well as situations) were strongly associated with one and only one emotion, either positive or negative. In contrast, the ambiguous facial reactions were strongly associated both with a positive emotion and with a negative emotion. Based on this information, subjects were asked to either identify the emotion that the face expressed or to infer the target's emotional dispositions (see Trope, 1986).

The results showed that the identification of the emotions expressed by the unambiguous faces was unaffected by the situation. Consistent with our model, dispositional inferences from such facial expressions showed strong subtractive effects. In contrast, the identification of the ambiguous facial expressions largely depended on the situational context. The same facial expression was perceived as conveying a positive emotion when the situation was pleasant and a negative emotion when the situation was unpleasant. As predicted, dispositional inferences from these reactions did not yield subtractive effects. On the contrary, subjects attributed to the target person higher levels of any given disposition if its expression was elicited by the situation than if its expression was not elicited by the situation.

These results suggest that the contextual effect of the situation extends beyond the identification of the immediate behavior. Our subjects used the situation to identify the emotion of the ambiguous faces. But, then, they used this contextually derived identification as new, independent evidence regarding emotional dispositions. The contextual effect of the situation on behavior identification thus undermined the situation's own effect on dispositional judgment.

Trope, Cohen, and Maoz (1988) extended these findings to the attitudinal domain. Subjects heard person A making an evaluation (behavioral cues) of a likable or dislikable person B (situational cues). The evaluation was either ambiguous or unambiguous. Based on this information, some subjects judged the favorability of A's evaluation (behavior identification), whereas other subjects judged A's leniency toward people in general (dispositional judgment). As expected, B's likability had a much stronger (contextual) effect on the perceived favorability of the ambiguous evaluation than on the perceived favorability of the unambigious evaluations. Moreover, the inferences of A's leniency from the unambiguous evaluations showed subtractive effects of B's likability. That is, A was attributed less dispositional leniency for any given evaluation if it pertained to a likable person than if pertained to a dislikable person. In contrast, B's likability had little or no effect on the inferences from the ambiguous evaluations.

These results are consistent with our earlier research on emotion judgment in showing that behavioral ambiguity has opposite effects at identification and inference. On one hand, it increases the situation's contextual effect on behavior identification and, on the other hand, it decreases the situation's subtractive effect on dispositional judgment.

Although the preceding studies provide convergent evidence for the present analysis, their generalizability is limited by the fact that they all used intrinsic stimulus properties as situational inducements. In the emotion judgment studies, the situational inducements were the emotion-eliciting properties of the situation, and in the interpersonal evaluation study, they were likable or dislikable characteristics of the evaluated person. In a recent study, Trope, Cohen, and Giladi (1989) sought to extend the test of the model to extrinsic situational constraints of the kind commonly used in the attitude attribution paradigm (see, e.g., Jones, 1979).

The situational inducements in this study were instructions to provide a positive or a negative evaluation of another person. The experiment initially described a workshop on interpersonal communication for a group of corporate executives. Subjects were told that, as part of the workshop, each executive was asked to prepare either a positive or a negative report about a predesignated employee. Subjects then received a report written by one of the executives. The report was either unambiguously positive, unambiguously negative, or ambiguous.

These manipulations were made possible by using information pertaining to the trait pairs persistent-stubborn and serious-gloomy. Like other evaluatively different but descriptively similar traits, each of these trait pairs have opposite evaluative connotations but partially overlapping behavioral features (see Peabody, 1967). The positive instructions asked the executive to describe the employee as persistent and serious, whereas the negative instructions asked the executive to describe the employee as stubborn and gloomy. We used common features of these trait pairs to construct ambiguous reports and distinctive features to construct unambiguous reports. The choice of features was based on pretest data from a group of judges. Specifically, the unambiguous positive report included features that were seen as associated with persistence and seriousness, for example, "If Dan starts something, you can be sure he'll complete it" (persistent); "He gives thorough consideration to problems he is faced with" (serious). The unambiguous negative report included characteristics that were seen as associated with stubbornness and gloominess, for example, "Dan doesn't change his mind, even when he is clearly wrong" (stubborn); "He creates a melancholic and pessimistic atmosphere" (gloomy). The ambiguous report included features that were seen as associated both with the positive and the negative traits, for example, "Dan rarely changes his mind" (persistent-stubborn); "In meetings, Dan is always quiet. He expresses his opinion at the end and always in a low voice" (serious-gloomy).

After presenting the information about the instructions and the executive's report, we assessed subject's perceptions of the report (behavior identification) and their inferences regarding the executive's true attitude toward the employee (dispositional judgment). Let us consider first the identification data. As predicted, the positive report was perceived as highly favorable and the negative report as highly unfavorable, regardless of the instructions. In contrast, the perception of the ambiguous report strongly depended on the instructions. This report was perceived as favorable in the context of the positive instructions and as unfavorable in the context of the negative instructions. An open-ended measure of identification yielded similar results. Specifically, we asked our subjects to summarize from memory the content of the report. Two judges performed a content analysis of these summaries. They first determined whether the items in the summary pertained to the trait pairs persistent-serious and stubborn-gloomy and then rated the favorability of the items. As before, we found that the instructions had a stronger impact on the favorability of the summaries of the ambiguous reports than on the favorability of the summaries of the unambiguous reports. Moreover, we found that almost all of the items in the summaries (96%) pertained to our two trait terms. This finding suggests that the instructions affected the perceived descriptive content of the ambiguous reports, not only their general evaluative tone.

Let us turn now to the dispositional judgment data, namely, subjects' inferences regarding the executive's true attitude toward the employee. We found that the instructions produced consistent subtractive effects on inferences from the unambiguous positive and unambiguous negative reports. In both cases, subjects made weaker correspondent attitude inferences when the report conformed to the instructions than when the report violated the instructions. In contrast, inferences from the ambiguous report showed no such effect of situational inducements. Thus, ambiguity of the report increased the contextual effect of the instructions but decreased their subtractive effect.

These results demonstrate that the two-stage model is applicable to identification and dispositional judgment of attitudinal behavior under extrinsic constraints. Like the results of our earlier studies, they suggest that subjects do utilize situational information in dispositional inference. However, to the extent that the behavior is ambiguous, situational inducements affect dispositional inference via their contextual effect on behavior identification. This effect, in turn, may mask the utilization of situational inducements. Indeed, extensive research initiated by Jones and his colleagues has found that perceivers show little sensitivity to the magnitude of situational inducements and that they are willing to attribute behavior-correspondent dispositions to actors who are constrained by strong situational demands (see Gilbert & Jones, 1985; Jones, 1979). Several studies even reported reversals of the subtractive rule, that is, stronger dispositional attributions for situationally congruent behavior than for situationally incongruent behavior (see, e.g., Ross & Olson, 1981; Snyder & Frankel, 1976).

These findings were interpreted as reflecting a "failure to discount"—a tendency to underutilize information about situational inducements when provided with behavioral evidence. It has been argued that perceivers pay little attention to situational inducements and give them little weight when drawing inferences from behavior (Jones, 1979). The present two-stage model suggests that, even if fully subtracted at the inferential stage, situational inducements may have little or no effect on attribution because of identification stage processes. Behavioral cues are frequently ambiguous, and the resulting contextual effect of the situation may counteract its subtractive effect in dispositional judgment.

THE ORDER OF SITUATIONAL AND BEHAVIORAL INFORMATION

It has been suggested that the subtractive effect depends on the temporal order with which situational and behavioral information are presented (see Jones, Riggs, & Quattrone, 1979; Snyder, 1974; Snyder & Frankel, 1976). Specifically, Snyder and Frankel found a subtractive effect when situational information followed behavioral information. Subjects saw a videotape with no soundtrack of an interviewee reacting either to anxiety-provoking or to neutral questions. The questions, serving as situational inducements, were presented to subjects either before or after viewing the videotape. Snyder and Frankel found that when the questions were presented last, subjects attributed less dispositional anxiety to the interviewee reacting to the anxiety-eliciting questions than to the interviewee reacting in the same manner to neutral questions, as required by the subtractive rule. In contrast, when the questions were presented first, the questions produced an additive effect. That is, subjects attributed more dispositional anxiety to an interviewee reacting to anxiety-eliciting questions than to an interviewee reacting to neutral questions (see also Snyder, 1974).

The results of a subsequent study by Jones, Riggs, and Quattrone (1979) led to different conclusions. That study presented subjects with a student's essay on minority quotas in university admissions. Either before or after reading the essay, subjects were informed that the writer had or had not been free to choose which side of the issue to support. Based on this information, subjects judged the writer's true attitude on the issue of minority quotas. Jones et al. found that situational inducements produced situational subtractive effects when they preceded the essay, but not when they followed the essay.

How can we reconcile these seemingly contradictory findings? To answer this question in terms of the two-stage model, it is necessary to examine the effects of temporal order at the identification stage and at the inferential stage. Consider first the identification stage. As noted earlier, any given contextual factor is more likely to affect the identification of a stimulus if it precedes the stimulus than if it follows the stimulus. When the stimulus is presented first, its meaning will be determined by the information it contains and by contextual factors other than that under consideration. As a result, any given contextual factor that appears later will not have as much impact as it could have had if it were presented first (see Higgins & Stangor, 1988; Trope, 1986). In our case, then, situational inducements are more likely to shift the identification of behavioral cues if they appear before, rather than after, the behavioral cues.

Temporal order has different implications for the inferential stage. When situational information is presented last, behavioral information is likely to have a salience advantage over situational information. Behavioral information may simply draw more attention under these circumstances. Moreover, behavioral information is more likely to serve as a strong anchor for dispositional inference. Specifically, in the absence of information about situational constraints, perceivers may start with the judgment that the target person possesses the behavior-correspondent disposition. Later, when perceivers learn about situational constraints, they may adjust their initial impression. However, as evidenced in various domains, the adjustment of initial judgments, once made, is typically insufficient (Tversky & Kahneman, 1974; Ross, Lepper, & Hubbard, 1975). Indeed, the salience and anchoring processes have been proposed by Jones and his colleagues as explanations for the correspondence bias in dispositional attribution (see Jones, 1979). Here, salience and anchoring are viewed as properties of the inferential stage that act to increase the inferential weight of situational inducements when they are presented before, rather than after, behavioral information.

Figure 6.2 summarizes in schematic form the preceding analysis. The presentation of situational inducements first, rather than last, has two opposite effects on dispositional judgment at the inferential stage and at the identification stage. At the inferential stage, earlier presentation of situational inducements acts to increase their subtractive effect due to salience and anchoring processes. In contrast, at the identification stage, the same temporal order acts to decrease the subtractive effect of situational inducements due to their contextual effect on behavior identification. Depending on the magnitude of these identification and inferential factors, the net result of presenting situational information first, rather than last, can be an increase in the subtractive effect, as in the Jones, Riggs, and Quattrone (1979) study, or a decrease in the subtractive effect, as in the Snyder (1974) and Snyder and Frankel (1976) studies.

Examination of the materials used in past research suggests that the conflicting results are explainable in terms of behavioral ambiguity. Specifically, Snyder (1974) and Snyder and Frankel (1976) presented an interviewee's nonverbal reactions, whereas Jones et al. (1979) presented a short written essay arguing strongly for or against minority quotas. It seems reasonable to suppose that the nonverbal reactions were more ambiguous than the written essay. If so, Snyder and Frankel's finding that the earlier presentation of situational inducements decreases subtractive effects and Jones et al.'s finding that the same temporal order increases subtractive effects are both predictable within the two-stage model.

A recent study by Trope, Cohen, and Giladi (1989) was designed as a direct test of the preceding analysis. This study presented either ambiguous or unambiguous behavior that was either preceded or followed by situa-

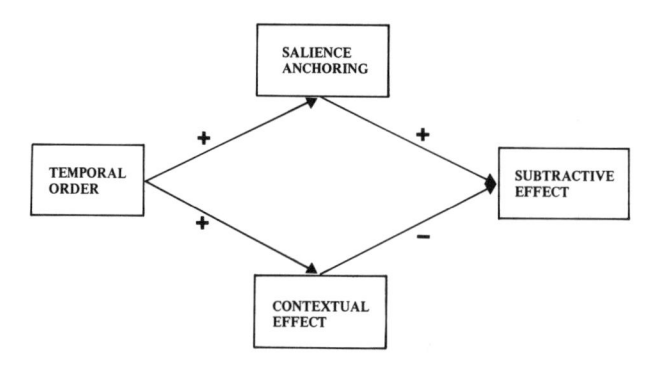

FIG. 6.2. Identification and inferential effects of temporal order (earlier presentation of situational information).

6. ROLES OF CONTEXT IN DISPOSITIONAL JUDGMENT 133

tional information. More specifically, subjects heard, through a tape recorder, person A making either an ambiguous or an unambiguous evaluation of person B. In addition, subjects received "objective information" that indicated that person B was either likable or dislikable. The objective information was designed to create a situational demand for a favorable or an unfavorable evaluation. This information was presented either before or after hearing the tape-recorded evaluation. Based on this information, subjects were asked to recall and rate the content of the evaluation (behavior identification) and to judge A's leniency toward people in general (dispositional judgment).

These manipulations were made possible by using information pertaining to the trait pair cheerful-frivolous. Subjects heard person A reporting either unambiguous frivolous characteristics, or ambiguous cheerful-frivolous characteristics about a target person B, who was described as having either unambiguous cheerful or unambiguous frivolous characteristics.

Let us consider first the identification data, that is, subjects' ratings of the positivity of the evaluation. As expected, we found that the contextual effect on identification depended on temporal order when the evaluation was ambiguous, but not when it was unambiguous. Specifically, B's likability produced little or no contextual effect on the perception of the unambiguous evaluation, regardless of whether the information about B was presented first or last. In both cases, subjects thought that A described B as a frivolous, negative person. In contrast, the ambiguous evaluation yielded substantial context effects when preceded by information about B, but not when followed by information about B. When the information about B was presented first, subjects who knew B was a likable person thought that the evaluation described him as a cheerful person, whereas subjects who knew B was dislikable thought that the evaluation described him as a frivolous person. However, as predicted, this contextual effect vanished when the information about B was presented last. Regardless of B's likability, subjects perceived A's evaluation as mixed.

Subjects' judgments of dispositional leniency were also consistent with our predictions. B's likability always produced a subtractive effect on inferences from the unambiguous evaluation. That is, A's unambiguous negative evaluation led to weaker attributions of dispositional harshness when B was dislikable than when he was likable. However, this subtractive effect was stronger when the information about B was presented first than when it was presented last. The ambiguous evaluation yielded the opposite pattern of results: When presented first, B's likability produced little or no subtractive effect, as in our earlier studies. However, when presented last, B's likability produced a significant subtractive effect, similar to that obtained for the unambiguous evaluation.

This study demonstrates the importance of distinguishing between identification and inferential processes. Temporal order represents an informational variable that may produce inconsistent effects on judgment, not because of judgmental incoherence, but because it operates differently at the identification and inference stages. By increasing the situation's context effect at the identification stage, earlier presentation of situational information may reduce the situation's subtractive effect. But by increasing the situation's inferential weight, the same temporal order may enhance the subtractive effect. Our study systematically varied the relative importance of the identification stage and inferential stage processes, thus allowing us to predict a priori the different effects of temporal order on dispositional judgment.

TYPES OF NONDIAGNOSTIC BEHAVIOR

In the studies discussed thus far, the ambiguous behaviors consisted of cues each of which was highly associated with two different categories. Each category, when rendered probably by the situational context, provided a good match for *all* of the behavioral cues. Subjects could therefore identify these cues in terms of the situationally invoked category without considering any alternative. We contrasted this behavior with unambiguous behavior, namely, behavior consisting of cues that are all highly associated with one and only one category. Situationally invoked categorizations are unlikely to affect the categorization of such behavior, as our research actually showed.

However, in real life, many behaviors are neither fully ambiguous (highly associated with different categories) nor fully unambiguous (highly associated with one and only one category). One class of such behaviors may be termed *conflictual*. Behavior of this kind consists of cues, each of which is highly associated with a *different* category. In their totality, these cues cannot fully match any single situationally invoked category and, therefore, are unlikely to be perceived with confidence in terms of that category. For example, a speech containing strong liberal arguments and equally strong conservative arguments is unlikely to be perceived with confidence as a liberal or as a conservative speech, even when situational expectancies (e.g., a biased audience) favor one possibility or the other.

Another kind of nondiagnostic behavior is *vague* behavior. In this case, all the cues are *weakly* associated with the various categories. The vagueness may stem from impaired perception or memory of the cues or from their low prototypicality with respect to the categories at hand. Like conflictual cues, they cannot fully match any given situationally invoked category and, therefore, are unlikely to be perceived with confidence in terms of any one of these categories.

Although ambiguous cues should yield stronger contextual effects than should both conflictual and vague cues, the latter should yield stronger contextual effects than should fully unambiguous cues. The two-stage model would therefore predict that the likelihood of subtraction should be greatest for fully unambiguous behavior, the smallest for fully ambiguous behavior, and intermediate for conflictual and vague behavioral cues.

The distinction between ambiguous, conflictual, vague, and unambiguous behaviors has implications for the role of memory processes in dispositional judgment. At encoding, conflictual and vague behaviors may yield weak contextual effects, at least in comparison to ambiguous behavior. However, over time, the identification of conflictual and vague behavior may become increasingly assimilated to situational expectancies and, thus, yield increasingly larger contextual effects. Depending on the time interval between the initial encoding of the situational and behavioral information and the subsequent dispositional judgment, the contextual effect on conflictual behavior may come to resemble the contextual effect on ambiguous behavior. Like the latter behavior, conflictual and vague behavior may then fail to show subtractive effects.

The preceding analysis assumes that perceivers make identifications *on-line* and only later, if required, do they apply dispositional inference operations to the retrieved identifications. The delay may allow stronger contextual effects and, therefore, result in weaker subtraction. It is possible, however, that dispositional inferences are made at encoding. Such factors as instructions, task demands, and the perceiver's own need to predict the target's behavior in the future may encourage perceivers to make dispositional inferences on-line, when behavioral and situational information is initially processed (see Bargh, 1989; Hastie & Park, 1986). In fact, recent work by Bassili and Smith (1986) and Winter and Uleman (1983) suggests that, even in the absence of any instructions or other instrumental considerations, perceivers make dispositional judgments spontaneously.

If dispositional judgments are made at encoding, then a later dispositional judgment, when requested, will rely on the retrieval of the initial dispositional judgment, rather than on retrieval of the behavioral and situational identifications. Any changes in identification of conflictual and vague behavior over time will not affect dispositional judgments at recall and, therefore, will not attenuate the subtractive effect on these judgments. Thus, if dispositional inferences are made on-line, then, at recall, conflictual and vague behavior will show stronger subtractive effects than will ambiguous behavior, but if dispositional inferences are based on retrieved identifications, then the difference between these behaviors in subtractive effects will be relatively small. These predictions suggest interesting directions for future research.

THE ROLE OF BEHAVIOR AS DISAMBIGUATOR OF SITUATIONS

This chapter focused on the role of the situation as a disambiguator of the meaning of behavior. The assumption was that the situation is always unambiguous, eliciting one and only one kind of emotional or evaluative response. Many real-life situations, however, are more ambiguous. Norms are sometimes contradictory, instructions vague, and incentives multivalent. In the extreme case, the same situation may be perceived as eliciting opposite behaviors. For example, positive results of a pregnancy test may be perceived as a happy or as a sad event, a stare may be seen as a pleasant or as an unpleasant stimulus, and so on.

In such cases, the actor's behavior, if unambiguous, will serve as context that determines the meaning of the situation. The two-stage model suggests that this contextual effect may counteract the behavior's effect on dispositional judgment. Specifically, in context, ambiguous situations will be perceived as facilitating the actor's behavior. The subtraction of the situation, thus perceived, will attenuate or even reverse inferences of behavior-correspondent dispositions. If perceivers identify what the situation demands according to what the actor does, then the actor's behavior cannot have much impact on dispositional judgment. Thus, just as behavioral ambiguity attenuates the effect of the situation on attribution, so does situational ambiguity attenuate the effect of behavior on attribution. Empirical support for this analysis is provided by a recent paper by Trope and Cohen (in press).

CONCLUDING REMARKS

This chapter reaffirms the importance of context in the processing of behavioral information. Because behavior is always embedded in a situational context, contextual effects, small or large, are inevitable. Past research on dispositional judgment has focused on the inferential use of the situational context. The present two-stage model takes into account both the inferential use of the situation and its use in the initial identification of behavioral information. The research that I reviewed suggests that situationally derived behavior identifications are subsequently treated as independent rather than as conditional information, as inherent properties of the behavior rather than as situational derivatives. In essence, *the inference starts from a point where behavior is already identified as indicative of the very disposition that the situation discounts.* In this way, behavior identification counteracts the inferential implications of the context from which it was originally derived.

At a more general level, the present research illustrates violation of the requirement for independence between people's inferential rules and the procedures they use for identifying the data to which the rules are applied. Specifically, the subtractive rule for dispositional inference derives from people's causal models of behavior as caused by certain situational and dispositional properties. But the same model also underlies the situation's context effect on behavior identification. This use of the same model both for inference and for identifying behavioral evidence represents identification-inference nonindependence and produces judgments that disagree with people's own inferential rules.

I proposed several determinants of the situation's contextual effect: the ambiguity of the situation, the ambiguity of the behavior, the fit between the categorizations of the two kinds of information, and the order in which they are presented. Our research focused on two of these determinants: the ambiguity of the behavior and the order of situational and behavioral information. We found that ambiguity increases the contextual effect of the situation on behavior identification but decreases and even reverses the subtractive effect of situational information on dispositional judgment (Trope, Cohen, & Maoz, 1988). Our findings help explain inconsistencies in past research on the utilization of situational information. These inconsistencies may reflect, at least in part, the opposite effects of situational information at the identification and inferential stages.

Temporal order may also have opposite effects on dispositional judgment, depending on its influence at the identification and inferential stage. Earlier presentation of situational information increases its contextual effect at the identification stage and its weight at the inferential stage. Because these effects influence subtraction in opposite ways, it is not surprising that manipulations of temporal order yielded mixed results in past research (see Jones, Riggs, & Quattrone, 1979; Snyder, 1974; Snyder & Frankel, 1976). Close examination of the stimulus materials used in past research and the results of our own study (Trope, Cohen, & Giladi, 1989) suggest that behavior ambiguity plays a crucial role. When behavior is unambiguous, earlier presentation of situational information does not affect the situation's contextual effect. Therefore, earlier presentation can increase the situation's subtractive effect. In contrast, behavior ambiguity introduces contextual effects that counteract the inferential advantage (and, therefore, the greater subtractive effect) of the situation when it is presented earlier.

Memory-based dispositional judgments raise interesting questions regarding the interaction of identification and inferential processes. One question is whether dispositional judgments are made on-line and later retrieved or, alternatively, that they are made on the basis of retrieved situational and behavioral identifications (see Bassili & Smith, 1986; Hastie & Park, 1986; Winter & Uleman, 1983). I argued that this question is particularly important for the precessing of conflictual and vague behaviors. Contextual effects on such behaviors may increase over time. This, in turn, should affect dispositional judgments that are based on retrieved situational and behavioral identifications, but not those based on retrieval of on-line dispositional judgments. Unlike contextual effects on conflictual and vague behaviors, the contextual effects on unambiguous and ambiguous behavior are unlikely to change much over time. Hence, whether or not dispositional judgments are memory-based or made on-line should be less important for inferences from unambiguous and ambiguous behavior.

A related question is whether awareness of the role of the situational context in behavior identification eliminates subsequent use of these identifications for dispositional inference. A study by Trope (1978) suggests that awareness may be insufficient. In that study, subjects made dispositional inferences on the basis of behavioral information retrieved from memory. The difficulty of the retrieval task was manipulated experimentally. Our subjects were fully cognizant of the inaccuracy with which they retrieved the original behavior information. In fact, when the memory task was hard, subjects expressed great uncertainty as to what the target person had really done. Nevertheless, these same subjects proceeded to make dispositional inferences *"as if"* the retrieval of information was errorless. The confidence with which they made dispositional inferences was no less than that of subjects who knew that their retrieval was perfect.

Because each and all of the cues comprising ambiguous behavior are strongly associated with different categories, contextual resolution of the ambiguity may occur without awareness. Perceivers may identify the situationally invoked meaning without considering alternative ones. This is less likely to occur when behavioral cues are conflictual or vague. Because vague cues are weakly associated with the situationally invoked category, and because some of the conflictual cues are strongly associated with the alternative category, perceivers are likely to be sensitized to the role of context in their behavior identifications. However, the Trope (1978) study suggests that such sensitization will not necessarily eliminate perceivers' reliance on the situationally invoked category in subsequent inferences. They may be aware of the alternative interpretation of the behavioral cues but, nevertheless, proceed to dispositional inference *"as if"* the situationally invoked interpretation is valid.

The preceding analysis obviously requires direct empirical tests beyond those reported in this chapter. If such tests indeed show that the processing of conflictual and vague information resembles the processing of ambiguous information, then inferences from a wide range of behaviors are likely to show contextually produced biases.

REFERENCES

Ajzen, I., & Fishbein. M. (1975). A Bayesian analysis of the attribution process. *Psychological Bulletin, 82,* 267-277.

Bargh, J. A. (1989). The power behind the throne of judgment: Varieties of automatic inferences in social perception and cognition. In J. S. Uleman & J. A. Bargh (Eds.), *Unintended thoughts: Limits of awareness, intentions, and control.* New York: Guilford.

Bassili, J. N., & Smith, M. C. (1986). On the spontaneity of trait attribution: Converging evidence for the role of cognitive strategy. *Journal of Personality and Social Psychology, 50,* 234-245.

Darley, J. M., & Fazio, R. H. (1980). Expectancy confirmation processes arising in the social interaction sequence. *American Psychologist, 35,* 867-881.

Frijda, N. H. (1969). Recognition of emotion. In L. Berkowitz (Ed.), *Advances in experimental social psychology* (Vol. 4, pp. 167-223). New York: Academic Press.

Gilbert, D. T., & Jones, E. E. (1985). Perceiver induced constraint: Interpretations of self-generated reality. *Journal of Personality and Social Psychology, 50,* 269-280.

Ginossar, Z., & Trope, Y. (1980). The effect of base-rates and individuating information on judgment about another person. *Journal of Experimental Social Psychology, 16,* 228-242.

Ginossar, Z., & Trope, Y. (1987). Problem solving in judgment under uncertainty. *Journal of Personality and Social Psychology, 52,* 464-476.

Hastie, R., & Park, B. (1986). The relationship between memory and judgment depends on whether the judgment task is memory based or on-line. *Psychological Review, 93,* 258-268.

Higgins, E. T., & King, G. (1981). Accessibility of social constructs: Information-processing consequences of individual and contextual variability. In N. Cantor & J. F. Kihlstrom (Eds.), *Personality cognition, and social interaction* (pp. 69-121). Hillsdale, NJ: Lawrence Erlbaum Associates.

Higgins, E. T., & Lurie, L. (1983). Context, categorization, and memory: The change in standard effect. *Cognitive Psychology, 15,* 525-547.

Higgins, E. T., & Stangor, C. (1988). Context-driven social judgment and memory: When "behavior engulfs the field" in reconstructive memory. In D. Bar-Tal & A. Kruglanski (Eds.), *Social psychology of knowledge.* Cambridge, England: Cambridge University Press.

Jones, E. E. (1979). The rocky road from acts to dispositions. *American Psychologist, 34,* 107-117.

Jones, E. E., Riggs, J. M., & Quattrone, G. A. (1979). Observer bias in the attitude attribution paradigm: Effect of time and information order. *Journal of Personality and Social Psychology, 37,* 1230-1238.

Kahneman, D., & Miller, D. T. (1986). Norm theory: Comparing reality to its alternatives. *Psychological Review, 93,* 136-153.

Kelley, H. H. (1972). Causal schemata and the attribution process. In E. E. Jones, D. E. Kanouse, H. H. Kelley, R. E. Nisbett, S. Valins, & B. Weiner (Eds.), *Attribution: Perceiving the causes of behavior* (pp. 151-174). Morristown, NJ: General Learning Press.

Marcel, I. (1980). Conscious and preconscious recognition of polysemous words: Locating the selective effects of prior verbal context. In R. S. Nickerson (Ed.), *Attention and performance* (Vol. 8, pp. 435-457). Hillsdale, NJ: Lawrence Erlbaum Associates.

Miller, D. T., & Turnbull, W. (1986). Expectancies and interpersonal processes. *Annual*

Review of Psychology, 37, 233-256.
Nisbett, R. E., & Wilson, T. D. (1977). Telling more than we can know: Verbal reports on mental processes. *Psychological Review, 84,* 231-259.
Peabody, D. (1967). Trait inferences: Evaluative and descriptive aspects. *Journal of Personality and Social Psychology,* Monograph 7, No. 4. (Part 2, Whole No. 644), 1-18.
Ross, L., Lepper, M. R., & Hubbard, M. (1975). Perseverance in self-perception and social perception: Biased attribution processes in the debriefing paradigm. *Journal of Personality and Social Psychology, 32,* 880-892.
Ross, M., & Olson, J. M. (1981). An expectancy-attribution model of the effects of placebos. *Psychological Review, 88,* 408-437.
Schvaneveldt, R. W., & McDonald, T. E. (1981). Semantic context and the encoding of words: Evidence for two modes of stimulus analysis. *Journal of Experimental Psychology: Human Perception and Performance, 7,* 673-687.
Snyder, M. L. (1974). The field engulfing behavior: An investigation of the attributing emotional states and dispositions. *Dissertation Abstracts International, 34,* 625g-6260.
Snyder, M. L., & Frankel, A. (1976). Observer bias: A stringent test of behavior engulfing the field. *Journal of Personality and Social Psychology, 34,* 857-864.
Trope, Y. (1974). Inferential processes in the forced compliance situation: A Bayesian analysis. *Journal of Experimental Social Psychology, 10,* 1-16.
Trope, Y. (1978). Inference of personal characteristics on the basis of information retrieved from one's memory. *Journal of Personality & Social Psychology, 36,* 93-106.
Trope, Y. (1986). Identification and inferential processes in dispositional attribution. *Psychological Review, 93,* 239-257.
Trope, Y., & Burnstein, E. (1975). Processing the information contained in another's behavior. *Journal of Experimental Social Psychology, 11,* 439-458.
Trope, Y., & Cohen, O. (in press). The perceptual and inferential determinants of behavior-correspondent judgment. *Journal of Experimental Social Psychology.*
Trope, Y., Cohen, O., & Giladi, O. (1989). *Perceptual and inferential mediators of order effects in dispositional judgment.* Unpublished manuscript. Hebrew University, Jerusalem, Israel.
Trope, Y., Cohen, O., & Maoz, I. (in press). The perceptual and inferential effects of situational inducements. *Journal of Personality and Social Psychology.*
Tversky, A., & Kahneman, D. (1974). Judgment under uncertainty: Heuristics and biases. *Science, 85,* 1124-1131.
Winter, L., & Uleman, J. S. (1983). When are social judgments made? Evidence for the spontaneousness of trait inferences. *Journal of Personality and Social Psychology, 49,* 904-917.
Wyer, R. S., Jr., & Srull, T. D. (1986). Human cognition in its social context. *Psychological Review, 93,* 322-359.

7

On-Line Processes in Category-Based and Individuating Impressions: Some Basic Principles and Methodological Reflections

Susan T. Fiske
Janet B. Ruscher
University of Massachusetts at Amherst

Much of the work of impression formation, in natural settings, occurs at encoding. The more we study impression formation processes in our laboratory, the more we are impressed by what perceivers accomplish as they are encountering information. Moreover, people possess on-line strategies for impression formation that prove to be quite functional for social purposes. For the past several years, we have focused on how people make sense of other people at the moment of the encounter itself and the functions served by those impressions. From various studies over time, we are beginning to distill general principles and useful methods for examining such functional, on-line impression formation processes; some of these principles and methods may prove useful to other researchers.

By way of preview, consider this scenario: A stranger walks into your office. Perhaps even upon hearing the character of the person's footsteps (uncertain) or knock (tentative), and then immediately upon seeing the person (young, female, blue-jean jacket, red lipstick), you categorize the person as an undergraduate student. Depending on whether you are a faculty member, graduate student, or a fellow undergraduate, and depending on whether you are having office hours, a bad day, or difficulty recruiting coders, you may seek much or little additional information about her. Suppose she volunteers that she is a junior psychology major, has heard fascinating things about your work, and she is interested in applying to graduate school. Open to the possibility that she is a budding psychologist, you invite her to sit down. Upon further questioning, however, you discover that she knows nothing about social psychology, has no research experience, has mediocre grades, and simply wants to "work with people."

You may then recategorize her as an unlikely prospect for graduate school and steer her elsewhere.

This example serves to illustrate a few basic principles in our approach to impression formation. First, one attempts to form a coherent impression, good enough for present purposes and given the information at hand. That is, one forms an impression that is functional under the current practical and motivational circumstances. To do this, diverse strategies are available, as indicated by initially categorizing and recategorizing the student, as well as by more individuating processes to be described. Second, one uses diverse information, from appearance to behaviors to self-reported traits to inferred traits, but some information tends to organize the remaining information better than vice versa. In this example, the student's vagueness might organize the remaining cues (innocence about the field, inexperience in research, mediocre performance, unfocused interest in graduate school, tentative behavior, etc.). Third, one attends to the most informative cues; this, too, is functional. In this instance, one attends more to her interests and abilities than to her clothing because of what is relevant in context. And one attends to the discrepancy between her initially apparent sophistication (supposed fascination with your work) and her total innocence of the field itself. Fourth, one forms a surprising amount of the impression rapidly and without much thought, but in ways that also prove functional. A professor, for example, is usually adept at categorizing students according to the type of information they need or the favor that they want and how long it will take. Fifth, impression formation processes are controllable: People respond to incentives and instructions. The initial possibility that the student might be a hot prospect for graduate school creates an incentive that affects the amount of attention and type of interpretations that, in turn, shape subsequent impression formation.

The agenda for this chapter, then, is to elaborate each of these points, drawing heavily on our own previous research, and then to discuss some methodological issues that have arisen in our studies of on-line impression formation. Throughout, we note the ways in which on-line impression formation processes appear quite functional, in the sense of practical and useful, under the circumstances.

SOME PRINCIPLES OF ON-LINE IMPRESSION FORMATION

People Use Diverse Strategies to Form Coherent, Good-Enough Impressions

A series of papers has developed a continuum model of impression formation, describing the range of strategies that perceivers use to make sense of other people (Fiske, 1982; Fiske & Pavelchak, 1986; Fiske & Neuberg, in press-a; cf. Brewer, 1988; Fiske, 1988). As described in this model, the range and priority of on-line strategies appears to be useful, adaptive, and functional under most circumstances. The continuum model assumes that initial categorization occurs automatically upon first perceiving the person or encountering a verbal label (see Fig. 7.1). In the prior example, tentative footsteps and a telltale hesitant knock at the office door together trigger the category "student" for at least one professor. Then, depending on the circumstances, the perceiver may pay more or less attention to the target, and the nature of the additional attention and interpretation determines which of several strategies of impression formation predominates.

The subsequent impression formation strategies can be ordered along a continuum, beginning with *category confirmation* (upon entering one's office, the person's age, dress, and demeanor confirm that she is a student). Category confirmation is favored by a general paucity of information, either: limited information beyond the category label; category-consistent information that is essentially redundant with the category label; mixed category-consistent and category-inconsistent information that can be resolved in favor of the category; or irrelevant, nondiagnostic information that can be interpreted as bolstering a strong, well-established stereotype (see Fiske & Neuberg, in press-a or Higgins & Bargh, 1987, for a review). Various motivational conditions, to be noted later, can also affect category confirmation processes.

Alternatively, if the category cannot easily be confirmed or is insufficient for the interaction at hand, the process may turn to *recategorization* (the generic student becomes more specifically a potential graduate school applicant or simply an unfocused people-oriented psych major). Recategorization includes finding a subcategory or an altogether new category, as well as using the self or another specific exemplar as a standard of comparison. It is favored by category-inconsistent information, or by irrelevant, nondiagnostic information accompanied by a weak stereotype (the "dilution" effect; Nisbett, Zukier, & Lemley, 1981).

Finally, if none of these categories suffice, impression formation may proceed by relatively attribute-oriented processes (combining the evaluations of the features: young, female, blue-jean jacket, red lipstick, junior, psychology major, interested in your research, mediocre grades, and so on). Such *piecemeal,* attribute-oriented processes are favored by information that does not easily fit any accessible category or by the judgmental conditions of high-quality, routinized decision-making, as in initially screening graduate applications.

Essentially, whatever the process, the perceiver searches for a good-enough impression to organize the available information in a satisfactory

144   FISKE AND RUSCHER

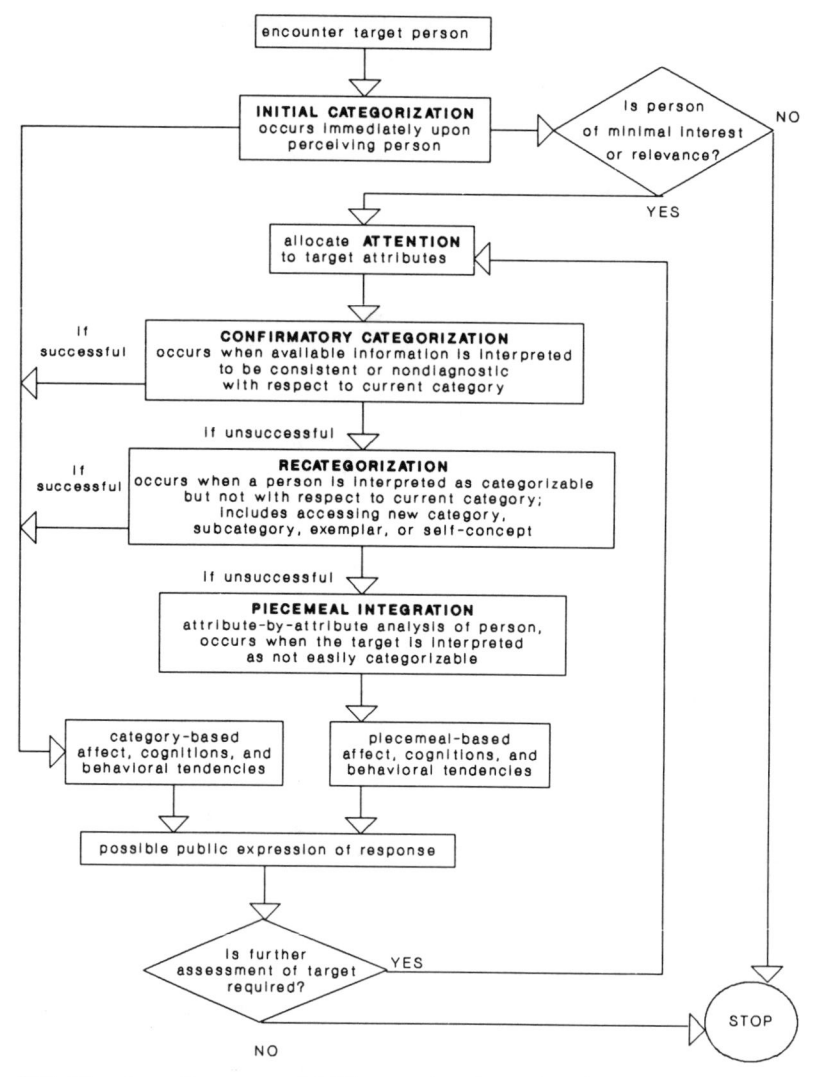

FIG. 7.1. A continuum model if impression formation, from category-based to individuating responses: The impact of information and motivation on attention and interpretation. From Fiske & Neuberg, in press[a]. Figure copyright Susan T. Fiske, 1986.

way, favoring the more category-oriented types of impressions over the more attribute-oriented types. If the initial category cannot be confirmed, then the perceiver recategorizes by generating a subcategory, an exemplar, or an altogether new category. If it is not possible to recategorize, then the perceiver will move to an attribute-by-attribute response to the other person. It is functional for perceivers to use the more category-oriented processes when sufficient, as such processes are efficient, being rapid and based on accumulated prior experience.

In positing the impression formation continuum, we have drawn heavily on traditional person perception research (e.g., Anderson, 1974) for an understanding of relatively attribute-based processes, but on the categorization literature in social cognition (e.g., Taylor & Crocker, 1981) and in stereotyping (e.g., Allport, 1954) for an understanding of relatively category-based processes (see Fiske & Neuberg, in press-a, for a review). The initial impetus in this effort was to combine the two supposedly competing models of impression formation first defined by Asch (1946), the holisitic and the elemental approaches, which were then studied subsequently by others as mutually exclusive frameworks (Ostrom, 1977). In our view, the elemental, attribute-oriented mode and the holistic, category-oriented mode anchor the two ends of a theoretical continuum. Moreover, our own research bears out this diversity of processing strategies (Fiske & Neuberg, in press-b), as does that of other laboratories (e.g., Brewer, 1988; see Fiske & Neuberg, in press-a for others).

The basic premises of our continuum model are straightforward and support the functional qualities of on-line impression formation. First, category-based processes have priority over more attribute-oriented processes, in three respects: (a) Initial categorization is posited to occur early and fairly automatically, affecting any processes that follow. This is useful, as noted, because category-based processes are often efficient and effective. Moreover, (b) the more category-based processes precede the more attribute-based processes in the sequence of impression formation. This also makes sense because of the functional value of category-based processes. Finally, (c) whenever an earlier, more category-oriented process allows a good-enough fit to the information, then the perceiver stops proceeding along the continuum. People do not ordinarily elaborate their impressions beyond what suffices under the circumstances.

The second premise of the model is that the perceiver's interpretation of category–attribute fit influences how the continuum of strategies is used. Depending on how the perceiver views the consistency of the remaining cues with regard to an initial category, a subcategory, a new category, or an exemplar, the perceiver will assess the fit as adequate or look for a better fit. The variability across perceivers and across situations in what constitutes good-enough fit depends, in part, on the function of the impression for the perceiver, as is elaborated later.

The continuum model's third basic premise states that attention to attributes beyond the initial category mediates use of the continuum. Without attention after initial categorization, the subsequent processes cannot unfold. And it is attention to attributes, specifically, that is necessary here; our research indicates that the more attribute-oriented processes are not mediated by decreases in attention to the category, but rather by increases in use of the attribute information (Fiske, Neuberg, Beattie, & Milberg, 1987; Fiske, Neuberg, Pratto, & Allman, 1986).

All these points are discussed at length elsewhere, along with related models and the relevant research (Fiske & Neuberg, in press-a). In the current context, the continuum model simply serves to illustrate the diversity of strategies that occur in on-line impression formation, to suggest that some (more category-based strategies) are likely to have priority over others (more attribute-based strategies), all else being equal, and that the range and diversity of strategies seems functional. One might ask at this point whether the perceiver's on-line strategies could be anything but functional. After all, the strategies develop for a reason, and they would not survive if they were not among the fittest. In arguing that people use functional strategies, we merely intend to provide a counterpoint to the view that people are simply cognitive misers who are efficient at the cost of all accuracy. Instead, people seem to be reasonably efficient in arriving at reasonable impressions, under many circumstances.

People Use Diverse Information for Specific Purposes

Perceivers attend to a variety of features in trying to make sense of another person. From a structural perspective, they use both categories and attributes, as well as the relationships between them. From a content perspective, they use a wide range of features, including traits, behavior, appearance, relationships, origins, and contexts. Next, we examine structure and content in turn and also the relationship between them. In each case, particular functions or purposes are served by each type of information.

Structure: Categories and Attributes. A central distinction in the continuum model is between features considered *categories* and features considered *attributes*. In the process of impression formation, perceivers inevitably treat some features as more central organizing principles than others (cf. Asch, 1946), and one type of central feature is that which operates as a cue to a social category. Category labels are distinguished from other features by having more and stronger conceptual links to those other features than these features do to each other. Cognitively, categories cue attributes better than vice versa, categories frame interpretation of attributes, and categories connect the attributes to each other.

Which features operate as category labels and which as attributes depends on context and on the perceiver (Fiske & Neuberg, in press-a). Contextual configurations influence the organization of impressions in various ways indicated by prior research. Features that come early in the flow of information are most likely to serve as a basis for categorization (Jones & Goethals, 1972). For instance, physically manifested features are likely to serve as category labels, in part because they often come early in the available information, and in part because they are relatively fixed features of the person (cf. McArthur, 1981). Contextually novel features that set the person apart from others are also a likely basis for categorization (Taylor & Fiske, 1978). And recent research indicates that social roles or stereotypes, rather than personality traits, are likely categories, when both are available (Andersen & Klatzky, 1987; Bond & Brockett, 1987). Similarly, personality traits are likely to serve as categories for specific behaviors, when both are available (Carlston, 1980; Ebbesen & Allen, 1979). Essentially, it is a matter of specificity in both cases: Roles and stereotypes can summarize a series of traits, and traits can summarize a series of behaviors, so the less specific feature organizes the more specific ones.

The perceiver's idiosyncracies also influence category choice. For example, dimensions that are chronically accessible to the perceiver or acutely accessible in context are likely bases for categorization (Higgins & King, 1981; Wyer & Srull, 1981). Similarly, features that have the same valence as the perceiver's current mood are likely to be used as category labels (Erber, 1985), as are features that are relevant to the current judgmental task. Hence, what the perceiver has in mind, as well as what surrounds the perceiver, will jointly influence which features operate as category labels and which as attribute information.

Given the conceptual utility of this category–attribute distinction, it is important that we have found it operationally workable as well. In some studies, we have provided category labels consisting of the target's self-reported task-relevant trait information (i.e., competence), either alone (Ruscher & Fiske, 1988) or embedded among miscellaneous task-irrelevant demographics (age, hometown, major, college; Erber & Fiske, 1984). This was followed in each case by comments about the target's task-relevant behaviors, made either by the target (Ruscher & Fiske, 1988) or by others (Erber & Fiske, 1984). The operational principles here were the level of specificity of the information (traits are more general than behaviors), its judgment relevance (likely competence matters most in a joint task), and its sequential primacy in the flow of information (first, or at least early, makes it salient). All of these factors led us to predict which information would act as a category label and which as attributes, and our results supported this interpretation.

In other studies, we have relied on the distinction between roles and traits as levels of specificity, expecting that the roles would serve as category labels for the traits. In some cases, we have combined primacy with the role-trait distinction (Fiske et al., 1987; Fiske et al., 1986). In other cases, we have combined novelty and primacy with role (e.g., hospital patient status, schizophrenic or paraplegic) to suggest the category label. In these cases, the attributes consisted of comments about the target's traits and behaviors, made by the target (Neuberg & Fiske, 1987) or by others (Fiske & Von Hendy, 1988). Across studies, category and attribute information have been presented in oral, written, or videotaped formats, with no discernable differences among modalties. In sum, then, we have successfully operationalized the category-attribute distinction within the stimulus configuration, using a variety of the defining features of each.

Moreover, the distinction has proved feasible to operationalize on the dependent variable side, in our coding of subjects' open-ended responses. The range of comments made about the categories and attributes is particularly interesting. As Table 7.1 indicates, comments about the category itself are primarily evaluative in nature. Other category comments relate the category to specific attributes (see following). In our experience, the number of comments about the category is usually higher than the number of comments about any given attribute (Fiske et al., 1987; Fiske et al., 1986). Moreover, the level of commenting about the category does not typically vary across manipulations designed to increase or decrease category-based responding. Hence, the focus on category information appears to be fairly constant and high.

What varies, in our research, is the level of commenting about attribute information. Thus, there is increased or decreased responsiveness to the potentially individuating attributes, which alters the role of the category only relative to the total information attended. The types of attribute-oriented comments are also more varied than the category-oriented comments. Some are trivial with regard to underlying processes, as when a subject merely repeats the attribute or provides a synonym.

However, interpretive comments about the attributes are more informative. Perceivers may compare the attribute to any of the following: what they know about people in general (*population-attribute comparison*), what they know about the category (*category-attribute comparison*), the overall impression they are developing about the individual (*target-attribute comparison*), what they know about themselves (*self-comparison*), or what they know about another specific attribute of the target (*attribute-attribute comparison*).[1] In each case, the perceiver is building links, on-line, to prior knowledge, from the most general to the most specific. Some prior knowledge may be of longstanding duration (population, category, self),

---

[1] Our ordering of these types of prior knowledge borrows from the Jones and McGillis (1976) distinction between expectancies that are category-based and target-based.

TABLE 7.1
Coding Guide for Structure of Impressions

General Instructions: This coding system requires a clear a priori distinction between category and attribute, as determined by experimental manipulations or the particular context (see text).

Category Comments (C): Comments only about the category itself.
    Note: This code may be scored with different valences: positive, negative, and neutral.
    Examples: "People who aren't confident get on my nerves."(C-)
    "There aren't many British people on campus." (C)
    "Iranians are great people." (C+)

Attribute Comments (A): Comments concerning a particular attribute.
    Repetition (AR).
        Examples: *"Watched TV.* He watched TV." (AR)
    Synonyms (AS).
        Examples: *"Gets angry easily.* He gets mad at people." (AS)
    Interpretations.
      1. *Population-attribute comparison or consensus* (AP).
          Note: This code may be scored according to its commonality or uniqueness (+,-).
          Examples: *"Gets angry easily.* A lot of people are like that; everyone does that." (AP+)
      2. *Category-attribute comparison* (AC)
          Note: This code may be scored according to its consistency or inconsistency (+,-).
          Examples: *"Gets angry easily.* Iranians are like that." (AC+)
          "That doesn't go with being British." (AC-)
          "Watched TV. People who don't have a lot of confidence like to do that." (AC+)
      3. *Target-attribute comparison* (AT).
          Note: This code may be scored according to its consistency or inconsistency (+,-).
          Examples: *"Gets angry easily.* That sounds like something he'd do." (AT+).
          "Watched TV. She doesn't seem like the kind of person who'd do that a lot." (AT-)
      4. *Me/Self comparison* (AM)
          Note: This code may be scored according to its consistency or inconsistency (+,-).
          Examples: *"Gets angry easily.* So do I." (AM+)
      5. *Situational* (AS).
          Examples: *"Gets angry easily.* Must have had a bad day." (AS)
          "Watched TV. Must have been in the evening." (AS)
      6. *Dispositional* (AD)
          Note: This code may be scored with different valences: positive, negative, and neutral (+,-,0).
          Examples: *"Gets angry easily.* Must have a bad temper." (AD)
          "Gets angry easily. I don't like people who have bad tempers." (AD-)
          "Watched TV. Lonely." (AD)

7. *Attribute-attribute comparison* (AA)
   Note: This code may be scored according to its consistency or inconsistency (+,-).
   Examples: "*Gets angry easily.* That doesn't go with *is often cheerful.*" (AA-)
   "*Watched TV.* And she reads journals too!" (AA)
8. *Elaboration of attribute* (AE).
   Examples: "*Gets angry easily.* Throws books and stuff." (AE)

Evaluations (AV)

Note: This code may be scored with different valences: positive, negative, and neutral (+,-,0).
Examples: "*Gets angry easily.* That's not good." (AV-)
Comment: Sometimes one does not always get a straightout evaluation ("Not good." "I like that.") Often it is mixed with an interpretation ("*Gets angry easily.* People who are always picking fights with others are a pain.") One has to decide whether to keep these separate (People who are always picking fights with others (AE) are a pain (AV-)) or to make one category (AE or AV) more inclusive than the other.

---

whereas other knowledge may be more recently acquired (overall impression of the target so far, or the target's other specific attributes).

In addition, there are attribute-oriented interpretations that make *attributions of causality,* either to the person's particular circumstances (situational) or to the person's inferred personality traits (dispositional). We have found the usual distinction in the attribution literature workable in coding our subjects' open-ended comments during impression formation.

There are also some attribute-oriented interpretations that merely *elaborate* the attribute to a more specific level or a concrete image. These may be akin to merely stating the obvious, or they may involve considerable meaning change to fit a developing impression, subcategory, or evaluative bias (cf. Asch, 1946; Asch & Zukier, 1984).

Finally, sometimes there are simple *evaluations* provided in isolation from interpretations. These are the clearest evidence, in our protocol data, for an attribute-by-attribute or piecemeal type of impression formation (cf. Anderson, 1974, 1981), although they are compatible with other processes of impression formation as well. Such pure responses are also rather rare in our data. Usually, they occur in combination with interpretations that draw heavily on prior knowledge.

This range of comments, then, reflects the structural diversity of category and attribute usage in on-line impression formation, each type functional for particular purposes.

Content: Traits, Behavior, Appearance, Relationships, Origins, and Contexts. In addition to the different structural types of category and attribute comments, people use a wide range of content as well. In open-ended descriptions of others, people refer to a range of content, and each type arguably has a functional relationship to subsequent interactions with that other person (Fiske & Cox, 1979; see Table 7.2). For example, considerable parts of some descriptions are taken up by appearance information; how another person looks is obviously crucial, at a minimum, to identifying the person in the future. Moreover, because physical information is available immediately upon encountering the other, as well as constantly during the interaction, it is not surprising that so many meaningful social categories are communicated by appearance (fixed physical features, as well as clothing and other changeable artifacts; cf. McArthur, 1981).

Interactions also require that one know what the other is doing; in any interaction, observation of the other's behavior is the *sine qua non* for coordinating, communicating, reacting, and so on. However, open-ended descriptions do not reflect as much raw behavioral content as on-line processing probably would. The on-line encoding of another's behavior would be difficult to measure, for on-line encoding is doubtless a highly automated process. The observation and immediate interpretation of another's speech acts and nonverbal behavior has to be rapid enough not to disrupt the flow of interaction. It will be difficult to demonstrate the functional value of encoding another's behavior. But the point is so obvious that perhaps empirical demonstration is unnecessary.

Inferred, internal properties such as personality traits and attitudes generally predominate in open-ended descriptions, and they, too, have a functional purpose. Attributing patterns of behavior to stable dispositions allows the perceiver a sense of prediction over the other's future behavior; this clearly is more functional than taking each behavior as it comes, without generalizing and forming hypotheses.

Appearance, behavior, and traits form the "Big Three" of open-ended descriptions, and each has its functional value. Less common types of features also have functional value. For example, information about relationships tells what one does or can do with the other; relationship information includes roles, shared history, social networks, and personal reactions. Information about the contexts for encountering the other person tells where one finds the other; this can include both interpersonal and physical settings. And information about the other's origins tells how the person reached his or her present state, by including the other's individual history.

Other coding schemes for open-ended impressions identify similar components. For example, Park (1986) found that traits and behaviors predom-

TABLE 7.2
Coding Guide for Content of Impressions

General instructions: Score each adjective or phrase that falls into one of the following categories. A unit may be double scored. For example, "He is my postman" would receive one score under "role" and a second score under "occupation."

Appearance: How They Appear
Note: For this section, score each adjective as one mention.
Body
1. *Physique*: any mention of body type or build except as below
2. *Weight*: mention of a specific weight estimate or adjective such as "heavy"
3. *Height*: mention of a specific height estimate or adjective such as "tall"
4. *Posture*: any chronic or habitual body carriage, e.g. "slumped," "erect"
5. *Specific Parts*: mention of abnormalities or elaborations on particular parts of the body, e.g., "He has beautiful hands."

Face
1. *Features*: fixed physiognomic attributes
2. *Eyes*: color, size, but not movement of the eyes or eye contact
3. *Skin*: color, texture, complexion, etc.
4. *Hair*: color, curliness, style, etc.

Voice: fixed attributes of the voice, e.g., pitch

Grooming
1. *Clothing*: style, color, specific items carried (cane, shopping bag), jewelry
2. *Make-up*: any mention of cosmetics
3. *Glasses*: presence of, and any elaboration of description
4. *Other grooming clues*: neatness, cleanliness, odor

Overall attractiveness: evaluation of overall impact of appearance, e.g., "good-looking"

Age: specific age estimate or adjective

Race: specific racial category mentioned

Sex: specific gender category mentioned, but not including the use of a pronoun; i.e., "girl, man, lady" would be scored, but not "she"

Behavior: What They Do
Note: For this section, score adjectives, such as "He moves gracefully," and phrases, such as "He moves as if he were dancing." These attributes are all directly observable.

Chronic nonverbal
1. *Speech*: accent, language use, dialect, vocabulary, style, paralinguistic cues
2. *Facial behavior*: mention of transient expressions, e.g., smiles, winks, laughs
3. *Eye contact*: visual attention, glances, stares
4. *Gestures*: hand movements while talking, head nods
5. *Movement*: gait, general style of movement, fluidity, amount of movement

Activities
1. *Habits*: smoking, nail biting, finger drumming
2. *Hobbies*: avocations, sports played
3. *Occupation*: usual job

Scripts: chronic behavior patterns or behavior sequence used to illustrate an attribute, e.g., "He never says hello when you see him on the street."

Relationship: What One Does With Them
Note: This section involves nonobservable attributes.
Role: social position, e.g., "my mother, my friend, his student, her lawyer"
History: past interpersonal experiences with perceiver, e.g., "She lent me a dime"
Social network: person's relationships to people in general, e.g., "He has a lot of friends," "He never goes out," "She is married"
Perceiver's reaction: "He makes me nervous," "I like her," or other comments that state how the person being described makes the observer feel or react

Context: Where One Finds Them
Note: This includes observable and nonobservable settings.
Situation: interpersonal setting, e.g., a cocktail party, phone conversation, interview
Location: physical place, e.g., office building, the suburbs, New York

Origins: How They Got This Way
Note: This includes characteristics from the past.
Nationality and ethnicity: country or group origins or affiliations
Class: economic standing
Educational and occupational background: training and work experience, resume items
Drastic events: traumas, accidents, honors, life events of major impact

Properties: What Makes Them Up
Note: This includes inferred, internal characteristics.
Traits: adjectives or descriptive phrases of dispositional attributes, e.g., "He's friendly"
Causality: intentionality, environmental constraints, luck, personal effort or any explanation of influences over the person's life events
Attitudes: opinions, political stance, evaluations of objects or ideas
Interests: orientations or nonevaluative involvement, e.g., "He is into personal growth," "She is interested in children"

Note: From Fiske and Cox (1979).

inated over physical characteristics (essentially appearance), demographics (essentially origins and the role aspect of relationships), and attitudes (the attitudes and interests aspects of properties) (cf. Beach & Wertheimer, 1961; Ostrom, 1975). Hence, there is some generality to the finding that people use a diversity of information to describe others, although they concentrate on traits, behaviors, and perhaps appearance. One limiting aspect to all these data, for present purposes, is that they show what people communicate to an experimenter, rather than the pattern of what people necessarily encode on-line during impression formation. Nevertheless, they provide a reasonable index of the variety of content that perceivers record about another.

As noted previously, although perceivers have available diverse information, from appearance to behaviors to traits, some information tends to organize the remaining information better than vice versa. The prior section, in drawing the distinction between features that act as category labels and features that act as attributes, described some of the factors that make particular features more likely to organize the remaining features. One such factor is level of specificity, as when roles organize traits, or when traits organize behaviors. A major link, then, between the content of impressions and their structure is that category labels often consist of certain typical types of content (roles and traits), relative to the other content available (respectively, traits and behavior).

People Attend to the Most Informative Cues

Thus far, we have argued that people use diverse on-line strategies, depending on the ease of fitting attributes to an initial category, and that they do so in order to form coherent, good-enough impressions. This flexibility qualifies as functional and responsive to the environment. Moreover, people's use of that diverse information seems to be functional as well. They rely on a range of information, but particularly stable traits that predict what the other person may do next. This responsiveness to a range of cues, but particularly to predictive cues, also seems functional, in that it strikes a balance between predictive information bound to be interactively useful and more miscellaneous information that must be monitored for disruption of the perceiver's current prediction or operating assumptions.

The types of cues that must be monitored for disruption will, almost by definition, be the most informative cues. That is, information that disputes previous assumptions is more informative than information that merely confirms them. Both types of information can alter one's confidence, but only the unexpected information can potentially alter the direction or basic nature of one's prediction. It is not a new idea that social perceivers rely heavily on the unexpected (Jones & Davis, 1965). But social cognition research is now well positioned to examine the processes by which this occurs, as it is happening.

Information may be unexpected with regard to several levels of prior knowledge. It may be unexpected with regard to people in general. For example, extreme behavior departs from modal behavior, by definition, as the most common type of behavior is more moderate. If perceivers typically expect modal, moderate behavior, then extreme behavior disrupts that expectancy, is potentially informative, and requires attention. And perceivers indeed do attend to extreme behavior (Fiske, 1980). Similarly, people expect moderately positive behavior from others, so negative behavior often disrupts that expectation and attracts attention (Fiske, 1980; but see Skowronski & Carlston, 1987). And finally, physical features that are unusual for people in general (e.g., physical disability, prominent scars, and the like) attract attention, at least in part, because they are unusual and therefore seem informative (Langer, Taylor, Fiske, & Chanowitz, 1976).

Information may also be unexpected with regard to the category of person (Jones & McGillis, 1976). That is, given an operative category, inconsistent information disputes the potential accuracy of that category, so inconsistency is informative and attracts attention. Numerous studies support the observation that expectancy-inconsistent information requires attention to synthesize into a developing impression (Brewer, Dull, & Lui, 1981; Burnstein & Schul, 1982; Fiske et al., 1987; Fiske et al., 1986; Fiske & Pavelchak, 1986; Neuberg & Fiske, 1987; Srull, 1981; Sujan, 1985).

Moreover, some information is unexpected and informative with regard to a particular individual; when a person behaves in a way that is unusual for that person, that incident violates target-based expectancies (Jones & McGillis, 1976). To our knowledge, no one has directly assessed attention as a function of target-based expectancies, as opposed to category-based expectancies. One would have to examine target-based expectancies built up from consistent patterns of behavior and then demonstrate the impact of unexpected behavior that contradicts the previous pattern. In any event, it should have the same impact as any inconsistency in being informative and attracting attention.

Information can also be informative in context. For example, the first information received about another person represents a bigger proportional gain in knowledge than does the 20th piece of information, all else being equal. Accordingly, impression primacy effects follow the informativeness principle (Jones & Goethals, 1972). If impression weight reliably reflects attention (Fiske, 1980), then any of the studies assessing the relative weight of initial information constitutes evidence for attention to early information as a function of its informativeness (Anderson, 1981). Primacy clearly contributes to information value.

Another way in which information can be informative in context depends on the characteristics of the other people present. If a person stands out from the group, the dimension of difference (race, sex, etc.) attracts perceivers' attention (Kanter, 1977; Taylor, Fiske, Etcoff, & Ruderman, 1978; Wolman & Frank, 1975). It is also the dimension along which people describe themselves to another; if describers follow the conversation rule of reporting what they perceive to be the most informative content first, that suggests that they see the difference as most informative, or they expect that the audience of the communication would view it that way (cf. McGuire, McGuire, Child, & Fujioka, 1978; McGuire & Padawer-Singer, 1976).

To summarize, perceivers often encounter social material that is unexpected, based on what they know about people in general, particular categories of people, or the specific target. Information can also be informative in context, for example by coming early in the information received, or by distinguishing the person from others that are present. A social perceiver functions adaptively by attending to these kinds of informative cues because they potentially impinge on the perceiver's ability to predict and control future interactions.

People Form a Surprising Amount of the Impression Rapidly and Without Much Thought, But in Ways that Prove Functional

Categories serve adaptive functions, as we have noted. Hence, it is not surprising that people categorize quite quickly: Impressions of another person are affected by social stereotype categories from the earliest moments of the encounter (Dovidio, Evans, & Tyler, 1986; Klatzky, Martin, & Kane, 1982), seemingly without intent (Taylor et al., 1978). People quickly categorize behavior according to the relevant traits (Gilbert, Pelham, & Krull, 1988; Quattrone, 1982; Trope, 1986), and such categorizations occur spontaneously and without awareness (Uleman, 1987). Even when people control subsequent stages of impression formation, they appear not to control initial categorization (Neuberg & Fiske, 1987).

The rapid initial categorization could be mistaken as showing that people are dominated by cognitive economy at the price of accuracy, but as the continuum model indicates, initial categorization is only the first (albeit important) step. The bulk of impression formation depends on attention to and interpretation of the information configuration and, as we see next, it depends on motivation.

People Have Some Control Over the Impression that is Formed: They Respond to Instructions, Incentives, and Feedback

Impression formation processes are functional in yet another way. Impression formation—subsequent to initial categorization—requires attention to attributes that go beyond the initial category cues. Recent work suggests that both the amount of attention and the types of interpretation that perceivers make are at least somewhat under the perceivers' control. If this is the case, it also would be functional, in that perceivers adapt better by responding to environmental contingencies. People form impressions for a purpose (cf. Swann, 1984), so it is important that the impressions are responsive to the demands placed upon them. In our opening example, the professor may have formed an impression for the purpose of evaluating the student's potential as a research assistant. The criteria in this case revolved around the person's competence in psychology. If the professor had been forming an impression of the student for another purpose, other attributes would have demanded attention. There is a variety of evidence that people have control over how they form impressions, in ways that prove functional.

People also respond to situational incentives of various kinds. In effect, if it's worth it, people can control at least some of the processes by which they form impressions. In our laboratory, we have manipulated interdependence, both cooperative (Erber & Fiske, 1984; Neuberg & Fiske, 1987) and competitive (Ruscher & Fiske, 1988). We have found that interdependent perceivers more consistently attend to the most informative attributes (i.e., expectancy-inconsistent attributes) than do nondependent perceivers, and that they do so in the service of forming dispositional attributions. Attention to potentially disconfirming attributes and making dispositional inferences both fit with a functional analysis of perceivers enhancing their sense of prediction and control. Related results have been obtained by other investigators (Berscheid, Graziano, Monson, & Dermer, 1976; Omoto & Borgida, 1988).

Other types of situational incentives include self-presentation or accountability (Kruglanski & Freund, 1983; Snyder, Campbell, & Preston, 1982; Tetlock, 1983a, 1983b; Tetlock & Kim, 1987), time pressure (Bechtold, Naccarato, & Zanna, 1986; Jamieson & Zanna, 1989; Kruglanski & Freund, 1983), and self-esteem threats (Crocker & Gallo, 1985; Crocker, Thompson, McGraw, & Ingerman, 1987). Clearly, the list of possible motivational influences on impression formation processes is far from exhausted. Various pressures exerted on impression formation processes by such incentives are discussed at length by Fiske and Neuberg (in press-a) and by Kruglanski (in press). And Fiske (in press) argues that the perceiver's degree of intentional control can be responsibly defined.

In sum, people control some aspects of impression formation, subsequent to initial categorization, as shown by their response to instructions and incentives.

Interim Summary

Ten years of research in our laboratory have identified some basic principles of impression formation, which support research by others, and our image of the social perceiver has evolved from merely a cognitive miser to a more broadly functional interaction participant. Clearly, there is more to be done, as we have noted throughout. The remainder of the chapter discusses some methodological techniques and pitfalls that are part and parcel of this line of work.

METHODOLOGICAL REFLECTIONS

Some methods that have been particularly useful to us include measuring visual attention, in concert with measuring judgment weight or judgment impact; think-aloud protocols; and requests for information, prior to interactions and during interactions.

Measuring Visual Attention

Because of its central position in our framework as the mediator determining which information is encoded, and because of its functional value for person perceivers, attention has been a central variable in our investigations. Although not invariably, we have generally operationalized attention as looking time. Subjects view serially presented stimuli at their own pace, proceeding to a subsequent stimulus when they no longer wish to attend to the current one. The rationale behind this measure of attention is quite simple: People tend to fixate what they are currently processing. Looking time is, therefore, a rough indicator of how long people take to process each stimulus.

In addition to duration, the specific location where gaze fixates is also proper to attention, although somewhat unwieldy to measure in social settings (Taylor & Fiske, 1981). Looking time can serve as an elegant, essentially equivalent alternative to charting gaze location. This is because the potential locations of interest on a complex social stimulus, such as items on a job application, are often smaller, separable stimuli. Individual presentation of these stimuli merely breaks a single complex stimulus into several manageable pieces that can be presented serially, with gaze duration measured. Looking time also has convenience, elegance, and simplicity to recommend it. Armed with a carefully concealed stopwatch, a simple computer program, or a remote-controlled slide projector, researchers may easily capture attention without subjects' knowledge.

Although looking time implies that individuals are indeed processing information, measured alone it is insufficient evidence of this. Rather, looking time should be considered in concert with at least one other measure. Crucial to our own research is the premise that the stimuli most demanding of attention are those that individuals find most informative. By employing other measures in tandem with looking time, the informativeness premise is spared the problem of circularity. If stimuli are indeed informative, they should do more than merely increase attention. Informativeness should manifest itself through the impact of a stimulus on judgment and on behavior.

Visual Attention and Judgment Weight. As noted earlier, stimuli encountered early in the impression formation process, as well as stimuli that are extreme, are maximally informative and attention getting. Almost by definition, informative stimuli ought to be weighted heavily in the impressions being formed. For example, a target's sole extreme behavior or trait, presented along with moderate ones, should exert proportionately more influence in on-line impression formation and behavior. That is, if the extreme information is taken seriously, observers may attribute additional extreme characteristics to the target, or may choose not to interact with the target. To the extent that informative stimuli receive more weight, they may be thought about more often, or may frequently form the basis for inferences about the target. None of these effects of informativeness have been extensively studied, however.

More significantly, although all predicted by increased weighting, these outcomes do not precisely indicate the degree to which informative stimuli influence on-line impressions. To address this issue, Fiske (1980) used Anderson's (1974) model of information integration to ascertain which types of stimuli are indeed weighted most heavily in final impressions. This method essentially enables one to mathematically determine the weights given to various types of stimuli, most commonly providing that evaluations of all stimuli are determined in advance. In addition to doing this, Fiske measured the amount of time that subjects looked at each stimulus, showing that subjects looked longest at those types of stimuli also weighted most heavily in their impression judgments. In and of itself, this method is quite cumbersome, requiring either a massive within-subjects design, or prior estimation of each subject's evaluation of each behavior or trait. The primary advantage in this particular case was its demonstration that looking time can serve as a valid behavioral indicator of judgment weight.

One of the issues remaining for future research is that this method cannot address the exact nature of the relationship between judgment weight and attention. Increased attention may directly cause increased judgment weighting, or a third factor, such as the extremity of the information, might effect an increase in both looking time and weight. However, manipulations designed to increase attention (e.g., explicit instructions to pay attention, accuracy goals, outcome dependency) often also result in judgment change (see Fiske & Neuberg, in press-a for a review). As considered in greater detail hereafter, the evidence suggests that attention is a mediator of judgments and impressions, not a mere side effect of informative stimuli.

Visual Attention and Judgment Impact. To reiterate, impressions are not formed in a vacuum. Despite an onslaught of new information, impressions formed by person perceivers are heavily influenced by the prior knowledge that they bring into situations. Consider the following: You know Ward detests lawyers, but adores people who are assertive, intelligent, or socially aware. After encountering Ann, a lawyer possessing all these qualities, Ward tells you that he dislikes her. Apparently, Ward's evaluation is based primarily on Ann's being a lawyer, rather than on her individual attributes.

By analogy, prior independent evaluations of attributes and of a relevant category label can be compared with final evaluations of a target, when all those pieces of information appear together. In doing so, one can ascertain the extent to which the category or the attributes exert primary influence on the subsequent judgment. Correlational techniques (Fiske, et al., 1987; Pavelchak, in press) and analyses of the discrepancies between final evaluations and those predicted by the category or attributes (Pavelchak, in press) are relatively uncomplicated ways to assess under what circumstances stereotypes and other prior judgments are predictive of later impressions. Thus, liking of a stereotyped target should better reflect the likableness associated with the stereotype, rather than the attributes accompanying it. As in the previous vignette, the presence of the category results in the attributes affecting the final impression differently than they would otherwise.

Unfortunately, knowing the relationship between prior independent judgments and later impressions offers little insight into the encoding process. Predicting *when* attributes are encoded differently is perhaps less interesting than *how* this occurs. Recently, combining a measure of attention with the spirit of the methods discussed earlier, Neuberg and Fiske (1987) addressed this process issue. Analogous to assessing subjects' individual evaluations of a category and attributes, Neuberg and Fiske used consensual evaluations (likability) estimated through pretesting. After recording subjects' attention to target attributes, the experimenters obtained subjects' liking judgments about the target. As expected, these findings corroborated results found in studies of judgment impact. Furthermore, attention to attributes was minimal when judgments reflected the category. It appears that attention to attributes mediated judgments, because decrements in attention to those attributes resulted in more category-based evaluations.

One issue worth considering, however, is the adequacy of the prior measures (individual or consensual) of categories and attributes in determining subsequent impact. Conceivably, when judged independently, attributes are phenomenologically different than when they appear in the context of other attributes and a category label. As discussed in detail elsewhere (Fiske & Pavelchak, 1986), we have essentially followed Asch's (1946) germinal lead in maintaining that, in context, attributes can change meaning. What is meant by change of meaning is, of course, not always agreed on, however, (see Schneider, Hastorf, & Ellsworth, 1979 for a review). One common interpretation is that, depending on context, attributes can change in evaluative flavor. Rated in isolation, "clever," for example, may be moderately positive, but it may lose this evaluation in the context of a negative category label such as "thief." An alternative interpretation, and more in line with our own thinking, is that context imposes change in semantic meaning. Indeed, a word may have several meanings that nevertheless all possess similar evaluations. "Clever" in reference to a social scientist is likely to mean ingenious, whereas "clever" in reference to a comedian means witty. Although similarly positive, "clever" connotes something different in each context. We are well aware of the controversies around the change-of-meaning issue, but present purposes and space simply do not allow repeating them all here (see Ostrom, 1977).

More to the point, what constitutes change of meaning is important from a practical methodological standpoint. If evaluations of trait attributes change dramatically from prior testing to the actual experiment, any statistical relationships detected might be unduly biased. For instance, if prior independent ratings of certain traits are positive, but become negative in particular contexts, a final impression cannot be expected to reflect those earlier ratings. Although this may be somewhat rectified by using trait-attributes that have a rather narrow range of evaluations (a strategy used in our lab), or perhaps trait-attributes with a narrower range of definitions, the meaning-change issue can not entirely be dismissed. In fact, because semantic meaning comprises potency and activity dimensions as well as the evaluative one (Osgood, Suci, & Tannenbaum, 1957), all these dimensions are potentially altered by context as well. Thus, "clever" with respect to comedian is somehow light and quick, whereas with respect to social scientist, "clever" conjures images of original insight followed by slow, Herculean (Sisyphean?) efforts. Failure to demonstrate that target *evaluation* does not reflect independent ratings of attributes or of a category does not dismiss the possibility of meaning change along other dimensions. We raise this issue not to solve it, but rather to suggest that, if an impression is more than the sum of its evaluative parts, potential research projects remain wide open for examining various types of meaning change.

Using Think-Aloud Protocols

Despite some of the theoretical and methodological difficulties stemming from measures of attention and judgment impact, the evidence on the whole convinces us that individuals' impressions of a target are directly influenced by attention to information about that target. Unfortunately, elegant though they are, simple measures of attention invariably leave several interesting questions unanswered: How are individuals using the information they are encoding? Do individuals think much about the information as they encode it, and, if so, what are they thinking about? And, if they are indeed attempting to form an impression, how much and what kind of effort are they investing in this endeavor? In several studies, we have addressed these questions by examining subjects' think-aloud protocols. In this technique, subjects simply state their current thoughts while reading information about a target person.[2] Gathered in this fashion, think-aloud data avoid the retrospective nature of many self-reports, which often rely as heavily on retrieval as on encoding. Moreover, because they are concurrent and open-ended, think-aloud protocols are rich, lending themselves to the testing of many different types of hypotheses.

In the past, think-aloud methods were charged with being introspective, as if subjects were asked to report on their thought processes. This criticism is invalid in properly used methods. Although retrospective think-aloud procedures may encourage introspection by providing subjects opportunities to theorize about how a particular thought or impression arose (cf. Nisbett & Wilson, 1977), concurrent protocols prompt subjects merely for the contents of their thoughts. By thinking aloud, subjects do little more than make covert verbalizations into overt ones. Concurrent think-aloud methods thus assume thought processes to be inaccessible to subjects, and subjects are in fact discouraged from analyzing their own thoughts. Essentially, subjects furnish the raw data from which, on the basis of theory, researchers endeavor to infer process (Taylor & Fiske, 1981).

Whether thinking aloud affects the encoding process is another issue entirely. It is conceivable that simply by creating a demand for subjects to talk, thinking aloud may elicit qualitatively different thoughts. For example, such a demand might encourage subjects to ponder more or different information than they would otherwise have considered. Alternatively, insofar as a recording device might increase self-awareness or self-consciousness, the nature of subjects' thoughts might be transformed. Hence, this concern is not merely a matter of self-presentational reporting bias. Rather, to the extent that subjects' thoughts change as a result of

---

[2]Because subjects are verbalizing by thinking aloud, using stimuli likewise in verbal code makes the task simpler and yields more interpretable results (cf. Ericsson & Simon, 1980).

thinking aloud, the type of encoding might also change. For example, if the self is made salient, target information may be processed in reference to the self rather than with respect to the target's category. Quite plausibly, then, think-aloud procedures may alter the very process researchers purport to study.

In our own experience, this criticism of think-aloud methods is too harsh. First, of course, all these points pertain to the more traditional retrospective measures. Second, our use of verbal, rather than nonverbal, stimuli decreases the likelihood that cognitive processes are substantially altered by thinking aloud (Ericsson & Simon, 1980). Third, the attentional patterns demonstrated in studies that do not use protocols (e.g., Neuberg & Fiske, 1987; Fiske & Von Hendy, 1988) are identical to those that do (e.g., Erber & Fiske, 1984; Ruscher & Fiske, 1988). Under conditions of outcome dependency, for example, attention increases to expectancy-inconsistent information, whether subjects are thinking silently or aloud. This suggests that subjects' processing of information is none too different. Finally, in a study directly comparing subjects who read silently with subjects who thought aloud (Erber & Fiske, 1984), the attentional patterns were identical. Admittedly, these findings only indicate that the same stimuli received proportionately equivalent attention. Encoding, as noted earlier, impacts on judgments. Thus, if think-aloud and silent reading conditions result in similar encoding, subsequent impressions of a target should be indistinguishable. This, however, still needs experimental validation.

Procedures: Some Advice. Researchers electing to use think-aloud protocols should decide in advance whether or not they are interested in capturing subjects' thoughts as information is encountered. If so, stimuli should be presented serially to prevent subjects from being distracted by subsequent information while they are considering prior information. This recommendation, of course, holds whenever control over order is desirable; in the case of thinking aloud, it specifically enables the protocol to be concurrent with impression formation. Consider the alternative, when relevant information is received all at once, as with an on-campus job application. Although they might ordinarily glance immediately at GPA and test scores, subjects thinking aloud will likely state their thoughts in a top-to-bottom, left-to-right fashion. It would be a mistake to assume that the protocols necessarily mirrored natural impression formation. Nevertheless, insofar as people often encounter a wealth of information all at once, protocols of simultaneously presented information are worthwhile in their own right.

Instructions for thinking aloud are a deciding factor in the data obtained. For instance, subjects can be given a specific task, such as forming an impression of the target person. Although subjects' protocols consequently will be both focused and codable, such instructions could seriously bias the data. Individuals perhaps do not ordinarily form spontaneous impressions, but such instructions may compel them to do so. Alternatively, more vague instructions might be given, such as simply asking subjects to comment about information. In the absence of task instructions, theoretical bias (if any) might be reduced, only to leave subjects to their own random devices. Some subjects' protocols may yet reflect impression formation, whereas other protocols may more resemble free association. For example, in a study without specific task instructions, one subject, upon learning that the target person enjoyed writing, spoke at length about a poem she wrote for her boyfriend, then proceeded to discuss her boyfriend, their relationship, and so on. The focus provided by a specific task attenuates such tangents (and coder headaches). More importantly, if the hypothesized difference is between groups (e.g., impressions differ among groups) rather than a prediction about a population (e.g., people form spontaneous impressions), potential bias introduced by a task is obviously less a concern. Furthermore, people's "normal" thought processes do indeed range from task-focused decision-making to meandering free-association, and what one attempts to elicit in an experiment depends on which type of thought one wishes to simulate.

Uses and Analyses. The diverse uses of think-aloud data include generating new hypotheses and supporting both qualitative and quantitative predictions. For instance, one might anticipate that information being encoded more thoroughly might be referenced frequently. Along this vein, Fiske et al. (1987) found that when final evaluations reflected the attributes rather than the category label, analyses of impression formation protocols revealed that subjects also mentioned the attributes more often.

Protocols may also serve as evidence for process and/or stage models. Subjects can be assigned to conditions in which a theory predicts particular types of processing or thoughts peculiar to each given stage. For example, in Fiske et al.'s (1987) study, qualitative analyses demonstrated that subjects in conditions that were predicted to elicit category-based processing frequently made category-based inferences by adding new attributes suggested by the category. In our experience, think-aloud data are invaluable for inspecting the extent to which people are actually doing the encoding that a model predicts they will do.

A compelling method of analyzing protocols is content-coding statements on the basis of a priori predictions. Earlier, we discussed the functional significance of making dispositional inferences in response to unexpected or inconsistent information. The value of dispositional inference is exaggerated when perceivers are motivated to predict another's behavior. Under such conditions, a disproportionate number of dispositional comments should be evident in subjects' protocols. And this is indeed the case. Both Erber and Fiske (1984) and Ruscher and Fiske (1988) content-coded protocols to demonstrate that, for interdependent individuals, dispositional inferences increased in response to inconsistent information. Moreover, in both studies, the pattern of attention was strikingly similar to the pattern of dispositional inferences only. Thus, in combination, the two measures suggest that people attend to inconsistencies in order to predict the behavior of relevant others. Clearly, encoding of information in such cases serves adaptive functions for interdependent perceivers.

In summary, think-aloud protocols can be an excellent data resource, although not devoid of theoretical and methodological complications. While the typical expenses of coding, transcribing, and the like still persist, think-aloud data may be well worth the added trouble. Moreover, they even form a personal archival resource. Conceivably, we might eventually wish to reexamine the tape recordings in light of new hypotheses. We are reminded of early twentieth-century anthropological films, analyzed at that time from a wholly Western, narrowly masculine perspective, reinterpreted in more recent years from the standpoint of cultural relativism. Likewise, there are, undeniably, data embedded in think-aloud protocols not known because not looked for; this legacy may be left to future generations of researchers or to ourselves in subsequent incarnations of theoretical interests.

Assessing Requests for Information

Experimental situations prod subjects at least to glance at researcher-selected information about target persons. However, if they had their druthers, subjects might favor different information or might even prefer no information at all. In numerous real-world settings, people essentially choose the information they wish to encode through gaze direction and through information seeking. Whether loading questions to confirm their expectancies (Snyder & Swann, 1978) or proceeding in a relatively unbiased fashion (Trope & Bassok, 1982), people are more than merely the passive recipients of social information. Rather, they are active selectors of impression-relevant data.

Written and Self-Report. The potential range of data for selection is constrained when perceivers find themselves in a psychological experiment. In addition to the impact of manipulations designed to influence what kind of information they seek, the experimental situation itself affects the nature of requests made. Because the interaction between experimenter and subject is a negotiated communication (the experimenter makes certain kinds of queries and the subject responds accordingly), experimental subjects are, with few exceptions, unlikely to request information unless expressly prompted to do so. Thus, the framing of the experimenter's prompts is crucial. For example, asked "if" additional information is desired, a resounding "no" might be the reply. On the other hand, though profitable when theoretical predictions are precise, forced choice formats (e.g., "Would you rather know the target's grade-point average or race?") can induce subjects to make requests that might otherwise not have occurred to them.

Open-ended questions are a viable alternative and, as always, they place fewer theoretical constraints on subjects' responses than do forced choice formats. Nevertheless, they, like vague instructions for think-aloud, can procure both drivel and data. For this reason, hints or guidelines to guide subjects' requests for information can be quite useful. For instance, rather than solely asking *what* information is desired, researchers can provide a few broad categories of potential issues for subjects to consider (Fiske & Von Hendy, 1988). Again, as with think-aloud data, if a between-groups difference is the primary concern, assisting subjects in focusing their requests can prove invaluable to coding.

In addition, because the information sought might be based on subjects' idiosyncracies, "why" questions can be included as corollaries to "what" questions, in order to help clarify ambiguous responses. Though potentially helpful in simple cases (such as self comparisons), such data need to be interpreted with caution; subjects' reasons for their requests are likely to reflect their own prior theories. An anecdote from our own research might illustrate this point. Asked what further information she wanted concerning a target who was her opponent in a competition, one subject wrote, "Does she do drugs?" Curious as to whether this subject was searching for a supplier or anticipating a moral debate, the experimenter inquired about this response during the debrief. The subject grinned and said, "Simple. If she was too wasted, I'd win." In retrospect, whether such insight was indeed the impetus for the request is, of course, moot.

As with any self-report measures, issues surrounding validity are not easily ignored. Subjects' requests may be self-presentational or may reflect their perceptions of experimenter expectations. Alternatively, subjects' responses may indeed reflect information that they desire, but they may or may not wish to ask the target about it directly. Researchers might employ different measures to tease apart such nuances. For example, separate questions concerning what information is desired and other questions concerning how subjects plan to approach a conversation with the target (Fiske & Von Hendy, 1988) might differentiate between information that would or would not be directly requested from a target. As with the other measures discussed, requests for information might be combined with measures of attention. Theory might predict, for example, that individuals who attend primarily to individuating information about the target might also ask more individuating questions, or may plan to be more open-minded in their conversations. Although combining self-reports with another measure does not eliminate the issue of validity, confidence in such data of course increases as they corroborate other predictions and findings.

Information-Gathering in Interactions. Measuring the questions that individuals intend to ask is somewhat hypothetical and may not reflect behavior in true interactions; intentions may be thwarted by diverse obstacles. For example, people respond to incoming information by generating new questions and abandoning old ones. More importantly, information seeking involves more than the mere content of requests. People may expend considerable effort in obtaining information. And, as information is acquired, people devote differing degrees of attention to it. An inquirer may attend closely to a response, cut it off mid-sentence, or encourage the target to elaborate. This is a slightly different phenomenon than attention as considered previously in one important respect: The information is that which subjects expressly desire.

Role-played interactions, combining the virtues of ecological validity with experimental control, are one provocative way to study information seeking. In one simulation of a job interview (Neuberg, in press), "employer" subjects interviewed "job applicant" subjects by telephone, with listening time functioning as a direct measure of interviewer attention. Unlike other attention studies discussed before, the "stimuli" consisted not of inanimate slides or information sheets, but of applicants' responses to interviewer questions. Analogous to turning the page or pressing a slide projector switch, interviewers issued or withheld verbal encouragements in order to maintain their attention to a particular response. Neuberg also computed an index of each question's quality, based on whether the question was open- or closed-ended, the extent to which it sought new information, and the extent to which it was positive. Interviewers with a goal to form accurate impressions asked better questions, encouraged respondents to continue, and listened more. As a result, those subjects encoded richer information, and more of it, and their impressions of the applicants were duly influenced. Thus, this particular study combines duration and direction of attention with measures of judgment impact. Moreover, it does so in a setting that is similar to ones that perceivers regularly encounter in the real world.

In short, information seeking, or the lack of it, is vital to impression formation. Although people certainly are exposed to unsolicited information in their daily lives, much information integrated into impressions is garnered through information seeking. Moreover, a good deal of real-world information seeking is accomplished through third-party sources, rather than through direct interaction with targets themselves. Although an experimenter technically counts as a third party source, the relationship between subject and experimenter is highly proscribed, as mentioned earlier. How the perceiver investigates a target by requesting information from the target's peers "behind the back" is one interesting research question. Perhaps more intriguing is the notion that information seeking is manifested through "hypothesis testing," not only through questions asked, but in "experimental" situations of the person perceiver's own creation (cf. Kelly, 1955). For example, suspicious that Chad might be an office gossip, Sophia might, in feigned confidence, divulge a harmless rumor to see how far it travels through the grapevine. Analogous to nonreactive measures in the psychology lab, person perceivers, if clever enough, may obtain information without the knowledge of the target person or cohorts. Intuition (and experience) suggests that much real-world information seeking proceeds in such a fashion. We leave it to the imagination of our colleagues to devise ways to investigate this.

Summary

Several interrelated, recurrent themes have emerged in our musings about methodology. Because encoding is largely inaccessible, we have stressed the need to combine potentially convergent measures of encoding. To the extent that results from those measures agree, we can express greater confidence in our models and theories. And, just as each theory has its focus of convenience, so too with the methodologies described herein. The methods we have reviewed here are sufficiently broad to be flexibly applied to a wide range of research questions, but each has its own proper domain. Related to this point, we have urged careful consideration of what each measure does and does not do. This last point perhaps reaffirms the importance of combining measures, measures that complement each other and thereby tell a complete, coherent story.

CONCLUSION

We are heartened by progress in both knowledge and techniques for studying on-line impression formation in situations. Coming full circle to the professor and the denim-clad student at the beginning, this area of research has progressed beyond a vague interest in impression formation, but, like the rather unfocused psychology major, we also have some distance to go. We are also encouraged by findings that stress the functional value of impression formation "on the fly," in the office and on the street, showing some of the sensible strategies employed by ordinary person perceivers.

ACKNOWLEDGMENT

The research described herein and the second author were supported by NIMH grant MH 41801 to the first author. The authors thank various collaborators, particularly Ralph Erber, Steven Neuberg, Mark Pavelchak, and Holly Von Hendy, for their contributions to this work.

REFERENCES

Allport, G. W. (1954). *The nature of prejudice.* Reading, MA: Addison-Wesley.
Andersen, S. M., & Klatzky, R. L. (1987). Traits and social stereotypes: Levels of categorization in person perception. *Journal of Personality and Social Psychology, 53,* 235-246.
Anderson, N. H. (1974). Information integration: A brief survey. In D. H. Krantz, R. C. Atkinson, R. D. Luce, & P. Suppes (Eds.), *Contemporary developments in mathematical psychology* (pp. 236-305). San Francisco: Freeman.
Anderson, N. H. (1981). *Foundations of information integration theory.* New York: Academic Press.
Asch, S. E. (1946). Forming impressions of personality. *Journal of Abnormal and Social Psychology, 41,* 258-290.
Asch, S. E., & Zukier, H. (1984). Thinking about persons. *Journal of Personality and Social Psychology, 46,* 1230-1240.
Beach, L., & Wertheimer, M. (1961). A free-response approach to the study of person cognition. *Journal of Abnormal and Social Psychology, 62,* 367-374.
Bechtold, A., Naccarato, M. E., & Zanna, M. P. (1986, September). *Need for structure and the prejudice-discrimination link.* Paper presented at the annual meeting of the Canadian Psychological Association, Toronto, Ontario.
Berscheid, E., Graziano, W., Monson, T., & Dermer, M. (1976). Outcome dependency, attention, attribution, and attraction. *Journal of Personality and Social Psychology, 34,* 978-989.
Bond, C. F., Jr., & Brockett, D. R. (1987). A social context-personality index theory of memory for acquaintances. *Journal of Personality and Social Psychology, 6,* 1110-1121.
Brewer, M. B. (1988). A dual process model of impression formation. In T. K. Srull, & R. S. Wyer, Jr. (Eds.), *Advances in social cognition, Vol. 1: A dual model of impression formation* (pp. 1-36). Hillsdale, NJ: Lawrence Erlbaum Associates.
Brewer, M. B., Dull, V., & Lui, L. (1981). Perceptions of the elderly: Stereotypes as prototypes. *Journal of Personality and Social Psychology, 41,* 656-670.
Burnstein, E., & Schul, Y. (1982). The informational basis of social judgments: Operations in forming impressions of other persons. *Journal of Experimental Social Psychology, 18,* 217-234.
Carlston, D. E. (1980). The recall and use of traits and events in social inference processes. *Journal of Experimental Social Psychology, 16,* 303-328.
Crocker, J., & Gallo, L. (1985, August). *The self-enhancing effect of downward comparison.*

Paper presented at the meeting of the American Psychological Association, Los Angeles, CA.

Crocker, J., Thompson, L., McGraw, K. M., & Ingerman, C. (1987). Downward comparison, prejudice and evaluations of others: Effects of self-esteem and threat. *Journal of Personality and Social Psychology, 52,* 907–916.

Dovidio, J. R., Evans, N., & Tyler, R. B. (1986). Racial stereotypes: The contents of their cognitive representations. *Journal of Experimental Social Psychology, 22,* 22–37.

Ebbesen, E. B., & Allen, R. B. (1979). Cognitive processes in implicit personality trait inferences. *Journal of Personality and Social Psychology, 37,* 471–488.

Erber, R. (1985). *Choosing among multiple categories: The effects of moods on category accessibility, inference, and interpersonal affect.* Unpublished doctoral dissertation, Carnegie Mellon University, Pittsburgh, PA.

Erber, R., & Fiske, S. T. (1984). Outcome dependency and attention to inconsistent information. *Journal of Personality and Social Psychology, 47,* 709–726.

Ericsson, K. A., & Simon, H. A. (1980). Verbal reports as data. *Psychological Review, 87,* 215–251.

Fiske, S. T. (1980). Attention and weight in person perception: The impact of negative and extreme behavior. *Journal of Personality and Social Psychology, 38,* 889–906.

Fiske, S. T. (1982). Schema-triggered affect: Applications to social perception. In M. S. Clark & S. T. Fiske (Eds.), *Affects and cognition: The 17th Annual Carnegie Symposium on Cognition* (pp. 55–78). Hillsdale, NJ: Lawrence Erlbaum Associates.

Fiske, S. T. (1988). Compare and contrast: Brewer's dual process model and Fiske et al.'s continuum model. In T. K. Srull & R. S. Wyer, Jr. (Eds.), *Advances in social cognition, Vol. 1: A dual process model of impression formation* (pp. 65–76). Hillsdale, NJ: Lawrence Erlbaum Associates.

Fiske, S. T. (in press). Examining the role of intent, toward understanding its role in stereotyping and prejudice. In J. S. Uleman & J. A. Bargh (Eds.), *Unintended thought: The limits of awareness, intention, and control.* New York: Guilford.

Fiske, S. T., & Cox, M. G. (1979). Person concepts: The effects of target familiarity and descriptive purpose on the process of describing others. *Journal of Personality, 47,* 136–161.

Fiske, S. T., & Neuberg, S. L. (in press-a). A continuum model of impression formation, from category-based to individuating processes: Influences of information and motivation on attention and interpretation. In M. P. Zanna (Ed.), *Advances in experimental social psychology* (Vol. 23). NY: Academic Press.

Fiske, S. T., & Neuberg, S. L. (in press-b). Stereotyping and individuating processes as a function of information and motivation: Evidence from our laboratory. In D. Bar-Tal, C. F. Graumann, A. W. Kruglanski, & W. Stroebe (Eds.), *Stereotyping and prejudice: Changing conceptions.* New York: Springer-Verlag.

Fiske, S. T., Neuberg, S. L., Beattie, A. E., & Milberg, S. J. (1987). Category-based and attribute-based reactions to others: Some informational conditions of stereotyping and individuating processes. *Journal of Experimental Social Psychology, 23,* 399–427.

Fiske, S. T., Neuberg, S. L., Pratto, F., & Allman, C. (1986). *Stereotyping and individuation: The effects of information inconsistency and set size on attribute-oriented processing.* Unpublished manuscript, University of Massachusetts at Amherst.

Fiske, S. T., & Pavelchak, M. A. (1986). Category-based versus piecemeal-based affective responses: Developments in schema-triggered affect. In R. M. Sorrentino & E. T. Higgins (Eds.), *Handbook of motivation and cognition: Foundations of social behavior* (pp. 167–203). New York: Guilford Press.

Fiske, S. T., & Von Hendy, H. (1988). Unpublished data, University of Massachusetts at Amherst. The shoe that fits: Personality feedback and situational feedback influence impression formation processes.

Gilbert, D. T., Pelham, B. W., & Krull, D. S. (1988). On cognitive busyness: When person perceivers meet persons perceived. *Journal of Personality and Social Psychology, 54,* 733-740.

Higgins, E. T., & Bargh, J. A. (1987). Social cognition and social perception. In M. R. Rosenzweig & L. W. Porter (Eds.), *Annual Review of Psychology,* (Vol. 38, pp. 369-425). Palo Alto, CA: Annual Review.

Higgins, E. T., & King, G. A. (1981). Accessibility of social constructs: Information-processing consequences of individual and contextual variability. In N. Cantor & J. F. Kihlstrom (Eds.), *Personality, cognition, and social interaction* (pp. 69-121). Hillsdale, NJ: Lawrence Erlbaum Associates.

Jamieson, D. W., & Zanna, M. P. (1989). Need for structure in attitude formation and expression. In A. R. Pratkanis, S. J. Breckler, & A. G. Greenwald (Eds.), *Attitude structure and function* (383-406). Hillsdale, NJ: Lawrence Erlbaum Associates.

Jones, E. E., & Davis, K. E. (1965). From acts to dispositions: The attribution process in person perception. In L. Berkowitz (Ed.), *Advances in experimental social psychology* (Vol. 2, pp. 219-266). New York: Academic Press.

Jones, E. E., & Goethals, G. R. (1972). Order effects in impression formation: Attribution context and the nature of the entity. In E. E. Jones, D. E. Kanouse, H. H. Kelley, R. E. Nisbett, S. Valins, & B. Weiner (Eds.), *Attribution: Perceiving the causes of behavior* (pp. 27-46). Morristown, NJ: General Learning Press.

Jones, E. E., & McGillis, D. (1976). Correspondent inferences and the attribution cube: A comparative reappraisal. In J. H. Harvey, W. J. Ickes, & R. F. Kidd (Eds.), *New directions in attribution research* (Vol. 1, pp. 389-420). Hillsdale, NJ: Lawrence Erlbaum Associates.

Kanter, R. (1977). *Men and women of the corporation.* New York: Basic Books.

Kelly, G. A. (1955). *The psychology of personal constructs.* New York: Norton.

Klatzky, R. L., Martin, G. L., & Kane, R. A. (1982). Influence of social-category activation of processing of visual information. *Social Cognition, 1,* 95-109.

Kruglanski, A. W. (in press). Motivations for judging and knowing: Implications for causal attribution. In E. T. Higgins & R. M. Sorrentino (Eds.), *Handbook of motivation and cognition: Foundations of social behavior* (Vol. 2). New York: Guilford.

Kruglanski, A. W., & Freund, T. (1983). The freezing and unfreezing of lay-inferences: Effects of impressional primacy, ethnic stereotyping, and numerical anchoring. *Journal of Experimental Social Psychology, 19,* 448-468.

Langer, E. J., Taylor, S. E., Fiske, S. T., & Chanowitz, B. (1976). Stigma, staring, and discomfort: A novel stimulus hypothesis. *Journal of Experimental Social Psychology, 12,* 451-463.

McArthur, L. Z. (1981). What grabs you? The role of attention in impression formation and causal attribution. In E. T. Higgins, C. P. Herman, & M. P. Zanna (Eds.), *Social cognition: The Ontario Symposium,* (Vol. 1). Hillsdale, NJ: Lawrence Erlbaum Associates.

McGuire, W. J., McGuire, C. V., Child, P., & Fujioka, T. (1978). Salience of ethnicity in the spontaneous self-concept as a function of one's ethnic distinctiveness in the social environment. *Journal of Personality and Social Psychology, 36,* 511-520.

McGuire, W. J., & Padawer-Singer, A. (1976). Trait salience in the spontaneous self-concept. *Journal of Personality and Social Psychology, 33,* 743-754.

Neuberg, S. L. (in press). Interpersonal expectancies and impression formation goals: Overriding the impact of negative expectancies on social interactions and impression formation. *Journal of Personality and Social Psychology.*

Neuberg, S. L., & Fiske, S. T. (1987). Motivational influences on impression formation: Outcome dependency, accuracy-driven attention, and individuating processes. *Journal of Personality and Social Psychology, 53,* 431-444.

Nisbett, R. E., & Wilson, T. D. (1977). Telling more than we can know: Verbal reports on mental processes. *Psychological Review, 84,* 231-269.

Nisbett, R. E., Zukier, H., & Lemley, R. E. (1981). The dilution effect: Non-diagnostic information weakens the implications of diagnostic information. *Cognitive Psychology, 13,* 248–277.

Omoto, A. M., & Borgida, E. (1988). Guess who might be coming to dinner? Personal involvement and racial stereotypes. *Journal of Experimental Social Psychology, 24,* 571–593.

Osgood, C., Suci, G. J., & Tannenbaum, P. H. (1957). *The measurement of meaning.* Urbana, IL: University of Illinois Press.

Ostrom, T. M. (1975, August). *Cognitive representation of impressions.* Paper presented at the meeting of the American Psychological Association, Chicago, IL.

Ostrom, T. M. (1977). Between-theory and within-theory conflict in explaining context effects in impression formation. *Journal of Experimental Social Psychology, 13,* 492–503.

Park, B. (1986). A method for studying the development of impressions of real people. *Journal of Personality and Social Psychology, 51,* 907–917.

Pavelchak, M. (in press). Forming impressions of others: A demonstration of two distinct processes using an idiographic measurement technique. *Journal of Personality and Social Psychology.*

Quattrone, G. A. (1982). Overattribution and unit formation: When behavior engulfs the person. *Journal of Personality and Social Psychology, 42,* 593–607.

Ruscher, J. B., & Fiske, S. T. (1988). *Competition can cause individuating impression formation.* Unpublished manuscript, University of Massachusetts at Amherst.

Schneider, D. J., Hastorf, A. H., & Ellsworth, P. C. (1979). *Person perception.* Reading, MA: Addison-Wesley.

Skowronski, J. J., & Carlston, D. E. (1987). Social judgment and social memory: The role of cue diagnosticity in negativity, positivity, and extremity biases. *Journal of Personality and Social Psychology, 52,* 689–699.

Snyder, M., Campbell, B. H., & Preston, E. (1982). Testing hypothesis about human nature: Assessing the accuracy of social stereotypes. *Social Cognition, 1,* 256–272.

Snyder, M., & Swann, W. B. (1978). Hypothesis-testing processes in social interaction. *Journal of Personality and Social Psychology, 36,* 1202–1212.

Srull, T. K. (1981). Person memory: Some tests of associative storage and retrieval models. *Journal of Experimental Psychology, 7,* 440–462.

Sujan, M. (1985). Consumer knowledge: Effects on evaluation strategies mediating consumer judgments. *Journal of Consumer Research, 12,* 1–16.

Swann, W. B., Jr. (1984). Quest for accuracy in person perception: A matter of pragmatics. *Psychological Review, 91,* 457–477.

Taylor, S. E., & Crocker, J. (1981). Schematic bases of social information processing. In E. T. Higgins, C. Herman, & M. P. Zanna (Eds.), *Social cognition: The Ontario Symposium* (Vol. 1, pp. 89–134). Hillsdale, NJ: Lawrence Erlbaum Associates.

Taylor, S. E., & Fiske, S. T. (1981). Getting inside the head: Methodologies for process analysis in attribution and social cognition. In J. H. Harvey, W. Ickes, & R. F. Kidd (Eds.), *New directions in attribution research* (Vol. 3, pp. 459–524). Hillsdale, NJ: Lawrence Erlbaum Associates.

Taylor, S. E., & Fiske, S. T. (1978). Salience, attention, and attribution: Top of the head phenomena. In L. Berkowitz (Ed.), *Advances in experimental social psychology* (Vol. 11, pp. 249–288). New York: Academic Press.

Taylor, S. E., Fiske, S. T., Etcoff, N. L., & Ruderman, A. J. (1978). Categorical bases of person memory and stereotyping. *Journal of Personality and Social Psychology, 36,* 778–793.

Tetlock, P. E. (1983a). Accountability and complexity of thought. *Journal of Personality and Social Psychology, 45,* 74–83.

Tetlock, P. E. (1983b). Accountability and the perseverance of first impressions. *Social*

Psychology Quarterly, 46, 285-292.
Tetlock, P. E., & Kim, J. I. (1987). *Journal of Personality and Social Psychology, 52,* 700-709.
Trope, Y. (1986). Identification and inferential processes in dispositional attribution. *Psychological Review, 93,* 239-257.
Trope, Y., & Bassok, M. (1982). Confirmatory and diagnosing strategies in social information gathering. *Journal of Personality and Social Psychology, 43,* 22-34.
Uleman, J. S. (1987). Consciousness and control: The case of spontaneous trait inferences. *Personality and Social Psychology Bulletin, 13,* 337-354.
Wolman, C., & Frank, H. (1975). The solo woman in a professional peer group. *American Journal of Orthopsychiatry, 45,* 164-171.
Wyer, R. S., Jr., & Srull, T. K. (1981). Category accessibility: Some theoretical and empirical issues concerning the processing of social stimulus information. In E. T. Higgins, C. P. Herman, & M. P. Zanna (Eds.), *Social cognition: The Ontario Symposium (Vol. 1).* Hillsdale, NJ: Lawrence Erlbaum Associates.

8
Functional Memory and On-Line Attribution

Norman H. Anderson
University of California, San Diego

The original distinction between "on-line" and "memory-based" was essentially that made by Anderson and Hubert (1963). This distinction has been popularized by Hastie and Park (1986), who introduced the quoted terms in place of those used by Anderson and Hubert. The term *verbal memory* hypothesis was used by Anderson and Hubert to refer to the then-unquestioned belief that judgments are based on memory for the given stimulus information. This term is equivalent to *memory-based,* which refers to the "relatively raw evidence information" as the base for judgment. The main result of Anderson and Hubert was that such a concept of memory was insufficient to account for person cognition: The strong recency in the verbal recall was not compatible with the weak recency or even primacy in the judgment of the person.

To account for the person judgment, Anderson and Hubert suggested a serial integration process. As each stimulus adjective was received, it was processed for its implications, which were integrated into the cumulative impression of the person. The judgment of the person at the end of the list was based on this *impression memory,* not on the verbal memory for the given adjectives. Anderson and Hubert concluded:

> The fundamental characteristic of the model is the representation that it gives of the internal state of the subject ... a representation of the impression memory which is consistent with the distinction between impression memory and verbal memory made above. In the model it is assumed that, as each adjective is received, its meaning is extracted and combined with the current impression, thus yielding a changed impression. (1963, p. 390)

This is the prototypical on-line model.

The two-memory formulation of Anderson and Hubert was the beginning of a more general distinction between *reproductive memory* and *functional memory*. Reproductive memory is the traditional conception, epitomized by reliance on recall and recognition measures, that is, by reproduction of the given stimulus materials. Memory researchers have almost unquestioningly assumed that the study of reproductive memory is all-sufficient. Functional memory, in contrast, is concerned with the nature and function of memory in on-going thought and action. The main functions of memory appear in processing given information for goal-oriented implications and in assemblage of operating memory. The study of these functions in social cognition required new theory and new methods, outside the reproductive tradition.

LIFE IS ON-LINE

In the functional perspective, life is on-line. Thought and action are dynamic, addressed to momentary goals, changing continuously as obstacles appear or are overcome, as the goal is approached, and as new goals arise. The nature of cognition is to be found in its on-line functions. The nature of memory is likewise to be found in its on-line functions.

The functional approach to memory has already been illustrated with the on-line person memory of Anderson and Hubert (1963). On-line memory is typically goal-oriented. It provides a working summary of given information, not ordinarily in its raw, reproductive form, but in the form of inferences relative to operative goals. An associated function appears with the storage of such on-line processing. Present processing is thus conserved for future use. This long-term memory function has special importance in social attitudes (Anderson, 1971, 1973a, 1981b).

This chapter considers several aspects of functional memory. A preview of the four main parts may be helpful. The first part discusses functional memory, first in general terms and then in relation to the central problem of serial curves. This treatment of serial curves makes concrete the reproductive–functional distinction and also makes concrete the fundamental problem of how to measure functional memory.

The second part takes up some aspects of the general problem of memory in social psychology. Of principal concern here are the concepts of *knowledge systems* as the basic form of long-term social memory and of *assemblage* as the basic form of operating memory.

The third part considers one of the more pervasive on-line activities, namely, attribution. This part argues that attribution ideas need to be reconstituted in a framework of cognitive theory. A promising beginning to a cognitive theory of attribution may be seen in the algebraic integration schemas.

The fourth part discusses selected issues in functional memory. The misdirection produced by the reproductive conception of memory is illustrated with critiques of the availability heuristic and of studies of recall of inconsistent information. Of more positive interest is a new method for analysis of functional memory.

The chapter concludes with the thesis that social-personality psychology needs to develop its own cognitive theory. The narrow insufficiency of mainstream memory theory brought out by the two-memory formulation reappears in mainstream cognitive theory. Social-personality psychology is unique in its focus on everyday thought and action. Theory development, correspondingly, needs to focus on how cognition functions in everyday life.

FUNCTIONAL MEMORY: A CASE HISTORY IN COGNITIVE THEORY

This chapter is, in part, a case history, in that it covers 25 years in the evolution of the concept of functional memory. The two-memory hypothesis of Anderson and Hubert (1963) meant that traditional memory theory was insufficient for social judgment. Qualitatively different theory and methods had to be developed for an effective analysis of functional memory. Two considerable difficulties had to be resolved.

One difficulty was theoretical, illustrated in the contrast between curve of judgment and the curve of recall (shown later in Fig. 8.1). Analysis of the judgment curve, which represents functional memory, requires a theoretical model. Fortunately, a *cognitive algebra* of functional memory was discovered. The averaging model, in particular, has provided a good account of a basic class of on-line processing in virtually every branch of social cognition. Only with this model can the judgment curve be obtained.

The second difficulty was technical, mainly problems of using the averaging model for measurement of functional memory. This problem has only recently reached a satisfactory plateau. Before taking up these two developments, however, some preliminary comments are needed to outline the functional perspective that underlies this research program.

Functional Perspective

A guiding goal of the theory of information integration (ITT) is to develop a cognitive theory of everyday life. This goal is reflected in the emphasis on person cognition in IIT, from Anderson (1988):

> A functional perspective is basic to information integration theory (IIT). This reflects its focus on judgment and action, which are goal-oriented in character. Interpersonal interaction, in particular, involves approaching others, avoiding them, doing things for them, getting them to do things for us, and so on. Such interpersonal goals are a major determinant of person cognition. This goal-oriented perspective entails a corresponding conception of functional memory. (p. 37)

Person cognition, as this quote indicates, is quintessentially functional. Social-moral attitudes constitute storehouses for values that help guide our interpersonal interactions. Social roles are action schemas that are readily available for assemblage into operating memory for social interaction. Attribution of traits, of purpose, or of obligation, represent on-line functioning that is pervasive in everyday life.

Attitudes, roles, and attribution schemas are part of functional memory. A basic problem for cognitive theory of everyday life is to find means for analysis of such memory function.

Memory Theory in Social Psychology

Two main attempts have been made to unify mainstream memory theory with social psychology. The first was that of the Yale school of attitude theory in the 1950s; the second appeared with the recent concern over social cognition. Both attempts, however, adopted the traditional conception of reproductive memory. Reproductive memory is inadequate for social cognition.

The Yale school deliberately took the verbal memory hypothesis as basic: Attitudes were considered to be based on the verbal stimulus materials available for recall. This approach had the high aspiration of basing a fledgling attitude theory solidly on the enormous mass of verbal learning studies. But this approach had little success, for reasons that became clear with the two-memory formulation of Anderson and Hubert (1963). A historical lesson is that theory of social cognition cannot be constructed on concepts and methods borrowed from nonsocial psychology.

Much the same lesson reappears in recent attempts to conjoin mainstream cognitive psychology and social psychology. This led to isolation of affect, which is hardly recognized in cognitive psychology (see Anderson, 1987, 1988, in press). And it led once again to a focus on reproductive memory, as in the volume on person memory by Hastie et al. (1980). Thus, the overview of memory measurement by Hastie and Carlston (1980) considers only traditioinal measures of memory, mainly recall and recognition. Similar narrowness appears in the handbook chapter by Srull (1984) and in the survey of methodology by Taylor and Fiske (1981). Traditional measures of memory are not sufficient, because they embody the reproductive preconception.

Formulations similar to the two-memory formulation of Anderson and Hubert (1963) were adopted by most investigators who contributed to the cited volume on person memory. Wyer and Srull (1980), for example, took as primary the proposition that "Once a judgment is made of a person, this judgment rather than the information on which it was based is more likely to be recalled and used as a basis for subsequent judgments and decisions involving the person" (p. 228). This echoes the two-memory formulation of Anderson and Hubert (1963). Similarly, Wyer and Srull's proposition that what is stored in memory will depend on objectives at the time of processing is a direct implication of the original on-line formulation, in which valuation of given stimulus information depends on the operative goal.

But although the foregoing investigators have made useful contributions, they did not develop a theory of judgment. To implement the functional memory perspective requires a theory of judgment that can be coupled to social cognition. This coupling is needed to deal adequately with valuation and integration, two central problems of social cognition. The foregoing investigators were hobbled by the traditional reproductive conception of memory, which could not resolve the problems of valuation and integration. Some made cogent use of traditional recall-recognition measures, and ingenious reaction studies by Ostrom, Lingle, Pryor, and Geva (1980) yielded notable support for the two-memory formulation of Anderson and Hubert (1963; see also Dreben, Fiske, & Hastie, 1979; Hastie, 1981, pp. 64–65; Riskey, 1979). None of this work, however, came close to the theoretical development needed to handle valuation and integration.

Actually, effective theory and method to deal with valuation and integration had been developed and applied in many areas of social-personality psychology (Anderson, 1971, 1974a) and in general judgment-decision theory (Anderson, 1974b). As noted in a treatise on integration methods (Anderson, 1982):

> Integration theory embodies a functional approach that considers memory as an aid to judgment and action. Whereas traditional approaches to memory focus on reproduction of given stimuli, the functional approach is more concerned with how memory is utilized for attaining goals. The person's prevailing goal orientation affects the processing of prior memory; it also affects the storage of new memory. Accordingly, this functional approach is a useful supplement to a narrow concern with reproductive memory. (p. 345)

Social memory *is* functional. The conference on on-line memory is a welcome attempt to put the study of social memory on track.

Functional Memory: Valuation and Integration

The difference between functional memory and reproductive memory is clear in the two processes of *valuation* and *integration*. Functional memory has primary concern with valuation processes that draw goal-relevant inferences or implications from given information. *Happy-go-lucky* could be a desirable trait in a picnic guest but undesirable in a statistical clerk; the same trait has quite different values for the two goals. Functional theory of memory must deal with such goal-dependent inferences.

On problems of inference, however, traditional memory theory has little to say. Retrieving the semantic meaning of given words is not sufficient, for the reason just indicated. In everyday life, moreover, inference may contain substantial affect or be based on nonverbal stimuli that lie outside the scope of traditional memory theory. To study inferences, which are central to functional memory, requires new concepts and methods.

A second problem of functional memory arises because on-line judgments are typically cumulative. As each new piece of information is received, it is evaluated and integrated into the current on-line judgment. Because of this cumulative integration process, any on-line judgment is an overall resultant of multiple pieces of information. This problem of information integration lies beyond the horizon of mainstream memory theory.

These two processes, valuation and integration, present two basic problems of functional memory. One concerns measurement of inferences for individual stimuli, the other concerns the integration of multiple inferences into an overall judgment. Both problems can be solved under certain conditions using the functional measurement methodology of IIT.

Serial Curves: Judgment and Recall

Two quite different kinds of serial curves need to be considered: *recall* curves and *judgment* curves. They differ theoretically, in that recall refers to the single adjectives, whereas judgment is based on all the adjectives. They may also differ empirically, showing opposite shapes. This empirical difference implies that verbal memory is not sufficient for cognitive theory.

This recall–judgment comparison is shown in Fig. 8.1. The subject heard a sequence of eight personality trait adjectives that described a person and, at the end of the sequence, rated the person on likableness and recalled the adjectives. The recall curve in Fig. 8.1 is essentially the same as reported by Anderson and Hubert (1963, Experiment 2). It shows a standard bowed-serial shape, except for one discordant point explained later, with a short initial downswing (primacy) and a long terminal upswing (recency).

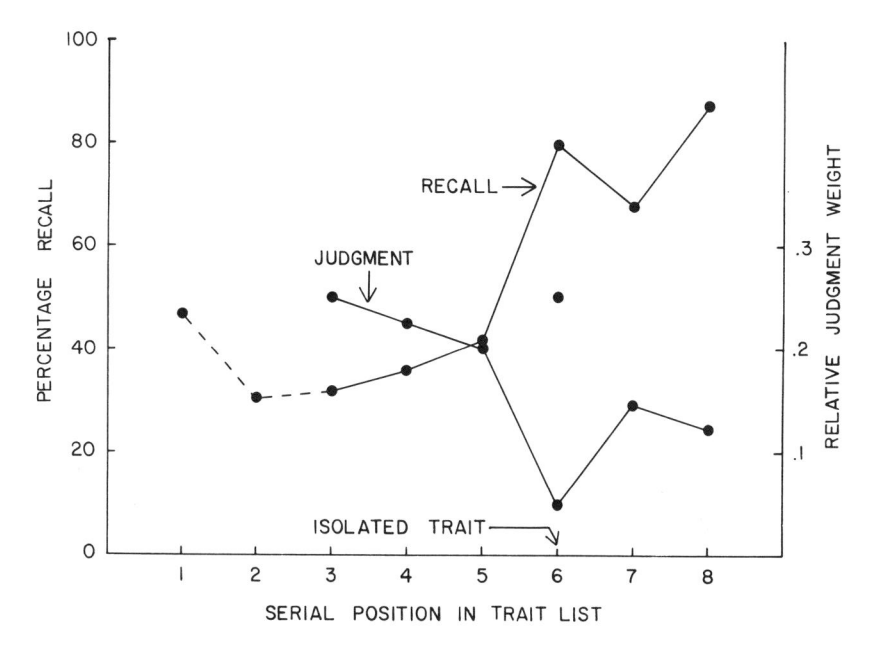

8. FUNCTIONAL MEMORY AND ON-LINE ATTRIBUTION 181

FIG. 8.1. Evidence for two memories. Recall curve for adjectives in person description shows strong recency over last six serial positions. Judgment curve for effect of these same adjectives in person impression shows marked primacy, with decreasing effects over serial position. Unreliable adjective written in red at serial position 6 shows increased recall and decreased effect. Both contrasts between recall and judgment imply that memory for the person impression is different from verbal memory for the trait adjectives. Recall data after Anderson and Hubert (1963); judgment data after Anderson and Hubert (1963) and Anderson (1965, 1973a). Effects of isolated adjective are hypothetical.

The serial curve of judgment, unlike the recall curve, is not observable. The judgment curve specifies how much influence the trait adjective at each serial position has on the single overall judgment at the end of the sequence. This single judgment must be dissected into several components, one from each serial position. Dissection can be accomplished in the manner described later, and the resulting curve is shown in Fig. 8.1. The first two adjectives in each sequence were fillers intended to factor out the initial primacy in the recall, so these first two positions do not appear in the judgment curve.

The contrast between the recall and judgment curves in Fig. 8.1 is absolute. The recall curve shows increasing recall over the last six serial positions, a large recency effect. The judgment curve shows decreasing effects of the adjectives over these same serial positions, a clear primacy effect. If the judgment depended solely on verbal memory, it would have to show primacy, like the recall curve. This recency–primacy contrast disproves the verbal memory hypothesis.

Anderson and Hubert (1963) did not actually have a complete serial curve of judgment as shown in Fig. 8.1. The theory and method for constructing such judgment curves did not then exist. Instead, they had to make do with a crude index of primacy–recency. This index, fortunately, was sufficient to reject the verbal memory hypothesis and argue for their on-line model.

Subsequent work has supported Anderson and Hubert (1963), both on the two-memory formulation and on the on-line model. The linear primacy curve for judgment was obtained in Anderson (1965) and, with improved methods, in Anderson (1973b). Further support for the two-memory formulation was provided by Dreben, Fiske, and Hastie (1979) and by Riskey (1979), both of whom found recency in the recall curve, primacy in the judgment curve.

For further study of functional memory, complete judgment curves like that of Fig. 8.1 are clearly desirable. Obtaining such curves depends on substantive theory, however, and certain associated methods that took quite some time to establish.

On-Line Model

To determine the judgment curve of Fig. 8.1 requires a theoretical model for the serial integration process. In the on-line model of Anderson and Hubert (1963), the judgment at any position in the sequence is considered a single number, the integrated resultant of all previous information. As each new item of information is presented, it is integrated with this previous judgment. This integration has been shown to obey an exact averaging rule in the personality adjective task and in many other tasks. At each position, in other words, the previous judgment is adjusted by averaging in the new information. This cumulative serial integration is an on-line process.

To formalize this model, let R denote the judgment, s the stimulus value, w a weighting factor, and let i index serial position. Then the model may be written as the average:

$$R_i = w_i s_i + (1 - w_i) R_{i-1}. \tag{1a}$$

It is also useful to rewrite this equation to express the change in judgment:

$$R_i - R_{i-1} = w_i(s_i - R_{i-1}). \tag{1b}$$

In this form, the amount of change on the left side is seen to be proportional to the difference between the given stimulus value, s_i, and the previous judgment, R_{i-1}. This could also be called an anchoring-and-adjustment model, because the previous judgment (= anchor) is adjusted towards the stimulus presented at each successive serial position (see Anderson, 1986, pp. 76–79).

This model is intended to apply even though the subject does not make an overt judgment until the end of the sequence, when all the information is in. Serial integration is still assumed to occur as an implicit on-line process. To obtain the serial curve for judgment, it is necessary to dissect this single judgment into the separate contributions from each serial position. This dissection is plotted in Fig. 8.1. A simple method for obtaining this judgment curve was developed in IIT and is illustrated in the following section.

Serial Curve of Judgment

The serial curve for judgment can be obtained very simply under certain conditions. The idea is to match scale values across serial positions. With such matching, the scale values need not be known. This markedly simplifies measurement of weights—which constitute the judgment curve.

This example uses hypothetical but realistic data based on previous experiments. Eight serial lists of High and Low adjectives are used, as shown in the following example. The High adjectives are matched in value and similarly for the Low adjectives. Filler adjectives are used in the first two positions so these first two adjectives can be ignored in the judgment curve. All adjectives are to be considered accurate and equally important, except one, written in red, which is stated to be uncertain and unreliable.

```
H H H H H H   4.50      L H L H H L   2.20
L H H L L H   2.70      H L L H L H   2.20
H L H L H L   2.90      L L L L H H   1.60
L L H H L L   1.50      H H L L L L   2.40
```

The eight lists constitute a factorial design, in which the serial positions are the design factors and the High and Low adjectives (e.g., *cheerful–gloomy* and *careful–careless,* Anderson, 1973b) are the levels of each factor. Strictly speaking, the eight lists constitute a fractional replication of a 2^6 design. This design can test the model and measure the judgment curve.

The problem facing the investigator is this: Given the response listed at the end of each sequence, dissect it into parts that represent the contributions from each serial position. The model makes this possible, thereby revealing the serial curve of judgment.

From Equation 1, it can be shown that the difference in marginal means at serial position i, denoted by $R_{Hi} - R_{Li}$, equals the weight, w_i, at position i times the difference in scale values for the High and Low adjectives at position i, namely, $(s_H - s_L)$. This last difference is constant over serial positions because of the matching. Hence, (Anderson, 1964, 1981a, Section 2.5):

$$R_{Hi} - R_{Li} = w_i(s_H - s_L). \tag{2}$$

Equation 2 defines the serial curve for judgment. Because adjective values are matched across serial position, any effect of serial position must appear in the weight parameter, w_i. And because $(s_H - s_L)$ is constant, the difference in observed response is proportional to, and hence an estimate of w_i. These estimates, obtained from the listed responses, are plotted as the *judgment curve* in Fig. 8.1.

The serial curve of judgment is thus visible in Fig. 8.1. The main trend is a linear primacy effect, with the weights decreasing linearly across serial position (Anderson, 1965, 1973b; see 1981a, Fig. 2.9 and Table 2.7). This linear primacy reflects a process of attention decrement, not processes of inconsistency resolution, as claimed in the gestalt position of Asch (1946, see Anderson, 1981a, chaps. 2 and 3). The one deviation from linearity stems from the one adjective designated as unreliable, which has much lower weight.

The corresponding recall data, plotted as the *recall curve* in Fig. 8.1, exhibit a quite different shape. The first two points represent the initial filler adjectives, which were included to factor out the initial primacy component of recall. The main trend over the six relevant serial positions is recency. This contrast between recency in recall and primacy in judgment implies that the person judgment is not based solely on the verbal memory.

Also notable is the contrast between the very low weight and very high recall at serial position 6. This position contains the one adjective in red, which was unreliable. The lower weight reflects the unreliability manipulation. The higher recall reflects the well-known Zeigarnik isolation effect. This particular recall manipulation has not actually been performed, although an analogous result has been obtained by Hastie and Kumar (1979), discussed later. Because the outcome can hardly be doubted, this contrast is taken as a thought experiment against the verbal memory hypothesis. Verbal memory is insufficient because recall is not a valid measure of weight. Hence, recall measures are basically inadequate for functional memory.

Averaging Theory

The judgment curve just considered in Fig. 8.1 is remarkable, in that it dissects the single overt judgment at the end of the trait list into the separate contributions from each past serial position. The scalpel for this dissection is the averaging model. Whereas the recall curve consists of observable frequencies, the judgment curve is a theoretical deduction from the data. The averaging model cannot be taken for granted, therefore, and, in fact, a substantial number of problems had to be resolved to discover and establish the averaging model (see Anderson, 1981a, chaps. 2–4). A few of these problems are noted here.

One assumption of the averaging model is that each trait adjective has a constant meaning, regardless of what other adjectives it is combined with. With the cited adjectives, for example, *cheerful* is assumed to have the same value, regardless of whether it is in a trait list with *careful* or *careless*. This assumption of meaning constancy is not free-floating; it is tested in the model analysis.

Meaning constancy, of course, is exactly contrary to the gestalt view of Asch (1946). Asch's conceptual analysis was faulty, however, so little of his evidence had any bearing on the problem (Anderson, 1981a, Section 3.6.3). Meaning constancy has been well established through demanding tests by many investigators.

A second problem for averaging theory concerned primacy–recency effects. Primacy could be interpreted to mean that the later adjectives were discounted to reduce their inconsistency with the earlier adjectives. Such discounting would violate the simple averaging model. However, extensive work by a number of investigators has shown that, in the personality adjective task, primacy–recency effects result from cognitive attentional factors.

A more quantititive problem was whether the integration rule was adding or averaging. In this case, the evidence has clearly favored averaging (Anderson, 1981a), although anachronistic summation models still persist in attitude theory (Anderson, 1981b). The averaging model has some notable properties. It accounts for certain "biases" in judgment (e.g., Anderson, 1974b, Section 7.2; 1981a, Section 2.3.6). It can measure personal values on true linear scales. It has the elusive, near-unique capability of measuring importance weights. This capability underlies the construction of the serial judgment curve of Fig. 8.1.

Finally, it should be noted that averaging processes are pervasive in social cognition. Although the personality adjective task, which was the primary domain for testing the model, involves small amounts of information, it taps directly into values and processes of everyday life. Hence, results obtained with it were expected to exhibit process generality (Anderson, 1981a, Section 2.1.1). This expectation has been justified: The averaging model has also had good success with attitudes, group discussion, wife–husband influence, moral judgment, and social attribution. The averaging model thus provides a solid theoretical base for studying social cognition.

Functional Measurement

A major obstacle in the development of functional memory theory was associated with certain technical problems in using the averaging model for measurement. To measure the serial curve for judgment with the method illustrated in Fig. 8.1 requires that adjective values be matched across serial positions. Matching allows easy analysis, but matching is not always feasible, especially when more than a single judgment is to be considered. The initial attempts to extend the averaging model ran into certain statistical difficulties that have only recently reached a satisfactory plateau. This section gives an overview of the averaging model and the AVERAGE program developed for using it.

Mathematically, the averaging model seems innocuous: a weighted sum of values divided by the sum of the weights. Consider a two-factor design in which each factor represents one source of information that bears on some judgment. Each cell of the design corresponds to two pieces of information to which the subject is to give an integrated response. Denote the values and weights of the row stimuli by s_{Ai} and w_A, those of the column stimuli by s_{Bj} and w_B. Denote the value and weight of the initial state by s_0 and w_0. The initial state is a knowledge system that represents prior information about the person or issue. For known persons and issues, the initial state would include long-term memory for prior on-line judgments that are integrated with present on-line information.

With this notation, the response, R_{ij}, to the combined information in row i and column j is the average:

$$R_{ij} = (w_A s_{Ai} + w_B s_{Bj} + w_0 s_0)/(w_A + w_B + w_0). \qquad (3)$$

The numerator on the right is the weighted sum of values; the denominator is the sum of the weights.

The obvious, natural way to test this model is the wrong way. The obvious way is to begin by measuring the stimulus values and their weights. This is pretty sure to fail, even if the model is correct, without a valid measurement theory to measure the stimulus values and weights.

The right way to test the model is with the *parallelism theorem*. If the model is correct, then the factorial plot of the data will be a set of parallel curves. This parallelism prediction provides a simple test of the model directly in terms of the observable response; no stimulus measurement is needed. On the contrary, the stimulus values can be derived from the data after the model has been verified.

The simplicity of this parallelism analysis depends on the assumption that the judgment response is a true linear scale. Fortunately, the ordinary rating method has proved generally capable of providing true linear scales. It is important to use stimulus end anchors and preliminary practice to establish a stable frame of reference, but these procedures are simple (Anderson, 1981a, Appendix A; 1982, chap. 1). Indeed, placing the rating method on a solid base in measurement theory is one contribution of IIT.

A major difficulty arises with the averaging model, however, when it comes to measuring weights. The parallelism theorem includes the assumption that all stimulus levels of each factor have equal weight. This assumption is not always true. The negativity effect discovered in one of the early tests of the model represents greater weight for more negative information. Differential salience, reliability, or amount of information can also produce differential weighting (Anderson, 1981a, Section 4.4), and hence systematic deviations from parallelism. In fact, the success of these predictions was important evidence for averaging in the averaging–adding controversy. Unfortunately, such differential weighting markedly complicates the use of the model for measurement.

The measurement problem involves a set of statistical difficulties that resisted solution for many years. These problems have now reached a reasonably satisfactory resolution, and a user-friendly AVERAGE program is available for functional measurement with the averaging model (Zalinski & Anderson, 1986, in prep.). Although not recommended for casual users, AVERAGE has broken a major roadblock to analysis of functional memory.

Judgment Curves as a Case History

This section may be concluded by commenting on the study of serial curves of judgment as a case history of scientific inquiry. Over the course of the research program on IIT, the averaging model has been transformed from speculation into solid theory, empirically grounded. Many obstacles had to be overcome, some theoretical, concerning the empirical validity of the model (Anderson, 1981a), some technical, concerning experimental procedure and methods of design and analysis (Anderson, 1982). Progress has been steady—and cumulative.

The work on the averaging model has opened up a new horizon in cognitive theory. This may be seen in its treatment of valuation and integration, two problems that are basic to the functional conception of memory. With the functional measurement methodology, the averaging model may be used as a minor but real parallel to Newton's laws, a working tool for cognitive analysis.

SOCIAL MEMORY

The discussion of functional memory is continued in this part with an overview of associated concepts. Social memory is a fitting framework for exposition because the concept of functional memory originated from the initial study of person memory by Anderson and Hubert (1963). These same concepts also apply to attitudes (Anderson, 1981b, in prep.-b) and indeed to general memory theory (Anderson, in prep.-a). The discussion of this section is oriented to the concepts of *knowledge system* and *assemblage*. Two preliminary sections are needed, however, to discuss the function of on-line processing in person memory. The first section, taken essentially verbatim from Anderson (1983b), points up similarity and differences between person memory and verbal memory. The second discusses on-line processing in long-term person memory.

Person Memory

Person memory has one basic similarity with and two basic differences from traditional verbal memory. The similarity is that both exhibit organization, whose understanding has been the primary goal of memory research since the time of Ebbinghaus. The two differences concern the form of this organization and the function of memory.

Form has typically been arbitrary in traditional verbal learning. This difference between list memory and person memory is highlighted by the nonsense syllable. The reasons that led to its adoption in traditional memory research render it inappropriate for understanding person memory. Even when meaningful, the words in a to-be-memorized list are typically unrelated to one another, while the list itself is typically unrelated to any real object.

The memory task is transformed when the list of words is said to describe a person. A person is a real object of a certain kind, and this imposes unifying constraints on the list. The single words are no longer arbitrary, for each should bear some relation to a person schema, which, in turn, may influence processing of the single words. Because the words are about one person, moreover, their interrelations are also constrained. *Bold* and *timid*, for example, may go well in the same list but not in the same person. Again, *dependable* and *reliable* may be largely redundant in a person description, but it would be an error to omit one in reciting a list. These are just two of many constraints that accompany processing aimed at valuation and integration into meaningful wholes.

Person memory is dominated by goal-directed processing for meaning. Our goals relative to our child, say, or our spouse, are variable, but they do not typically involve verbatim memory. Rather, each goal sets up valuation schemas that extract relevant meaning from present and memorial information.

Traditional verbal learning, in contrast, typically aims at verbatim reproduction—and at accuracy. Subjects are instructed to memorize—the list constitutes a standard of correctness that controls their behavior. Although memory research has been increasingly concerned with organization and meaning, it is still dominated by accuracy. What is to be learned is prescribed, even in studies of gist. The given stimuli provide feedback that controls the course of learning—and an accuracy standard for measuring memory. As useful as accuracy studies can be, they are insufficient for person memory, which is typically concerned with judgment and action rather than with reproductive memory.

Focus on judgment and action leads to perspectives that are different from focus on memory. Judgment and action are goal-directed in ways that memorizing is not. Instead of learning the prescribed stimuli, subjects need to evaluate them with respect to some goal, deciding how much to praise or blame the person, for example, or how far to push one's own position, and to integrate the valuations of the several stimuli to obtain a unified response.

The same set of stimuli may be processed rather differently, therefore, depending on the goal. This processing may itself affect the organization of memory. Such forms of organization, developed in daily life, may be significant even in traditional memory studies. Focus on judgment and action is thus a pertinent complement to the focus on memorization. (Further discussion is given in Anderson, 1983b, in prep.-a.)

Long-Term Memory and On-Line Function

The on-line formulation of Anderson and Hubert (1963) applies to persons and issues of everyday life. This section considers social interaction, as with family members or workmates. In place of the adjective list about a hypothetical person is episodic information from ongoing interpersonal interaction. This information is processed on-line in similar manner in both cases. For known persons, therefore, the two-memory representation still applies, referring to episodic interaction information, on one hand, and to impressions and judgments constructed from that information, on the other. For known persons, of course, memory structure is more complex (Anderson, 1976a, 1976b, 1981a, 1981b).

Long-term memory has two primary functions. The first is to assist in present on-line processing, which involves both valuation and integration. Long-term memory is clearly essential in valuation. The same word may mean quite different things when spoken by one's spouse, parent, child, or boss. A tone of voice or an emphasis may, when referred to that person memory, imply an unspoken reservation or disagreement. Similarly, the same information may have quite different implications relative to different goals.

Also in long-term memory are diverse affects, which function in valuation of goals for approach and avoidance (Anderson, in press). Such affects are included in the initial state construct, already discussed with Equation 3. An on-line judgment of helpfulness, say, results from an integration of current episodic information—together with a prior judgment derived from the long-term person memory.

More active elements also appear in long-term person memory, especially person-specific schemas and roles. Although some such schemas seem declarative in nature, as with sex stereotypes, others are active operators, as with integration schemas for attribution. Roles, similarly, have active functions in controlling ongoing interaction. Because they contain such active elements, long-term person memories are appropriately called *knowledge systems*.

The second primary function of long-term memory is to store information from present on-line processing. Some of this long-term storage follows the serial integration model, with judgments from on-line operating memory themselves being reintegrated into the long-term person memory. A mass of episodic information can be condensed into single on-line judgments, of helpfulness, for example, or of helplessness, and these judgments can be stored for future use.

This is an important implication of the two-memory representation, because it means that present interaction can take advantage of past processing. The continual updating provides a functional memory system that is adaptable for use in new interactions, efficient in utilizing the end products of past processing, and economical in memory demands, especially retrieval. This provides better biosocial economy than "memory-based" formulations, which would require retrieval—and reprocessing—of the original episodic information at each new interaction.

For everyday persons and issues, therefore, the two-memory formulation is even more important than with hypothetical persons. Long-term memory may include judgment memory from many dimensions, and the "verbal memory" may include diverse episodic information (Anderson, 1976a, 1981b). Similar views on person memory were adopted by most contributors to the volume on person memory by Hastie et al. (1980). Thus, the dual-code view of Ebbesen (1980) and others is quite similar to the Anderson-Hubert two-memory formulation in its distinction between memory for the given stimulus materials and for the more abstract implications of those materials. Ebbesen did not present evidence to establish this distinction, however, whereas Anderson and Hubert demonstrated that it was cognitively real.

Carlston (1980) also takes a two-memory position: "At the heart of the present approach is the assumption that a person may store in memory both a record of external events that he observes and a record of his accompanying, internal cognitive reactions to those events," (p. 92). This heart corresponds to the verbal memory and impression memory, respectively, of Anderson and Hubert (1963).

To pursue the analysis of functional memory requires cognitive theory of judgment and decision. Long-term memory representations of persons and attitudes are more complex than indicated in this brief overview. Fortunately, nature has provided one simple, effective path to deeper analysis. By the principle of molar unitization (Anderson, 1981a, Section 1.1.5), the operation of long-term memory of arbitrary complexity can be treated exactly and completely and measured with functional measurement. Cognitive algebra thus provides a precision method for study of memory function; this, in turn, provides a key to analysis of structure.

Knowledge Systems

Memory for any familiar person is a knowledge system, marked by goal-directed function. This should be expected on biosocial grounds. Our interactions with another person are goal-directed, and this functional character is impressed on person memory in several ways. First, present goals influence what is attended to and hence what is available for storage. Second, present goals influence what inferences are drawn and what integrations are made from available information; these also influence what is available for storage. Third, but not last, present goals influence what operators or procedures are used to process available information, and these operators may also be incorporated into the person memory. The transition from the feeling-out period of initial acquaintance to the facile roles of family interaction illustrate all three aspects of the functional character of person memory.

Knowledge systems, as just indicated, include processing operators. It is this dynamic aspect that warrants the term system rather than structure. The dynamic aspect of knowledge systems is nicely illustrated with the concept of role. In continued interaction between husband and wife, both develop sets of roles whose function, or dysfunction, is to routinize the interaction. These roles are active, controlling processes that are part of the corresponding person memories. The self concept, considered also as a memory system, may contain more abstract roles that can be assembled into operating memory for specific interaction episodes.

A knowledge system is more general than a schema. This is clear in the case of attitude memory, which is a prototypical knowledge system (Anderson, 1976a, 1976b, 1981a, 1981b, 1988, in prep.-a). Person memory, similarly, may contain schemas as components, but has more complex organization.

A beachhead on the study of schemas and knowledge systems has been provided by IIT. Judgments about persons and issues embody the functioning of the knowledge system. Hence these judgments constitute a base for analyzing function and structure of the knowledge system. Some of this potential can be actualized with the algebraic schemas studied in IIT.

Assemblage Theory

The concept of *assemblage* is central to functional memory. Assemblage refers to the construction of an operating memory that controls ongoing activity. Assemblage is on-line. The function of memory is not in retrieval per se, but in making inferences and in constructing assemblages. As stated in Anderson (1982, 1988):

> The pervasive role of background knowledge deserves emphasis. . . . This role of the background knowledge is constructive. . . . From this constructivist view, the full operative schema may be considered an *assemblage*. This term emphasizes the bringing together of diverse bits and pieces of background knowledge, which is a main cognitive activity in the task. (1982, p. 344)

> The functional approach entails a concept of assemblage. The operating memory for any judgment or action is typically assembled from diverse forms of memory storage, as already indicated, as well as from situational stimuli. Assemblage is not a simple matter of memory retrieval, but an active process of construction. . . . The necessity for an assemblage concept appears in the multiplicity of possible goals. A spouse, for example, may figure in many different motivations and goals. . . . Assemblage provides a base for goal-oriented judgment and action that is realistic in storage requirements as well as sensitive to social context. (1988, p. 39)

Functional memory is not a matter of retrieval or reproduction. The traditional conception of reproductive memory, taken over from mainstream memory theory, has dominated the study of person memory. For this purpose, however, it is not merely inadequate but largely inappropriate. Person memory requires a functional perspective and that requires a concept of assemblage.

Reproductive Memory

The strong grip of the traditional reproductive conception of memory is illustrated by Hastie and Park's (1986) use of "memory-based" in place of the equivalent "verbal memory" formulation discussed by Anderson and Hubert (1963). The term *"memory-based"* equates *memory* with the verbal memory for the given stimulus material. But person memory includes more than such verbal memory, and indeed has qualitatively different structure. Even for a hypothetical person described by a list of trait adjectives, person memory may be expected to include impressions about such reflex social judgments as sex and likableness. The term *"memory-*based" implicitly and explicitly conceptualizes *memory* as reproductive memory—as though *memory* had no other content.

The concept of reproductive memory has deep roots. It is epitomized in Ebbinghaus's lists of nonsense syllables, a paradigm that was long considered a prototype of human memory. The list paradigm also has roots in the associationist framework, in which paired associates and conditioning tasks are basic forms of learning.

Functional memory continues the direction of inquiry set up by Bartlett (1932), but leads into a new domain of judgment and decision. Bartlett emphasized memory as an active, constructive process, but he was still bound by the reproductive conception. His view of memory as *re*construction and his response measures both rest on the view that the function of memory is to reproduce. Recent concerns with "gist" memory have similar character, as shown by their reliance on accuracy criteria.

The functional perspective implies that memory should be studied in its natural mode, that is, as it functions in goal-oriented thought and action. But functional memory is quite different from reproductive memory, as already illustrated with the serial curves of Fig. 8.1.

Valuation and Inference

Functional memory requires processes of valuation and inference that seem beyond the scope of traditional memory theory. To illustrate with an attribution example, compare the two sentences, "The marine sergeant is afraid of the dog" and "The little girl is afraid of the dog." There is a clear implication that the first dog is more threatening than the second. This implication is not in the stimulus words, but depends on an attributional process that involves background memory information.

This functional perspective is basic to IIT. One facet appears in the concept of valuation. The function of the valuation operator is to process relevant information, whether from prior memory or present stimulus, to obtain implications for the operative goal. These implications must generally be constructed in relation to the goal, so the same stimulus will have different implications in relation to different goals.

This point may be carried farther by noting that the same stimulus will generally have different implications for different persons. As noted previously (Anderson, 1981a):

> It is a basic tenet of integration theory that stimuli must be considered in terms of their meaning and value to the individual. If two people hear the same message, they may disagree about what was actually said. If they agree about what was actually said, they may still disagree about its implications. And even if they agree about the implications, they may nevertheless disagree about their desirability. Valuation processes may be similar across individuals, but their outcomes will differ. (p. 7)

Functional measurement methodology makes it possible to measure meanings at the level of the individual within the situational context. Functional measurement thus provides an effective means for analysis of functional memory.

Episodic Information

An interesting question concerns the function of memory for specific items of information, which may be generically termed *episodic information* (Tulving, 1983). With hypothetical persons, the two-memory formulation of Anderson and Hubert (1963) downplays episodic information. With well-known persons, however, much more episodic information is generally available, especially for the self. But what it does is not clear.

Integration theory emphasizes judgment memory as a basic functional form. For known persons, therefore, operating memory in any on-line situation may derive largely from long-term judgment memory. Attitude memory is considered a prototype of such long-term storage.

Lingle and Ostrom (1981, pp. 399–400; Ostrom, Lingle, Pryor, & Geva, 1980) have erroneously criticized IIT on the grounds that it does not recognize the function of past judgments in making present judgments. Exactly the opposite is true: This was a primary theoretical implication of the two-memory formulation of Anderson and Hubert (1963). This implication was elaborated in the integration theory of attitudes (Anderson, 1971, 1973a, 1981b; Anderson & Farkas, 1973; Anderson & Graesser, 1976; Anderson, Sawyers, & Farkas, 1972).

For novel judgments, of course, episodic information may have some function (Anderson, 1976b, Section 7.2.1; 1981a, pp. 96, 310; 1981b, p. 365). Novelty means that little relevant judgment memory may be available, enforcing reliance on episodic memory. Two other functions of episodic information may be noted. One is as part of ongoing interaction, especially when valuation processing is spread out over time. The other is as a crystallization focus for judgment memory.

But even novel judgments may depend heavily on judgment memory rather than episodic memory. The much-discussed halo effects, for example, refer to reliance on general impressions rather than episodic information (Anderson, 1981a, Section 3.6.2). Similarly, people are facile at making inferences from almost any piece of information about almost any judgment.

It may be conjectured, therefore, that episodic memory typically has limited influence in on-line judgments of well-known persons. The adjective task with hypothetical persons favors operation of verbal memory: The adjectives are all the given information there is, and they are few in number and recent in memory. But even under these conditions, the general impression dominates. With known persons, judgment memory will be well developed, whereas episodic memory may be weakened by forgetting or interference over longer periods of time. The two-memory formulation thus leads to the paradoxical conjecture that episodic memory may be least important when it is most strongly developed.

Schema Theory

Cognitive algebra has surmounted the general criticism that schema formulations are vague and ineffectual. As noted by Anderson (in prep.-b):

> Schemas became suddenly fashionable around 1975 (see overview by Brewer and Nakamura, 1984), and some such concept seemed essential to represent organization of knowledge. For the most part, progress has been disappointing. There was a healthy liberation from traditional class-instance representations to bring out the importance of temporal, spatial, musical, motor, and other forms of organization. The concept of schema thus pointed to important problems, but most formulations remain almost where they began.
>
> With one class of schemas, however, real progress has been made. These are the integration schemas, whose structure has been exactly determined in a number of cases. This appears to be the only exception to the prevailing vagueness of schema theories.

The ineffectiveness criticism may be illustrated by the concepts of *slots* and *default values*, which were taken almost as defining characteristics in a number of schema formulations. Slots refer to relevant variables, and default values to values of these variables ready for use if relevant information is missing. An algebraic integration schema has explicit slots, as with Culpa and Damage in the blame schema, Blame = Culpa + Damage. Hence, the postulated default value should be used if information is missing on one variable. This implication has not been supported.

How people do handle missing information has been studied by a number of workers on integration theory (see *Imputations* in Anderson, 1983b, in prep.-b). These results, however, showed two serious shortcomings of the slot-and-default value formulations. First, when an imputation was made about the value of missing information, it was often not a constant default value, but variable, depending on situational information. Second, imputations were often not made, even when the task clearly called for them. In retrospect, it is apparent that the slot-and-default value conception relied on anecdotal examples, without theoretical firmness.

In social psychology, schema formulations have been even more vague. One example appears in the following discussion of attribution schemas. Another appears in persisting misconceptions about memory bias in studies of prototypes and stereotypes (e.g., Cantor & Mischel, 1977; Cohen, 1981; Hamilton & Rose, 1980; Snyder & Uranowitz, 1978) that had been resolved much earlier in the studies of meaning constancy (see Anderson, 1981a, Sections 3.6.3 and 4.1.8; 1983a, pp. 8-9, 26-29; 1988, p. 48).

The root of the problem is that current cognitive psychology is fundamentally inadequate for social-personality psychology. It neglects affect (Simon, 1982, p. 342) and it has little to say about judgment and decision, both of which are central to functional theory (Anderson, 1987).

Information integration theory provides a tested alternative to current schema formulations because it can diagnose operative schemas in certain cases. It is thus possible to demonstrate that the modal blame schema is an averaging rule—and to determine how people actually do handle missing information. More generally, the work on cognitive algebra has established the exact nature of one class of schemas.

Cognitive algebra provides a beachhead for study of schemas with nonalgebraic structure. Something can be learned about attitudes as knowledge systems, for example, because the derived attitudinal responses obey algebraic rules. Assemblage processes, similarly, can be studied by arranging for assemblage with algebraic rules as component operators. Cognitive algebra is no silver platter, but it does go beyond promissory notes to begin real work on schema analysis. The following main part illustrates this approach with attribution processes.

SOCIAL ATTRIBUTION

Attribution research needs reconstruction as part of general theory of social cognition. Current thinking is still dominated by the rational, normative conceptions of Jones and Davis (1965) and Kelley (1967, 1972a, 1972b). Jones and McGillis noted in 1976 that the growth of the original formulations had been stunted. This is even more obvious after a second decade. The main reason for lack of theory development suggested earlier (Anderson, 1978) was that "Previous work on social attribution has to a surprising degree neglected the study of cognitive process and general theory" (p. 109). This remains largely true.

The cited rational formulations represent a false start for attribution *theory*. Although they have led to some interesting empirical results, they are too narrow for growth of cognitive theory and are ineffective even within their own domain. Narrowness is seen in their restriction to causal attribution, whereas much social attribution is noncausal, as with blame and obligation. Ineffectiveness is apparent in the statement by Jones and McGillis (1976) that their formulation "is essentially a rational baseline model . . . the theory cannot be invalidated by experimental results" (p.

404). Similar lack of analytical power is clear also in the failure of the work with Kelley's ANOVA cube to determine the exact form of any causal schema.

A more cognitive foundation for attribution theory has been provided by IIT. This theory embodies a framework of cognitive process. It embraces the study of noncausal attribution and treats it in terms similar to causal attribution. And it has analytical power, as shown by the finding of a general cognitive algebra of attribution (Anderson, 1974a, 1978; Lopes, 1972; Shanteau, 1972; Singh, in prep.; Surber, 1981a, 1981b, 1985b, 1987).

On-Line Attribution

On-line processing is prominent in the attributions of everyday life. Inferring motives, estimating ability, distributing fair shares, judging obligation, and laying blame illustrate the pervasiveness of everyday attribution processes. They also illustrate the purposive character of everyday thought and action and the associated need for a functional perspective.

The foregoing treatment of functional memory applies directly to attribution. On-line attribution requires valuation and integration. These attributions guide on-line goal-oriented activity as their primary function. In addition, they will typically be incorporated into long-term memory. Long-term memory thus has two primary functions. One is to serve in assemblage of operating memory for current attribution, the other is to retain the end products of these attributions for future use. This role of functional memory may be illustrated with attribution of attitudes to another person, which, under some conditions, follows the on-line averaging model of Equation 1 (see later discussion of Himmelfarb & Anderson, 1975).

Other attempts to develop attribution theory cannot get very far, partly because they lack effective means of analysis, but more because they are too narrow to permit the growth of general theory. The following sections, accordingly, are mainly intended to set out the need for reconstruction in attribution theory. Most of this material on attribution is taken from Anderson (in prep.-b).

Causal Attribution

The prototypical question of causal attribution is "Why did she act that way?" Attribution theory is not primarily concerned with the actual causes, however, but with the causes imputed by some attributor, her husband, say, who seeks to make sense of her action. And although the accuracy of the husband's attribution is not without importance, cognitive theory is mainly concerned with his thought processes, that is, with his mental representation of his wife and her action.

A simple schema analysis would begin with the common sense formulation that has guided many studies of causal attribution (see Anderson, 1974a). The observed action, A, is considered to result from the operation of two causal forces, F and G, and may be symbolically represented as:

$$A = F \oplus G,$$

where $\oplus$ denotes a generalized integration operator. Some causation may be either/or, but in most social attribution, F and G act together so that A results from their integrated action. In one common social form, F refers to the real feelings or motives of the actor, and G refers to social constraints of politeness, for example, or ulterior motive that mask the real feelings.

This symbolic equation is a schema in several respects. Most obvious, it embodies an identification of the operative causal forces assumed in the attributor's causal conceptualization. Associated with this are valuation operations that process available information to determine the nature and strength of each causal force. These valuation operations correlate the present situation with the attributor's knowledge systems, as indicated in the discussion of functional memory. Also important to the causal schema is the nature of the integration operation itself, for this represents the attributor's understanding of the causal dynamics.

The uncertainty familiar from everyday attributions about another's real feelings is mirrored in this causal schema. Different configurations of the two causal forces can combine to produce the same observable action. To determine F requires knowledge of G. In practice, therefore, the attributor must also make an attribution about G from limited information about the actor–situation configuration.

Noncausal Attribution

Much attribution is noncausal. One prime example is the basic blame schema, in which blame attributed for a harmful act depends on the culpability of the actor and the harmful consequences of the act:

$$\text{Blame} = \text{Culpa} \oplus \text{Consequences}.$$

Although a preliminary causal attribution may or may not be needed to evaluate culpa, the attribution of blame itself is noncausal. The same applies for many other social attributions.

The blame schema also illustrates that attribution may depend on nonsocial factors, for the consequences term may refer to physical damage. In other attributions, similarly, nonsocial probability information may be important. Attribution theory must accordingly be developed as part of a general theory of judgment and decision.

Cognitive Algebra

Some attributions obey algebraic schemas. This cognitive algebra provides a beachhead for study of attribution. This approach includes causal and noncausal attribution, as well as prediction. It is programmatic in a good sense, in that it provides concepts and methods already found effective for schema analysis. This point may be illustrated with two basic schemas, for blame and for performance.

Fundamental developmental work by Leon (1980) has shown that the basic blame schema follows a modal averaging rule:

$$\text{Blame} = \text{Culpa} \oplus \text{Damage}.$$

This basic blame schema has been expanded to include mitigation (Leon, 1982), reparation (Hommers & Anderson, 1985), and applied in legal psychology (Hommers & Anderson, 1988). This schema analysis has also provided a new approach to the study of social learning (Anderson & Armstrong, in press; Leon, 1984). Important related work has been done by Surber (1982, 1985a). Aside from providing a theoretical base for blame attribution, this work has led to a conception of moral development that is quite different from the standard stage theories of Kohlberg (1976), Rest (1979, 1986), Damon (1977), and others.

The basic performance schema was studied by Anderson and Butzin (1974), who found the three algebraic rules:

$$\text{Performance} = \text{Motivation} \times \text{Ability},$$
$$\text{Motivation} = \text{Performance} - \text{Ability},$$
$$\text{Ability} = \text{Performance} - \text{Motivation}.$$

The mathematical inconsistency of these three rules indicates that the schema is not reversible, contrary to Heider's (1958) specific assumption and to Piaget's general claim of reversibility of formal operations. This nonreversibility is consistent with other work (e.g., Graesser & Anderson, 1974), including some outside the social domain (e.g., Wilkening, 1982). Incisive work by Surber (1985b, 1987) has added breadth and depth to this conclusion.

Cognitive algebra provides an essentially new foundation for attribution theory and unifies it with general theory of social cognition. The present focus on everyday life is similar to that of Heider (1958), but goes farther to establish a proper theory. Heider speculated that Performance = Motivation × Ability, but his balance theory proved ineffectual (Anderson,

1971, 1974a, Section III.G.1). The key to cognitive algebra lies in the associated capability for psychological measurement. Without this, the schemas would remain conjectual pseudoequations; with this, they become true equations of the mind.

Jones and Davis's Correspondent Inference Theory

Information integration theory began around the same time as Jones and Davis's (1965) correspondent inference theory, and both focused on judgments about personality disposition, the primary issue in the initial development of integration theory. The Jones–Davis formulation, however, addresses only one aspect of the judgment process, namely, valuation of single pieces of information. Although entitled, "From acts to dispositions," it only takes a first step. It cannot really arrive at a disposition because that generally requires integration; even a single act must generally be integrated with prior information about the person. Because it does not address the integration problem, the Jones–Davis formulation hardly qualifies as a theory of attribution.

Their formulation does have interest, however, with respect to the valuation process for single informers. If a person acts discourteously, for example, this information will be integrated into the observer's cognition of that person. But many acts cannot be taken at face value. Perhaps the person was not truly discourteous, but was sorely provoked. The face value of the act must be weighted by its credibility, that is, the degree to which it is considered to reflect the person's true disposition. It must then be integrated with other available information, including the initial state or prior expectation.

In integration theory, the weighting process itself is controlled by the foregoing causal schema.

$$A = F \oplus G.$$

In the present example, F represents the true disposition of the person, and G represents other causal forces. The schema implies that more undesirable behavior, such as discourtesy by a hostess, should be weighted more heavily in the person cognition. Because the other forces of social constraint operate to inhibit discourtesy, it must have been stronger to have occurred.

Even for valuation of a single informer, however, correspondent inference theory remains poorly developed. In discussing one problematic result, Jones and McGillis (1976) rejected the possibility of allowing some outcomes to be more important than others, saying "We view this as a defeatist alternative, however, because the problems of measuring effect importance are staggering" (p. 401). This problem had already been solved with functional measurement, as illustrated extensively in Anderson (1974a).

One of these illustrations concerned attitude attribution, which Jones and McGillis consider their most developed line of research. Attributions of attitude were found to obey the averaging model of information integration theory (Himmelfarb & Anderson, 1975; cited in Anderson, 1974a, Section III.D.3). A Jones–Davis type of manipulation was shown to affect the weight parameter in the averaging model, as implied by the foregoing causal schema. Integration theory goes farther by being able to measure the weight parameter, thereby solving the problem that staggered Jones and McGillis. Integration theory goes still farther with a well-developed theory of the integration process that is necessary to arrive at an attribution of disposition, which is not generally possible within the correspondent inference model. As Himmelfarb and Anderson (1975) said, "It is this emphasis on the underlying processes of information integration that distinguishes the present from previous approaches to social attribution . . . In a general and fundamental way, therefore, information integration theory provides a significant extension of work on attribution of opinion" (p. 1070).

Kelley's ANOVA Cube

Kelley (1967, 1972a,b) attempted to advance beyond Jones and Davis to consider the integration of multiple observations. This attempt was based on a rational concept of schema that misconstrues the operative cognitive schema. Kelley sought a theoretical basis for everyday causal inference by likening it to scientific causal inference. Accordingly, the covariation principle, that the mark of causality is coocurrence, was taken as basic. "Specifically, a causal schema is *an assumed pattern of data in a complete analysis of variance framework*" (1972b, p. 152). This analysis of variance was explicitly specified to have three factors: *Consistency,* which refers to past reactions of the given person in the same situation; *Consensus,* which refers to past reactions of other persons in the same situation; and *Distinctiveness,* which refers to past reactions of the given person to similar situations. These three *C-C-D* factors define Kelley's ANOVA cube, and this conception of attribution has been dominant in subsequent research.

As a definition of causal schema, the ANOVA cube seems a conceptual mistake. Three basic criticisms may be noted:

- The C-C-D factors are not causes, only information about causes.
- The ANOVA cube is a frequency table, not a causal schema.
- Other information that does not fit the ANOVA cube is essential.

These three criticisms may be illustrated by considering a prototypical attribution question: "Why was the person afraid of the dog?" Integration theory takes the causal schema to refer to the two indicated causal forces:

Behavior = Person ⊕ Dog,

or more specifically,

Fear = Fearfulness ⊕ Fearsomeness.

This, not the ANOVA cube, is the functional causal schema. The three C-C-D factors are just three kinds of information about the two causal forces.

Furthermore, other information that hardly fits the C-C-D factors is also necessary, such as salience, reliability, probability, base rates, and other prior knowledge. This point makes a good classroom demonstration, asking students to rate the dog on a 1–10, pussycat-killer scale and specifying the person only by occupation (fashion model, marine sergeant) or even by name (John, Percival). As pointed out previously (Anderson, 1978), "The restriction to distinctiveness, consensus, and consistency information is too narrow a base for theory construction" (p. 107). The need to allow other kinds of information has been acknowledged by Kelley and Michela (1980), but this implicitly acknowledges the inadequacy of the ANOVA cube. The integration schema, in contrast, explicitly recognizes the operation of diverse kinds of information as part of the first integration problem (Anderson, 1978, p. 107).

Discussions of the ANOVA cube, including that of Kelley (1972b), often refer to operative causal forces, as in the person–dog example, and implicitly or explicitly treat the C-C-D factors, not as causes, but as information about causes. This agrees with the integration schema. But it implies that Kelley's ANOVA cube is a misconception of schema. Despite this conceptual inconsistency, the ANOVA cube has retained its popularity as the foundation of Kelley's theory. Without it there would be no theory, only common-sense predictions about directional effects of various experimental manipulations (see similarly Fiedler, 1982).

The symbolic integration schema may seem just common sense, which it is. The problem is to transform common sense into cognitive theory. This requires concepts and methods that can assess when common sense claims are correct. Integration theory provides one base for such cognitive analysis. Functional measurement methodology goes beyond common sense to assess the actual schema structure, to establish cognitive reality of the causal forces, to measure their functional values, and to accomplish other cognitive analyses.

Kelley's C-C-D Patterns

In his experiment on causal schemas, Kelley defined them in a different way, as three specified patterns of high and low values of the C-C-D factors

(Orvis, Cunningham, & Kelley, 1975). Thus, the HHH pattern, in which all three factors have high values, was taken as one causal schema. "As such, the three patterns enter into the inferential process itself. Information is compared with them and is interpreted in terms of the pattern(s) with which it is consistent" (p. 606). This second definition, evidently inconsistent with the first, was introduced in an attempt to handle the obvious problem that people rarely possess the multiplicity of observations required to apply the covariation principle of the ANOVA cube.

This second definition, however, suffers the same three objections as the first, plus others of its own (Anderson, 1978, Section A.3.d; Wyer & Carlston, 1979). The most basic is that the C-C-D patterns are even farther from the concept of schema than the ANOVA cube. The HHH pattern, for example, represents just one cell of the ANOVA cube. This second definition thus confuses a particular instance of a concept with the concept itself.

The present definition of causal schemas as integration rules is closer to common knowledge than either of Kelley's definitions because the elements of the integration schema are cognitive entities from everyday knowledge. For the same reason, the concept of integration schema is closer to Heider, as with the basic performance schema considered earlier. The central problem, however, is to develop concepts and methods that can establish where the schema holds and where it does not. Balance theory, Heider's attempt to develop a formal theory, has done poorly in empirical tests and under conceptual scrutiny (Anderson, 1971, pp. 185–188; 1974a, pp. 81–82; Anderson, Lindner, & Lopes, 1973; see also Anderson, 1979; Gollob, 1979). Kelley's ANOVA is mere analogy; he has never used this or any similar method for schema analysis. The key to schema analysis lies in psychological measurement, which lies outside Kelley's formulation.

Future of Attribution Theory

Attribution theory needs to be reconstructed on a cognitive foundation. The growth of the rationalist formulations of Jones and Davis (1965) and Kelley (1967) was "stunted" (Jones & McGillis, 1976, p. 390) because the rational framework was infertile ground for psychological ideas. Even within the restricted domain of causal attribution, the basic phenomena were taken as biases, that is, deviations from presumptively rational behavior. As Harvey and Weary (1981) said in their overview, "The most potent challenges to basic attribution assumptions have evolved from arguments concerning people's cognitive limitations. These challenges relate to core attribution assumptions about how individuals are deliberative, analytic, and broad in their inferences" (p. 55).

Beginning with core assumptions about rational behavior was a mistake from which attribution research continues to suffer. That people have many cognitive limitations has long been known; that such core assumptions would fail could have been foreseen.

But the rationalist conception perpetuated itself by treating these biases as phenomena to be explained. This led to reification of "noneffects" that existed only in reference to a rational framework irrelevant to understanding the cognitive processes underlying the behavior (Anderson, 1974b, Section 7.2; 1986). Many attribution researchers have considered cognitive processes, of course, but their efforts have been obstructed by the ill-fitting rational framework. The attempts to pursue both directions of inquiry together have generally meant that both suffered, as with the attempts to adjoin psychological process to Kelley's ANOVA cube.

The strong preconception of the rational framework reappears in the conclusion of Harvey and Weary (1981) that future work should be devoted to "careful study of differentiating conditions" (p. 55) about cognitive limitations. This is ill-advised. Cognitive limitations can be important in practical affairs, but most attribution tasks have been unusually artificial, with little practical relevance. Nor is the focus on differentiating conditions likely to lead to theory, partly because the rational framework is antithetical to cognitive theory, partly because theory is needed to make sense of the differentiating conditions (see e.g., Anderson, 1982, p. 338).

A different objection is that the rational framework is too narrow. Not only does it slight many attributional phenomena, but it has fostered a provincial outlook that has largely ignored other areas (see similarly Eiser, 1983, pp. 91-93; Lloyd-Bostock, 1983, pp. 288-289). Attribution studies have had little concern with group dynamics or attitude theory, two central domains of social psychology, and have virtually ignored judgment-decision theory. Although these studies have made a variety of useful contributions, especially by widening the study of social judgment (Anderson, 1974a, p. 5), the rational formulations have outlived their usefulness. Development of attribution *theory* requires a new way of thinking.

ISSUES IN FUNCTIONAL MEMORY

The study of memory function involves the two processes of valuation and integration. Valuation processes construct the implications of the given stimulus information relative to the operative goal. Integration is required because several stimuli are generally operative, so their several implications need to be combined. Because memory function typically involves valuation and integration, its analysis is intimately bound up with general theory of judgment.

The reproductive conception of memory is insufficient for functional memory because it cannot handle valuation and integration. This point is illustrated in the first three sections with three issues that arose from the reproductive conception. The later sections illustrate some applications of IIT, including a new technique for studying functional memory.

Availability

The strong grip of the reproductive conception of memory appears in the availability heuristic (Tversky & Kahneman, 1973), which says that judgments of event frequency are determined by availability of instances. The availability heuristic is thus a special case of the verbal memory hypothesis disproved by Anderson and Hubert (1963) and by Dreben, Fiske, and Hastie (1979). The popularity of the availability heuristic reflects the grip of traditional thinking about memory, not any success in experimental tests. Indeed, as noted by Fiedler (1983), the availability heuristic has rested almost entirely on anecdotal evidence. Fiedler made an experimental test with instance information, but this disagreed with availability and led instead to an interpretation similar to the two-memory hypothesis of Anderson and Hubert (1963). More extensive discussion of availability, as well as other heuristics, is given in Anderson (1986).

Availability has been a blind alley. Once the on-line memory system of Anderson and Hubert (1963) is recognized, it becomes clear that much of long-term memory is derived from past on-line processing. It is mainly the end products of on-line processing that are stored, not the raw materials of verbal memory, as assumed in the availability heuristic.

Judgment-decision theory requires a broader conception of memory theory than availability or verbal recall. Starting from the original two-memory foundation, the theory of information integration was able to avoid this blind alley and proceed with the task of developing a theoretical foundation for functional memory.

Judgment Analysis of Verbal Memory

Judgment tasks may be useful for understanding recall and recognition. One illustration comes from the proposition by Reyes, Thompson, and Bower (1980) that unrecalled stimuli have no effect on judgment. This proposition reflects the strong grip of the reproductive conception of memory, for it disagrees with the two-memory formulation of Anderson and Hubert (1963). Unrecalled stimuli can affect judgment through mediation of on-line memory. Judgment theory is thus important in understanding recall.

A more interesting question is whether unrecalled stimuli can have direct effects on judgment. This question could be studied by presenting a rote memory task and asking for a judgment unexpectedly. The rote memory task could be a list of animal names, for example, or a list of trait adjectives. The unexpected judgment could be of average size of the animals or of average likableness of the adjectives or of average length of the words in the list. The working assumption is that preliminary practice with rote learning would prevent formation of any on-line memory for the indicated questions.

The hypothesis that only recalled words influence judgment implies that unrecalled words will have no predictive power. Assemblage theory, however, suggests that unrecalled words will have predictive power. Such effects might be largest with short lists followed by a standard interfering task, such as counting backwards (Peterson & Peterson, 1959). The hypothesis can readily be tested by regressing the judgment on the values of the unrecalled words.

Memory for Inconsistent Information

The strong grip of reproductive memory appears again in the much-discussed finding that inconsistent information in a person description may be better remembered than consistent information (Hastie & Kumar, 1979; Srull, 1981; see review by Hastie, Park, & Weber, 1984). This has seemed a puzzle to some, owing to belief that higher recall ought to reflect greater influence in the person impression. In light of the two-memory formulation of Anderson and Hubert (1963) there is no puzzle: Recall is dominated by the verbal memory, whereas the person judgment is dominated by the on-line impression memory. The superior recall of the inconsistent item is entirely consistent with lessened influence in the judgment of the person—as in Fig. 8.1.

The issue goes deeper: What function does the inconsistent information have in judgments about the person? On this question, recall data are silent. The various interpretations of the higher recall begin with the consideration that inconsistent information will receive more attention—more valuation processing, in present terms. An inconsistent item might be completely discounted, receiving zero weight in the person judgment, yet be well remembered because the discounting process required disproportionate time for this item. Alternatively, the inconsistent item could be seen as more revealing and receive higher weight. Recall data could not distinguish these two alternatives—even if the judgment was based on verbal memory.

The focus on reproductive memory thus seems to have caused the more important functional memory to be overlooked. The more important question about the inconsistent item is how it functions in judgments about the person, not how well it is recalled. With real people, it is such on-line judgments that are stored with long-term person memory. Functional memory analysis thus requires theory of judgment capable of dealing with the difficult problem of analyzing effects of inconsistency (Anderson & Jacobson, 1965; Anderson, 1981a, Section 3.4.1).

One point of agreement between judgment and recall deserves mention as a clue to cooperative analysis. A surprising finding of Anderson and Jacobson (1965) indicated that discounting was produced by affective but not semantic inconsistency, a finding supported by Kaplan (1973; see Anderson, 1981a, Section 3.4.1). Wyer and Gordon (1982, 1984, p. 128) provided further support for the Anderson-Jacobson finding by showing that the higher recall was facilitated by evaluative rather than semantic inconsistency. This agreement between judgment and recall measures suggests that recall measures may be able to provide helpful clues for analysis of functional memory.

Judgment Curves for Multiple Attributions

Little is known about the structure of on-line memory. The Anderson-Hubert study measured only the single dimension of likableness, but multiple dimensions may be studied simultaneously with integration methodology. An illustration comes from an unpublished study by Himmelfarb (cited in Anderson, 1974a).

In Himmelfarb's experiment, subjects saw six numbers that represented a person's test scores on successive examinations of equal difficulty in a mathematics course. These stimulus sequences were constructed according to a 2^6 design like that illustrated with Fig. 8.1. All six numbers were visible at once; the serial character reflected the temporal sequence of examinations. After viewing each sequence of six test scores, subjects judged (a) the ability and (b) the motivation of the student, and (c) predicted performance on a seventh examination.

Complete serial curves for each response were calculated, as illustrated with Fig. 8.1. These serial curves, shown in Table 8.1, represent the weight of each serial position in the integrated attribution. Attributions of *ability*

TABLE 8. 1
Judgment Curves for Three Attributions

Attribution	Serial Position					
	1	2	3	4	5	6
Ability	.21	.16	.16	.14	.15	.18
Motivation	.00	.06	.13	.20	.26	.35
Performance	.07	.10	.14	.17	.23	.29

Note: From unpublished study by Himmelfarb; cited in Anderson (1974a, p. 78).

show a fairly flat curve, with a small primacy effect at the first position. This equal weight across exams is consistent with the common view of ability as a relatively stable characteristic.

The attributions of *motivation* refer to the single overall judgment made on the basis of all the test scores. These show strong recency. The first test score gets zero weight; whether this score was high or low did not affect the attribution. The last test score determines 35% of the attribution. It should be realized that the serial curve does not measure the level of motivation at any position, but rather the relative weight of the test score at each position in the single overall judgment. Hence, the simplest interpretation is that motivation is considered naturally variable over time, so the more recent performance is a more reliable indicator. Predictions of *performance* on the seventh exam also show substantial recency. Again, the simplest explanation is that the more recent information is seen as a more reliable indicator.

This interesting study illustrates one way to get more detailed information on structure of functional memory. Related comments on this experiment are given as part of a general discussion of primacy-recency in Anderson (1974a, Section III.F). Also relevant is the basal-surface, two-component representation of attitudes (Anderson, 1981a, p. 152; 1986, pp. 93-96). Unfortunately, Himmelfarb's study seems never to have been followed up.

Serial Judgment Curves

Two relatively simple methods for construction of serial curves are available. Both depend on using auxiliary information about scale values to avoid having to estimate them in the analysis. One is the matching method illustrated with Fig. 8.1. Even simpler is the method of known scale values, which requires stimuli with objective numerical values that can be taken as equal to their subjective values. In an attitude study, for example, each argument could be quantified to denote, say, what percentage of the budget should be allotted to some program. If the percentages themselves could be substituted into the averaging formula, this would simplify weight estimation and also allow simpler design. Objective values will be available only in special cases, of course, and even then their equivalence to the subjective values cannot be taken for granted. Because of its simplicity and flexibility, however, the method of known scale values deserves consideration in further work on functional memory.

An interesting extension of the matching method appeared in Himmelfarb's study of Table 8.1. Matching applies directly to the prediction response, for it is on the same scale as the stimulus test scores. For the two attributions, however, the analysis actually assumes that the subjective values that subjects infer for ability (and for motivation) are a linear function of the given test scores. Although mild deviations from linearity would be expected, they would have little effect on the finding of the flat curve for attribution of ability or the strong recency for attribution of motivation. This linearity approximation might be applicable more generally when matching is not practicable.

Two-Memory Formulation

The distinction between two kinds of memory discovered by Anderson and Hubert (1963) was supported by similar results of Dreben, Fiske, and Hastie (1979). This distinction was repeated by Hastie and Park (1986): "In this article we have made the case for a distinction between two types of judgment tasks: on-line and memory-based" (p. 266). This distinction echoes the original distinction by Anderson and Hubert between impression memory (= on-line) and verbal memory (= memory-based).

Unfortunately, the article of Hastie and Park (1986) suffers from a misconception about on-line memory. They asserted, incorrectly, that the two-memory formulation of Anderson and Hubert (1963) implies no relation between memory and judgment, that it "postulates independence between judgment and memory processes, with no relationship expected between measures of memory and judgments" (p. 259), and that it "predicts no correlation between memory and judgment measures" (p. 263). But Anderson and Hubert explicitly stated the contrary: that judgment and recall may be correlated, that several indications of such correlation appeared in their data, and that such correlation would be expected when "stimulus variables tend to affect both memory systems in a similar way" (p. 388). The two memory systems are distinct functionally, but they will generally be correlated because both depend on the same given stimuli.

This issue is important for Hastie and Park. Their experiments rest on the assumption that their correlations between judgment and verbal recall could distinguish between "on-line" and "memory-based" formulations. Specifically, they have asserted that the former predicts zero correlation, whereas the latter predicts positive correlation. But positive correlations may well be obtained with the on-line model simply because some stimulus variable affects both forms of memory in the same way. The key argument of Hastie and Park is thus unwarranted.

It is not suggested, of course, that judgment never depends on verbal memory. Integration theory predicts such dependence when the judgment task is novel and/or unexpected (Anderson, 1981a, p. 96). Some support for this prediction is suggested by the recall–judgment correlations of Hastie and Park, which tend to be larger for judgments on an unexpected dimension. But such correlations have a number of weaknesses that trouble their interpretation.

The real problem is that both kinds of memory may act together. It is no longer very interesting to show that there are two memories. What is needed is a way to assess the separate and joint contributions of both types of memory. Recall–judgment correlations can hardly do this, because the two memories cannot be expected to be independent. Some progress is possible with IIT, as is illustrated in the next section.

Two-Memory Analysis with IIT

A simple method to demonstrate operation of two memories, a method that can also measure their relative influence, is presented here. The idea stems from the serial judgment curve of Fig. 8.1. If a second judgment is requested that depends solely on the on-line memory of the first judgment, it will yield a judgment curve of similar shape. Systematic deviations from this shape can be used to show the operation of a second form of memory. For present illustration, an even simpler design will be used, one that seems to have practical value.

Consider the two pairs of traits:

cheerful–unintelligent
gloomy–intelligent

Other adjectives are added to each pair to form two person descriptions, each being presented under instructions to judge likableness. Then, unexpectedly, judgments are requested of sociability and/or intelligence.

Both descriptions will yield roughly equal judgments of likableness. If the unexpected judgments of sociability are based solely on on-line likableness, then they will also be roughly equal for the two descriptions.

The alternative hypothesis is that sociableness will be judged substantially higher for the *cheerful-unintelligent* person than for the *gloomy-intelligent* person; and vice versa for judgments of intelligence. Such differences would be found if the judgment was based in part on verbal memory for the adjectives (but see also next section).

This task has some notable advantages. The test is simple, being made with the raw judgments to the two descriptions. The two observed differences can provide unambiguous evidence for the operation of a second memory, even while avoiding the difficulties that trouble recall-judgment correlations. Recall data are not even needed. The task thus avoids the arbitrary assumptions about scale values, about weights, and about the integration rule, that have been typical of previous recall-judgment analyses.

Not least important is that the task can measure the relative effects of the two forms of memory. A rough index is provided by the two observed differences themselves. This can be improved by adding a control condition with instructed judgments of sociability and intelligence. The unexpected judgment can be expressed as an average of the likableness judgment and the control judgment; the weight parameter will then measure the relative effects of the two forms of memory. This provides a useful method for assessing effects of various memory variables, such as forgetting intervals, repetition, and interference.

Molar Unitization

An interesting feature of the foregoing design, at once an advantage and a limitation, is that the second memory cannot be assumed to be the verbal memory. Instead, it might be a second on-line memory for a social judgment that people may make more or less spontaneously in social interaction (Winter & Uleman, 1984). The advantage of the analysis is that no assumption about the second memory is needed. It could be a composite of verbal memory and more than one additional on-line memory. Functional measurement can provide exact accounts of such complex processing without depending on assumptions about the structure of the complex. This concept of *molar unitization* was expressed by Anderson and Graesser (1976) in relation to attitudes formed on-line in group discussion:

> The informational flow in the group is complex and largely uncontrolled. The impact of any group member on the others is spread out in time, conditioned by his (her) motivations to influence and to conform, interlinked with the others' comments and silences, dependent on prior knowledge and on expressive factors from clarity of thought to eye contact and personal attractiveness. Thus, the attitude of each group member reflects an ongoing, time-dependent process in which the informational components seem close to unknowable.
>
> Nevertheless, any informational analysis must come to grips with the problem of specifying the effective information. The way in which this problem is handled determines how far the theoretical analysis can be taken. (p. 210)

This problem may be handled with the unitization principle (Anderson, 1981a, Section 1.1.5). A conglomerate of information can be treated in an exact and complete manner as a molar unit. In the quoted on-line attitude study, the three persons in the group were successfully treated as molar units. In the present application, the unitization principle may be applied to the components of second memory. Unitization thus allows progress without having to depend on uncertain assumptions about memory structure.

The reverse of the foregoing advantage is that the nature of the second memory remains ambiguous. This issue arose with the interpretation of the recall–judgment correlations of Hastie and Park (1986), which, as they observed, could reflect verbal memory or a second, implicit, on-line judgment. They attempted to resolve this ambiguity by asking for really unexpected judgments, such as the frequency with which the person engaged in cardiovascular exercise, and by showing higher correlations for unexpected judgments. The former method seems unsatisfactory because the judgment could be a halo of the on-line judgment memory and still correlate with recall; their argument seems to rest on their incorrect assumption that on-line memory is uncorrelated with verbal memory. The latter method seems plausible. At best, however, such correlations say little about the magnitudes of the operative memories or their relative importance.

An alternative approach would be to interpolate an interfering task between the list presentation and the unexpected judgment. This procedure was used by Riskey (1979), who found that it markedly lowered the recall curve but had little effect on the judgment curve (see Anderson, 1981a, Fig. 4.8). This contrast itself is supportive evidence against the verbal memory hypothesis, and this interference technique may be more generally useful.

Extensions

The task and design considered in the two previous sections can be extended in various directions. First is a direct extension to study more than two memory determinants. This would involve selecting three or more stimulus dimensions that, like sociability and intelligence, have relatively low intercorrelations. For this purpose, other judgment tasks might be desirable, such as tastiness of meals, in which different stimulus dimensions have little implicational relation.

A related consideration concerns the desirability of within-subject design. Although the foregoing 2 × 2 design is practicable with independent groups, within-subject design gives sensitivity that may be essential for more detailed analysis. The problem, of course, is that giving one unwarned trial may trigger expectancies for more. It may perhaps be practicable, however, to ask for judgments only on occasional, incidental trials, using signal lamps as suggested by Anderson and Hubert (1963). It might thus be possible to apply factor analysis to take out the general factor and enumerate the specific factors of memory.

A second extension is to study visual stimuli, using faces, or animals, or biomorphic shapes. This would allow tests of the two-memory hypothesis, because the concept of verbal memory has a direct analog in terms of given visual stimuli. Also of interest would be joint use of verbal and visual stimuli, which is characteristic of much social cognition. The little available evidence indicates that verbal and visual stimuli may have equivalent functions in judgment (Anderson, 1981a, Section 2.3.4). Hence, their effects could be compared on a measurement scale with a common unit, using the averaging model. Such judgment data might help in analysis of verbal and visual codes in reproductive memory.

The most important extension involves using the averaging model as a tool for deeper analysis. Instead of working with the overall judgment, the effect of each separate stimulus can be dissected to measure its twin parameters, weight and scale value. Serial judgment curves analogous to that of Fig. 8.1 could be obtained for each parameter. Simple design could be limited to two serial positions within a longer sequence, as in the task just considered. More complex design could obtain complete judgment curves, as in Fig. 8.1, not only for weight, but also for scale value.

This extension constitutes a milestone in the work on functional memory. It is practicable only because of the theoretical success of the averaging model, on one hand, and the recently completed statistical developments, on the other hand (Zalinski & Anderson, 1986, in prep.). To pursue this line of inquiry requires familiarity with model analysis that lies outside the scope of this chapter. It does, however, provide a new capability for analysis of functional memory.

Everyday Life and Cognitive Algebra

Cognitive algebra provides a base for developing a cognitive theory of everyday life. The efficacy of this thesis has been demonstrated with findings of algebraic rules in numerous studies of attitudes, attributions, and social affects, as well as in general judgment-decision. These algebraic rules provide a rigorous treatment of everyday life in something like its own terms.

This thesis is well illustrated in the foregoing discussion of attribution schemas. The basic blame schema, Blame = Culpa + Damage, originates in everyday phenomenology; the three terms of this schema are concepts from everyday life. Their cognitive reality cannot be taken for granted, however, nor can the integration rule be presumed to have any particular form. Cognitive theory is necessary to handle the two problems, valuation and integration, involved in determining the operative schema. This is what IIT has accomplished.

Cognitive algebra is only a first step, but an important one. The standard stereotypes about algebraic rules miss their main virtue, which lies in qualitative analysis. There is, to be sure, intrinsic interest in knowing that everyday cognition often has an algebraic form, even in young children. It is also important to use these algebraic rules in psychological measurement, as illustrated with functional memory in Fig. 8.1. More important, however, are their qualitative implications and applications.

In the blame schema, for example, the exactness of the averaging rule gives unique support to the cognitive reality of the three terms of the schema. The averaging rule itself rests on the qualitative property of meaning constancy, incidentally infirming the many once-popular theories of cognitive consistency. And the schema analysis of blame attribution provides a cogent new approach to social learning, as in Leon's (1984) remarkable mother-son study and in the husband-wife studies reported in Anderson and Armstrong (in press).

In its focus on everyday life, IIT stands out from mainstream cognitive theories, which have been far more concerned with letter-word recognition, short-term memory, and similar issues than with the attitudes, attributions, and affects of everyday life. Starting with everyday phenomenology, IIT was able to establish definite structure for one class of schemas. The functional perspective on memory, similarly, embodies the goal-directedness of everyday thought and action. New concepts and new methods are needed to study both schemas and functional memory, to which endeavor cognitive algebra has made a modest but worthwhile contribution. This same approach should also be useful in further work on the two basic problems of knowledge systems and assemblage.

SOCIAL COGNITION

Social-personality psychology needs to develop its own cognitive theory. Mainstream cognitive theory is fundamentally inadequate for social cognition. The present case history of functional memory is only one illustration of this narrow insufficiency. Neisser (1982a) has criticized the whole of mainstream memory research on grounds that it has been "accumulating the wrong *kind* of knowledge" (p. xii). Neisser (1982b) also argued for a functional approach to memory, although he remained bound within the reproductive framework. The present approach goes beyond Neisser to treat memory within a larger theory of judgment and action. As noted in a treatise on foundations of information integration theory (Anderson, 1981a):

> Few areas of psychology have received as intensive study as verbal learning and memory. From the standpoint of judgment theory, however, this body of work seems strangely incomplete, largely untouched by concern with the use and function of memory. Verbal learning is seldom an end in itself; memory is typically in the service of judgment and decision. Memory retrieval, for example, can hardly be understood without reference to the immediate goals of the person, as reflected in the valuation operation. (p. 96)

Many social psychologists have had the high aspiration of transposing conceptual frameworks from more developed and prestigious fields of psychology into a base for social-personality theory. Conceptual formulations, however, are not ready-to-wear ideas. These borrowed formulations could not fit social psychology because they had no place for basic social phenomena.

The fact is that cognition is the very stuff of social-personality psychology. Attitudes, attributions, roles, and social affects are embedded in cognitive psychology of everyday life. Theory of social cognition needs to base itself on its own phenomena.

To this endeavor, the theory of information integration has made useful contributions. It addresses social cognition in its own terms, yet provides a rigorous theory that can go below the phenomenology of everyday life. It provides a unified, general theory with demonstrated analytical power. It is well grounded empirically, as illustrated in the present discussions of attribution schemas and functional memory. It opens onto a new horizon.

ACKNOWLEDGMENTS

This work was supported in part by PHS Grant HD MH 22932-01 and by grants from the National Institute of Mental Health to the Center for Human Information Processing, University of California, San Diego.

REFERENCES

Anderson, N. H. (1964). Linear models for responses measured on a continuous scale. *Journal of Mathematical Psychology, 1,* 121-142.

Anderson, N. H. (1965). Primacy effects in personality impression formation using a generalized order effect paradigm. *Journal of Personality and Social Psychology, 2,* 1-9.

Anderson, N. H. (1971). Integration theory and attitude change. *Psychological Review, 78,* 171-206.

Anderson, N. H. (1973a). Information integration theory applied to attitudes about U.S. presidents. *Journal of Educational Psychology, 64,* 1-8.

Anderson, N. H. (1973b). Serial position curves in impression formation. *Journal of Experimental Psychology, 97,* 8-12.

Anderson, N. H. (1974a). Cognitive algebra: Integration theory applied to social attribution. In L. Berkowitz (Ed.). *Advances in experimental social psychology* (Vol.7, pp. 1-101). New York: Academic Press.

Anderson, N. H. (1974b). Information integration theory: A brief survey. In D. H. Krantz, R. C. Atkinson, R. D. Luce, & P. Suppes (Eds.), *Contemporary developments in mathematical psychology* (Vol. 2, pp. 236-305). San Francisco: Freeman.

Anderson, N. H. (1976a). *Integration theory applied to cognitive responses and attitudes* (Tech. Rep. CHIP 68). La Jolla, CA: Center for Human Information Processing, University of California, San Diego.

Anderson, N. H. (1976b). *Social perception and cognition* (Tech. Rep. CHIP 62). La Jolla, CA: Center for Human Information Processing, University of California, San Diego.

Anderson, N. H. (1978). Progress in cognitive algebra. In L. Berkowitz (Ed.), *Cognitive theories in social psychology* (pp. 1-126). New York: Academic Press.

Anderson, N. H. (1979). Indeterminate theory: Reply to Gollob. *Journal of Personality and Social Psychology, 37,* 950-952.

Anderson, N. H. (1981a). *Foundations of information integration theory.* New York: Academic Press.

Anderson, N. H. (1981b). Integration theory applied to cognitive responses and attitudes. In R. E. Petty, T. M. Ostrom, & T. C. Brock (Eds.), *Cognitive responses in persuasion* (pp. 361-397). Hillsdale, NJ: Lawrence Erlbaum Associates.

Anderson, N. H. (1982). *Methods of information integration theory.* New York: Academic Press.

Anderson, N. H. (1983a). A theory of stereotypes (Tech. Rep. CHIP 119). La Jolla, CA: Center for Human Information Processing, University of California, San Diego. In N. H. Anderson (Ed.), *Contributions to information integration theory.*

Anderson, N. H. (1983b). Schemas in person cognition (Tech. Rep. CHIP 118). La Jolla, CA: Center for Human Information Processing, University of California, San Diego.

Anderson, N. H. (1986). A cognitive theory of judgment and decision. In B. Brehmer, H. Jungermann, P. Lourens, & G. Sevón (Eds.), *New directions in research on decision making* (pp. 63-108). Amsterdam: North-Holland.

Anderson, N. H. (1987). Review of *Political cognition,* R. R. Lau & D. O. Sears (Eds.), *American Journal of Psychology, 100,* 295-298.

Anderson, N. H. (1988). A functional approach to person cognition. In T. K. Srull & R. S. Wyer, Jr. (Eds.), *Advances in social cognition* (Vol. 1, pp. 37-51). Hillsdale, NJ: Lawrence Erlbaum Associates.

Anderson, N. H. (in prep.-a). Functional memory in person cognition. In N. H. Anderson (Ed.), *Contributions to information integration theory.*

Anderson, N. H. (in prep.-b). Schemas in person cognition. In N. H. Anderson (Ed.), *Contributions to information integration theory.*

Anderson, N. H. (in press). The information integration approach to emotions and their measurement. In R. Plutchik & H. Kellerman (Eds.), *Emotion: Theory, research, and experience* (Vol. 4). New York: Academic Press.

Anderson, N. H., & Armstrong, M. A. (in press). Cognitive theory and methodology for studying marital interaction. In D. Brinberg & J. Jaccard (Eds.), *Dyadic decision making.* New York: Springer-Verlag.

Anderson, N. H., & Butzin, C. A. (1974). Performance = Motivation × Ability: An integration-theoretical analysis. *Journal of Personality and Social Psychology, 30,* 598-604.

Anderson, N. H., & Farkas, A. J. (1973). New light on order effects in attitude change. *Journal of Personality and Social Psychology, 28,* 88-93.

Anderson, N. H., & Graesser, C. C. (1976). An information integration analysis of attitude change in group discussion. *Journal of Personality and Social Psychology, 34,* 210-222.

Anderson, N. H., & Hubert, S. (1963). Effects of concomitant verbal recall on order effects in personality impression formation. *Journal of Verbal Learning and Verbal Behavior, 2,* 379-391.

Anderson, N. H., & Jacobson, A. (1965). Effect of stimulus inconsistency and discounting instructions in personality impression formation. *Journal of Personality and Social Psychology, 2,* 531-539.

Anderson, N. H., Lindner, R., & Lopes, L. L. (1973). Integration theory applied to judgments of group attractiveness. *Journal of Personality and Social Psychology, 26,* 400-408.

Anderson, N. H., Sawyers, B. K., & Farkas, A. J. (1972). President paragraphs. *Behavior Research Methods & Instrumentation, 4,* 177-192.

Asch, S. E. (1946). Forming impressions of personality. *Journal of Abnormal and Social*

Psychology, 41, 258-290.
Bartlett, F. C. (1932). *Remembering: A study in experimental and social psychology.* London: Cambridge University Press.
Brewer, W. F., & Nakamura, G. V. (1984). The nature and functions of schemas. In R. S. Wyer, Jr. & T. K. Srull (Eds.), *Handbook of social cognition* (Vol. 1, pp. 119-160). Hillsdale, NJ: Lawrence Erlbaum Associates.
Cantor, N., & Mischel, W. (1977). Traits as prototypes: Effects on recognition memory. *Journal of Personality and Social Psychology, 35,* 38-48.
Carlston, D. E. (1980). Events, inferences, and impression formation. In R. Hastie, T. M. Ostrom, E. B. Ebbeson, R. S. Wyer, Jr., D. L. Hamilton, & D. E. Carlston (Eds.), *Person memory: The cognitive basis of social perception* (pp. 89-119). Hillsdale, NJ: Lawrence Erlbaum Associates.
Cohen, C. E. (1981). Person categories and social perception: Testing some boundaries of the processing effects of prior knowledge. *Journal of Personality and Social Psychology, 40,* 441-452.
Damon, W. (1977). *The social world of the child.* San Francisco: Jossey-Bass.
Dreben, E. K., Fiske, S. T., & Hastie, R. (1979). The independence of evaluative and item information: Impression and recall order effects in behavior-based impression formation. *Journal of Personality and Social Psychology, 37,* 1758-1768.
Ebbesen, E. B. (1980). Cognitive processes in understanding ongoing behavior. In R. Hastie, T. M. Ostrom, E. B. Ebbesen, R. S. Wyer, Jr., D. L. Hamilton, & D. E. Carlston (Eds.), *Person memory: The cognitive basis of social perception* (pp. 179-225). Hillsdale, NJ: Lawrence Erlbaum Associates.
Eiser, J. R. (1983). Attribution theory and social cognition. In J. Jaspars, F. D. Fincham, & M. Hewstone (Eds.), *Attribution theory and research: Conceptual, developmental, and social dimensions* (pp. 91-113). London & New York: Academic Press.
Fiedler, K. (1982). Causal schemata: Review and criticism of research on a popular construct. *Journal of Personality and Social Psychology, 42,* 1001-1013.
Fiedler, K. (1983). On the testability of the availability heuristic. In R. W. Scholz (Ed.), *Decision making under uncertainty* (pp. 109-119). Amsterdam: North-Holland.
Gollob, H. F. (1979). A reply to Norman H. Anderson's critique of the subject-verb-object approach to social cognition. *Journal of Personality and Social Psychology, 37,* 931-949.
Graesser, C. C., & Anderson, N. H. (1974). Cognitive algebra of the equation: Gift size = Generosity × Income. *Journal of Experimental Psychology, 103,* 692-699.
Hamilton, D. L., & Rose, T. L. (1980). Illusory correlation and the maintenance of stereotypic beliefs. *Journal of Personality and Social Psychology, 39,* 832-845.
Harvey, J. H., & Weary, G. (1981). *Perspectives on attributional processes.* Dubuque, IA: William Brown.
Hastie, R. (1981). Schematic principles in human memory. In E. T. Higgins, C. P. Herman, & M. P. Zanna (Eds.), *Social cognition* (pp. 39-88). Hillsdale, NJ: Lawrence Erlbaum Associates.
Hastie, R., & Carlston, D. E. (1980). Theoretical issues in person perception. In R. Hastie, T. M. Ostrom, E. B. Ebbesen, R. S. Wyer, Jr., D. L. Hamilton, & D. E. Carlston (Eds.), *Person memory: The cognitive basis of social perception* (pp. 1-53). Hillsdale, NJ: Lawrence Erlbaum Associates.
Hastie, R., & Kumar, P. A. (1979). Person memory: Personality traits as organizing principles in memory for behaviors. *Journal of Personality and Social Psychology, 37,* 25-38.
Hastie, R., Ostrom, T. M., Ebbesen, E. B., Wyer, R. S., Jr., Hamilton, D. L., & Carlston, D. E. (1980). (Eds.). *Person memory: The cognitive basis of social perception.* Hillsdale, NJ: Lawrence Erlbaum Associates.
Hastie, R., & Park, B. (1986). The relationship between memory and judgment depends on whether the judgment task is memory-based or on-line. *Psychological Review, 93,* 258-268.

Hastie, R., Park, B., & Weber, R. (1984). Social memory. In R. S. Wyer, Jr. & T. K. Srull (Eds.) *Handbook of social cognition* (Vol. 2, pp. 151-212). Hillsdale, NJ: Lawrence Erlbaum Associates.

Heider, F. (1958). *The psychology of interpersonal relations*. New York: Wiley.

Himmelfarb, S., & Anderson, N. H. (1975). Integration theory applied to opinion attribution. *Journal of Personality and Social Psychology, 31,* 1064-1072.

Hommers, W., & Anderson, N. H. (1985). Recompense as a factor in assigned punishment. *British Journal of Developmental Psychology, 3,* 75-86.

Hommers, W., & Anderson, N. H. (1988). Algebraic schemes in legal thought and everyday morality. In H. Wegener, F. Lösel, & H. J. Haisch (Eds.), *Criminal behavior and the justice system* (pp. 136-150). New York & Berlin: Springer-Verlag.

Jones, E. E., & Davis, K. E. (1965). From acts to dispositions: The attribution process in person perception. In L. Berkowitz (Ed.), *Advances in experimental social psychology,* (Vol. 2, pp. 219-266). New York: Academic Press.

Jones, E. E., & McGillis, D. (1976). Correspondent inferences and the attribution cube: A comparative reappraisal. In J. H. Harvey, W. J. Ickes, & R. F. Kidd (Eds.), *New directions in attribution research* (Vol. 1, pp. 389-420). Hillsdale, NJ: Lawrence Erlbaum Associates.

Kaplan, M. F. (1973). Stimulus inconsistency and response dispositions in forming judgments of other persons. *Journal of Personality and Social Psychology, 25,* 58-64.

Kelley, H. H. (1967). Attribution theory in social psychology. In D. Levine (Ed.), *Nebraska symposium on motivation* (pp. 192-238). Lincoln, NE: University of Nebraska Press.

Kelley, H. H. (1972a). Attribution in social interaction. In E. E. Jones, D. E. Kanouse, H. H. Kelley, R. E. Nisbett, S. Valins, & B. Weiner (Eds.), *Attribution: Perceiving the causes of behavior* (pp. 1-26). Morristown, NJ: General Learning Press.

Kelley, H. H. (1972b). Causal schemata and the attribution process. In E. E. Jones, D. E. Kanouse, H. H. Kelley, R. E. Nisbett, S. Valins, & B. Weiner (Eds.), *Attribution: Perceiving the causes of behavior* (pp. 151-174). Morristown, NJ: General Learning Press.

Kelley, H. H., & Michela, J. L. (1980). Attribution theory and research. *Annual Review of Psychology, 31,* 457-501.

Kohlberg, L. (1976). Moral stages and moralization: the cognitive-developmental approach. In T. Lickona (Ed.), *Moral development and behavior: Theory, research, and social issues* (pp. 31-53). New York: Holt, Rinehart and Winston.

Leon, M. (1980). Integration of intent and consequence information in children's moral judgments. In F. Wilkening, J. Becker, & T. Trabasso (Eds.), *Information integration by children* (pp. 71-97). Hillsdale, NJ: Lawrence Erlbaum Associates.

Leon, M. (1982). Rules in children's moral judgments: Integration of intent, damage, and rationale information. *Developmental Psychology, 18,* 835-842.

Leon, M. (1984). Rules mothers and sons use to integrate intent and damage information in their moral judgments. *Child Development, 55,* 2106-2113.

Lingle, J. H., & Ostrom, T. M. (1981). Principles of memory and cognition in attitude formation. In R. E. Petty, T. M. Ostrom, & T. C. Brock (Eds.), *Cognitive responses in persuasion* (pp. 399-420). Hillsdale, NJ: Lawrence Erlbaum Associates.

Lloyd-Bostock S. (1983). Attributions of cause and responsibility as social phenomena. In J. Jaspars, F. D. Fincham, & M. Hewstone (Eds.), *Attribution theory and research: Conceptual, developmental, and social dimensions* (pp. 261-289). London & New York: Academic Press.

Lopes, L. L. (1972). A unified integration model for "Prior expectancy and behavioral extremity as determinants of attitude attribution." *Journal of Experimental Social Psychology, 8,* 156-160.

Neisser, U. (Ed.). (1982a). *Memory observed*. New York: Freeman.

Neisser, U. (1982b). Memory: What are the important questions? In U. Neisser (Ed.), *Memory observed* (pp. 3-19). New York: Freeman.

Orvis, B. R., Cunningham, J. D., & Kelley, H. H. (1975). A closer examination of causal inference: The role of consensus, distinctiveness, and consistency information. *Journal of Personality and Social Psychology, 32,* 606-615.

Ostrom, T. M., Lingle, J. H., Pryor, J. B., & Geva, N. (1980). Cognitive organization of person impressions. In R. Hastie, T. M. Ostrom, E. B. Ebbesen, R. S. Wyer, Jr., D. L. Hamilton, & D. E. Carlston (Eds.), *Person memory: The cognitive basis of social perception* (pp. 55-88). Hillsdale, NJ: Lawrence Erlbaum Associates.

Peterson, L. R., & Peterson, M. J. (1959). Short-term retention of individual verbal items. *Journal of Experimental Psychology, 58,* 193-198.

Rest, J. R. (1979). *Development in judging moral issues.* Minneapolis, MN: University of Minnesota Press.

Rest, J. R. (1986). *Moral development.* New York: Praeger.

Reyes, R. M., Thompson, W. C., & Bower, G. H. (1980). Judgmental biases resulting from differing availabilities of arguments. *Journal of Personality and Social Psychology, 39,* 2-12.

Riskey, D. R. (1979). Verbal memory processes in impression formation. *Journal of Experimental Psychology: Human Learning and Memory, 5,* 271-281.

Shanteau, J. (1972). Descriptive versus normative models of sequential inference judgment. *Journal of Experimental Psychology, 93,* 63-68.

Simon, H. A. (1982). Comments. In M. S. Clark & S. T. Fiske (Eds.), *Affect and cognition* (pp. 333-342). Hillsdale, NJ: Lawrence Erlbaum Associates.

Singh, R. (in prep.). Two problems in cognitive algebra: Imputations and averaging versus multiplying. In N. H. Anderson (Ed.), *Contributions to information integration theory.*

Snyder, M., & Uranowitz, S. W. (1978). Reconstructing the past: Some cognitive consequences of person perception. *Journal of Personality and Social Psychology, 36,* 941-950.

Srull, T. K. (1981). Person memory: Some tests of associative storage and retrieval models. *Journal of Experimental Psychology: Human Learning and Memory, 7,* 440-463.

Srull, T. K. (1984). Methodological techniques for the study of person memory and social cognition. In R. S. Wyer, Jr. & T. K. Srull (Eds.), *Handbook of social cognition* (Vol. 2, pp. 1-72). Hillsdale, NJ: Lawrence Erlbaum Associates.

Surber, C. F. (1981a). Effects of information reliability in predicting task performance using ability and effort. *Journal of Personality and Social Psychology, 40,* 977-989.

Surber, C. F. (1981b). Necessary versus sufficient causal schemata: Attributions for achievement in difficult and easy tasks. *Journal of Experimental Social Psychology, 17,* 569-586.

Surber, C. F. (1982). Separable effects of motives, consequences, and presentation order on children's moral judgments. *Developmental Psychology, 18,* 257-266.

Surber, C. F. (1985a). Applications of information integration to children's social cognitions. In J. B. Pryor & J. D. Day (Eds.), *The development of social cognition* (pp. 59-94). New York: Springer-Verlag.

Surber, C. F. (1985b). Developmental changes in inverse compensation in social and nonsocial attributions. In S. R. Yussen (Ed.), *The growth of reflection in children* (pp. 149-166). New York: Academic Press.

Surber, C. F. (1987). Formal representation of qualitative and quantitative reversible operations. In J. Bisanz, C. J. Brainerd, & R. Kail (Eds.), *Formal methods in developmental psychology* (pp. 115-154). New York: Springer-Verlag.

Taylor, S. E., & Fiske, S. T. (1981). Getting inside the head: Methodologies for process analysis in attribution and social cognition. In J. H. Harvey, W. Ickes, & R. Kidd (Eds.), *New directions in attribution research* (Vol. 3, pp. 459-534). Hillsdale, NJ: Lawrence Erlbaum Associates.

Tulving, E. (1983). *Elements of episodic memory.* New York: Oxford University Press.

Tversky, A., & Kahneman, D. (1973). Availability: A heuristic for judging frequency and probability. *Cognitive Psychology, 5,* 207-232.

Wilkening, F. (1982). Children's knowledge about time, distance, and velocity interrelations. In W. J. Friedman (Ed.), *The developmental psychology of time* (pp. 87-112). New York: Academic Press.

Winter, L., & Uleman, J. S. (1984). When are social judgments made? Evidence for the spontaneousness of trait inferences. *Journal of Personality and Social Psychology, 47,* 237-252.

Wyer, R. S., Jr., & Carlston, D. W. (1979). *Social cognition, inference, and attribution.* Hillsdale, NJ: Lawrence Erlbaum Associates.

Wyer, R. S., Jr., & Gordon, S. E. (1982). The recall of information about persons and groups. *Journal of Experimental Social Psychology, 18,* 128-164.

Wyer, R. S., Jr., & Gordon, S. E. (1984). The cognitive representation of social information. In R. S. Wyer, Jr. & T. K. Srull (Eds.), *Handbook of social cognition* (Vol. 2, pp. 73-150). Hillsdale, NJ: Lawrence Erlbaum Associates.

Wyer, R. S., Jr., & Srull, T. K. (1980). The processing of social stimulus information: A conceptual integration. In R. Hastie, T. M. Ostrom, E. B. Ebbesen, R. S. Wyer, Jr., D. L. Hamilton, & D. E. Carlston (Eds.), *Person memory: The cognitive basis of social perception* (pp. 227-300). Hillsdale, NJ: Lawrence Erlbaum Associates.

Zalinski, J., & Anderson, N. H. (1986). AVERAGE: A user-friendly FORTRAN-77 program for parameter estimation for the averaging model of information integration theory. La Jolla, CA: University of California, San Diego.

Zalinski, J., & Anderson, N. H. (in prep.). Parameter estimation for averaging theory. In N. H. Anderson (Ed.), *Contributions to information integration theory.*

Author Index

A

Abelson, R., 65, *88*
Adams, N., 44, 51, *59,* 102, *120*
Ajzen, I., 126, *139*
Alba, J. W., 82, *85*
Allen, R. B., 147, *170*
Allman, C., 146, 148, 155, *170*
Allport, G. W., 145, *169*
Andersen, S. M., 147, *169*
Anderson, J. R., 19, 21, 22, 23, 32, *36,* 44, 53, *57, 58,* 62, 64, 65, *85,* 94, *118*
Anderson, N. H., 1, 2, 11, 13, *15,* 57, *57,* 61, *85, 86,* 91, 93, 113, *118,* 145, 150, 155, 159, *169,* 175, 176, 177, 178, 179, 180, 181, 182, 183, 184, 185, 186, 187, 188, 189, 190, 191, 192, 193, 194, 195, 196, 197, 198, 199, 200, 201, 202, 203, 204, 205, 206, 207, 208, 209, 211, 212, 213, 214, *215, 216, 217, 218, 220*
Armstrong, M. A., 199, 214, *216*
Asch, S. E., 39, 53, *57,* 61, 73, *86,* 145, 146, 150, 161, *169,* 184, 185, *216*

B

Balota, D. A., 44, 49, *58*
Barclay, J. R., 102, *119*
Bargh, J. A., 10, *15,* 111, *118,* 135, *139,* 143, *171*
Baron, R., 80, *87*
Bartlett, F. C., 65, *86,* 193, *217*
Bassili, J. N., 43, *57,* 71, 74, 80, 82, *86,* 135, 138, *139*
Bassok, M., 165, *173*
Beach, L., 153, *169*
Beattie, A. E., 146, 148, 155, 160, 164, *170*
Bechtold, A., 157, *169*
Berscheid, E., 157, *169*
Birrell, P., 112, *120*
Bjork, R. A., 113, *118*
Bodenhausen, G. W., 62, 63, *89,* 97, *121*
Bond, C. F., Jr., 147, *169*
Borgida, E., 157, *172*
Bormann, C., 20, 29, *37,* 69, *88*
Bourne, L. E., 93, 112, *119*
Bower, G. H., 44, 53, *57,* 62, *85,* 113, *120,* 205, *219*
Bradshaw, G. L., 94, *118*
Brand, J. F., 94, *120*
Branscombe, N. R., 20, 27, 28, 29, 30, 32, *37,* 69, 79 84, *88*
Bransford, J. D., 102, *119*
Brewer, M. B., 97, *119,* 143, 145, 155, *169*
Brewer, W. F., 195, *217*
Brockett, D. R., 147, *169*
Brooks, L. R., 32, *36*
Brown, A. S., 31, *37*
Brunswik, E., 8, *15*

221

AUTHOR INDEX

Burnstein, E., 92, 96, 97, 102, 114, *119, 120,* 126, *140,* 155, *169*
Butzin, C. A., 199, *216*

C

Cacioppo, P E., 93, 116, *119, 120*
Campbell, B. H.,157, *172*
Cantor, N., 62, 80, 81, *86,* 102, *119,* 196, *217*
Carlston, D. E., 2, *15,* 25, *36,* 147, 155, *169, 172,* 178, 190, 203, *217, 220*
Chanowitz, B., 155, *171*
Chen, J., 24, *36*
Child, P., 156, *171*
Cohen, A. R., 97, *119*
Cohen, C. E., 113, *119,* 196, *217*
Cohen, O., 127, 128, 132, 136, 137, *140*
Cole, E., 97, *120*
Cook, T. D., 91, *119*
Corbett, A. T., 72, 73, 77, *86*
Cox, M. G., 61, *86,* 151, 153, *170*
Crocker, J., 102, *120,* 145, 157, *169, 170, 172*
Cunniff, C., 42, *59,* 70, 74, 78, 81, *88*
Cunningham, J. D., 203, *219*

D

Damon, W., 199, *217*
Darley, J. M., 126, *139*
Davis, K. E., 61, 64, 66, 67, 76, 79, *87,* 154, *171,* 196, 200, 203, *218*
Dawes, R. M., 8, *15*
Dellarosa, D., 93, 112, *119*
Dermer, M., 157, *169*
Dosher, B. A., 72, 73, 77, *86*
Dovidio, J. R., 156, *170*
Dreben, E. K., 1, *15,* 57, *58,* 93, 113, *119, 179, 182, 205, 209, 217*
Dull, V., 97, *119,* 155, *169*

E

Ebbesen, E. B., 2, *15,* 113, *119,* 147, *170,* 178, 190, *217*
Edwards, W., *15*
Einhorn, H. J., 14, *15*
Eiser, J. R., 204, *217*
Ekman, P., 80, *86*
Ellsworth, P. C., 161, *172*
Erber, R., 147, 157, 163, 165, *170*
Ericsson, K. A., 162, 163, *170*

Etcoff, N. L., 155, 156, *172*
Evans, N., 156, *170*

F

Farkas, A. J., 194, *216*
Fazio, R. H., 24, 25, *36,* 93, *119,* 126, *139*
Fiedler, K., 202, 205, *217*
Fishbein, M., 126, *139*
Fiske, S. T., 1, 2, *15, 16,* 56, 57, *58,* 61, 81, *86,* 93, 113, *119,* 143, 144, 145, 146, 147, 148, 151, 153, 155, 156, 157, 158, 159, 160, 161, 162, 163, 164, 165, 166, *170, 171, 172,* 179, 182, 205, 209, *217, 219*
Flay, B. R., 91, *119*
Flink, C., 40, *58*
Frank, H., 155, *173*
Frankel, A., 130, 132, 137, *140*
Franks, T. J., 102, *119*
Freund, T., 157, *171*
Friezen, W. V., 80, *86*
Frijda, N. H., 125, *139*
Fujioka, T., 156, *171*
Fulero, S., 112, *120*

G

Gallo, L., 157, *169*
Geva, N., 179, 194, *219*
Giladi, O., 128, 132, 137, *140*
Gilbert, D. T., 83, *86,* 130, *139,* 156, *171*
Ginossar, Z., 126, *139*
Goethals, G. R., 147, 155, *171*
Gollob, H. F., 203, *217*
Gordan, S. E., 55, *58, 59,* 97, *121,* 207, *220*
Grady, K., 91, *119*
Graesser, C. C., 194, 199, 211, *216, 217*
Grassia, J., 11, *15*
Graziano, W., 157, *169*
Greenwald, A. G., 91, 92, 93, 96, *119*
Grice, H. P., 114, *119*

H

Hamilton, D. L., 2, *15,* 92, 97, *119,* 178, 190, 196, *217*
Hamm, R. M., 11, *15*
Hammond, K. R., 11, *15*
Hansen, L. R., 39, *58*
Harvey, J. H., 203, 204, *217*
Hasher, L., 10, *15,* 82, *85*
Hass, R. G., 91, *119*

Hastie, R., 1, 2, 4, 5, 8, 9, 13, 14, *15, 16,* 57, *58,* 62, 64, 81, *86,* 92, 93, 94, 95, 96, 97, 106, 109, 111, 112, 113, *119,* 135, 138, *139,* 175, 178, 179, 182, 184, 190, 192, 205, 206, 209, 212, *217, 218*
Hastorf, A. H., 161, *172*
Hayes-Roth, B., 44, *58*
Heider, F., 61, 64, 66, 78, 80, 83, *86, 87,* 199, *218*
Higgins, E. T., 23, 27, *36, 27,* 79, 84, *87,* 123, 131, *139,* 143, 147, *171*
Himmelfarb, S., 197, 201, 207, *218*
Hintzman, D. L., 56, *58*
Hirt, E. R., 96, 110, 112, *120*
Hogarth, R. M., 14, *15*
Hogue, A., 14, *16*
Hommers, W., 199, *218*
Hovland, C. I., 91, *119*
Howard, J., 112, *120*
Hubbard, M., 114, *120,* 131, *140*
Hubert, S., 1, 2, *15,* 57, *57,* 91, 93, 113, *118,* 175, 176, 177, 179, 180, 181, 182, 187, 189, 192, 194, 205, 206, 209, 212, *216*

I

Ingerman, C., 157, *170*

J

Jacobson, A., 207, *216*
Jamieson, D. W., 157, *171*
Janis, I. L., 91, *119*
Jensen, C., 112, *120*
John, O. P., 33, *37*
Johnson, J., 96, 110, 112, *120*
Jones, C. R., 27, *36,* 79, 84, *87*
Jones, E. E., 61, 64, 66, 67, 76, 79, 83, *87,* 128, 130, 131, 132, 137, *139,* 147, 148, 154, 155, *171,* 196, 200, 203, *218*
Judd, C. M., 40, *58*

K

Kahneman, D., 2, 11, 14, *16,* 102, 112, *120, 121,* 123, 131, *139, 140,* 205, *219*
Kane, R. A., 156, *171*
Kanouse, D. E., 39, *58*
Kanter, R., 155, *171*
Kaplan, M. F., 207, *218*

Kardes, F. R., 25, *36,* 93, *119*
Katz, L. B., 92, 97, *119*
Keele, S. W., 56, *58*
Kelley, H. H., 66, 76, *87,* 91, *119,* 125, 126, *139,* 196, 201, 202, 203, *218, 219*
Kelly, C. W., 13, *16*
Kelly, G. A., 168, *171*
Kim, J. I., 157, *173*
King, G. A., 23, *36,* 84, *87,* 123, *139,* 147, *171*
Kintsch, W., 56, *58,* 64, *87*
Kitayama, S., 114, *119*
Klatzky, R. L., 147, 156, *169, 171*
Kohlberg, L., 199, *218*
Kolers, P. A., 19, 29, 31, *37*
Kruglanski, A. W., 157, *171*
Krull, D. S., 83, *86,* 156, *171*
Kumar, A. P., 4, *15,* 62, *86,* 95, 97, *119,* 184, 206, *217*

L

Langer, E. J., 155, *171*
Leirer, V. O., 92, 97, *119*
Lemley, R. E., 143, *172*
Leon, M., 199, 214, *218*
Lepper, M. R., 114, *120,* 131, *140*
Lerner, M., 20, 31, *37*
Leventhal, H., 97, *120*
Lewin, K., 93, *120*
Lichtenstein, M., 4, *15, 16,* 63, *88,* 96, 97, 103, 111, 112, 113, *120*
Lindauer, B. K., 72, *87*
Lindner, R., 203, *216*
Lingle, J. H., 7, *15,* 179, 194, *218, 219*
Lloyd-Bostock, S., 204, *218*
Lopes, L. L., 14, *15,* 42, *58,* 197, 203, *216, 218*
Lui, L., 97, *119,* 155, *169*
Lurie, L., 123, *139*

M

MacLeod, C. M., 74, *86*
Manis, M., 10, *16,* 113, *120*
Maoz, I., 127, 137, *140*
Marcel, I., 123, *139*
Marrs, S., 97, *120*
Martin, G. L., 156, *171*
Mavin, G. H., 84, *87*
McArthur, L. Z., 2, *16,* 80, *87,* 147, 151,

171
McClelland, J. L., 56, *58*
McDonald, T. E., 123, *140*
McDonel, E. C., 24, *36*
McGillis, D., 76, *87,* 148, 155, *171,* 196, 200, 203, *218*
McGraw, K. M., 157, *170*
McGuire, C. V., 156, *171*
McGuire, W. J., 2, 14, *16, 17,* 91, 114, *120,* 156, *171*
McKoon, G., 10, *16,* 44, *58,* 81, 82, *87*
Medin, D. L., 56, *58*
Michela, J. L., 202, *218*
Milberg, S. J., 146, 148, 155, 160, 164, *170*
Millar, M. G., 97, *120*
Miller, D. T., 123, 126, *139*
Miller, F. D., 10, *16,* 43, *59,* 67, 70, 77, *88*
Minsky, M., 65, *87*
Mischel, W., 62, 80, 81, *86,* 102, *119,* 196, *217*
Mitchell, D. B., 31, *37*
Moeser, S. D., 44, *58*
Monson, T., 157, *169*
Moskowitz, G., 71, 82, *87*
Myers, J. L., 44, 49, *58*

N

Naccarato, M. E., 157, *169*
Nakamura, G. V., 195, *217*
Neisser, U., 65, *87,* 214, *218*
Neuberg, S. L., 56, *58,* 143, 144, 145, 146, 148, 155, 156, 157, 160, 163, 164, 167, *170, 171*
Newell, A., 20, *37*
Newman, L., 71, 74, 78, 81, *88*
Newtson, D., 80, *87*
Nisbett, R. E., 123, *140,* 143, 162, *171, 172*
Norman, D. A., 64, *87*

O

O'Brien, E. J., 44, 49, *58*
Olson, J. M., 130, *140*
Omoto, A. M., 157, *172*
Orvis, B. R., 203, *219*
Osgood, C., 161, *172*
Ostrom, T. M., 2, 7, *15,* 20, *37,* 40, *58,* 145, 153, 161, *172,* 178, 179, 190, 194, *217, 218, 219*

P

Padawer-Singer, A., 156, *171*
Paris, S. C., 72, *87*
Park, B., 1, 2, 5, 8, 9, *15,* 34, *37,* 39, 40, *58, 59,* 61, *87,* 92, 96, 106, 109, 111, 112, *119,* 135, 138, *139,* 151, *172,* 175, 192, 206, 209, 212, *217, 218*
Pavelchak, M. A., 143, 155, 160, 161, *170, 172*
Payne, J. W., 11, *16*
Peabody, D., 128, *140*
Peak, H., 92, 93, *120*
Pearlston, Z., 94, *121*
Pearson, J., 11, *15*
Peevers, B. H., 61, *87*
Pelham, B. W., 83, *86,* 156, *171*
Pennington, N., 8, 13, 14, *16*
Peterson, L. R., 206, *219*
Peterson, M. J., 206, *219*
Petty, R. E., 93, 116, *119, 120*
Peynircioglu, Z. F., 10, *16,* 74, *88*
Posner, M. I., 56, *58*
Powell, M. C., 25, *36,* 93, *119*
Pratto, F., 146, 148, 155, *170*
Preston, E., 157, *172*
Pryor, J. B., 179, 194, *219*

Q

Quattrone, G. A., 83, *87,* 130, 131, 132, 137, *139,* 156, *172*

R

Ratcliff, R., 10, 14, *16,* 44, *58,* 81, 82, *87*
Reder, L. M., 44, *58*
Reed, S. K., 56, *58*
Rest, J. R., 199, *219*
Reyes, R. M., 113, *120,* 205, *219*
Rholes, W. S., 27, *36,* 79, 84, *87*
Riggs, J. M., 130, 131, 132, 137, *139*
Riskey, D. R., 179, 182, 212, *219*
Rosch, E., 65, *87*
Rose, T. L., 196, *217*
Rosenberg, S., 61, *87*
Rosenbloom, P. S., 20, *37*
Ross, B. H., 44, *58*
Ross, L., 83, *87,* 114, *120,* 131, *140*
Ross, M., 130, *140*
Rothbart, M., 33, 34, *37,* 39, *59,* 63, *88,*

97, 103, 112, *120*
Ruderman, A. J., 155, 156, *172*
Rumelhart, D. E., 56, *58,* 64, *87*
Ruscher, J. B., 147, 157, 163, 165, *172*

S

Sanbonmatsu, D. M., 25, *36,* 93, *119*
Sawyers, B. K., 194, *216*
Schacter, D. L., 30, 32, *37,* 74, *88*
Schaffer, M. M., 56, *58*
Schank, R. C., 65, *88*
Schneider, D. J., 161, *172*
Schneider, W., 70, *88*
Schorr, D., 44, 51, *59,* 102, *120*
Schul, Y., 7, *16,* 92, 96, 97, 102, *119, 120,* 155, *169*
Schum, D., 13, *16*
Schvaneveldt, R. W., 123, *140*
Secord, P. F., 61, *87*
Sedlak, A., 61, *87*
Shanteau, J., 197, *219*
Shedler, J., 10, *16,* 113, *120*
Sherman, S. J., 24, *36,* 96, 110, 112, *120*
Shiffrin, R. M., 70, *88*
Simmel, M., 80, *87*
Simon, H. A., 8, *16,* 162, 163, *170,* 196, *219*
Singh, R., 197, *219*
Skowronski, J. J., 155, *172*
Slovic, P., *16*
Smith, E. E., 44, 51, *59,* 102, *120*
Smith, E. R., 10, *16,* 20, 21, 25, 27, 28, 29, 30, 31, 32, 33, 34, 35, *37,* 43, *59,* 67, 69, 70, 77, 79, 84, *88*
Smith, M. C., 43, *57,* 71, 74, 82, *86,* 135, 138, *139*
Snyder, M., 157, 165, *172,* 196, *219*
Snyder, M. L., 130, 131, 132, 137, *140*
Sorrentino, R. M., 27, *37*
Srul, T. K., 4, 6, 7, *15, 16,* 23, 27, *37,* 62, 63, 64, 79, *88, 89,* 92, 94, 95, 96, 97, 103, 111, 112, 113, *120, 121,* 123, *140,* 147, 155, *172, 173,* 178, 179, 206, *219, 220*
Stangor, C., 131, *139*
Stark, H. A., 74, *88*
Stern, L. D., 97, *120*
Suci, G. J., 161, *172*
Sujan, M., 155, *172*
Surber, C. F., 197, 199, *219*
Swann, W. B., Jr., 157, 165, *172*

T

Tannenbaum, P. H., 161, *172*
Taylor, S. E., 2, *16,* 81, *86,* 102, *120,* 145, 147, 155, 156, 158, 162, *171, 172,* 179, *219*
Tesser, A., 114, *120*
Tetlock, P. E., 97, *121,* 157, *172, 173*
Thein, R. D., 111, *118*
Thomas, E. A. C., 14, *16*
Thompson, L., 157, *170*
Thompson, S. C., 2, *16*
Thompson, W. C., 113, *120,* 205, *219*
Thomson, D. M., 42, *59,* 70, *88*
Toyofuka, M. L., 44, 49, *58*
Trope, Y., 64, 79, *88,* 124, 126, 127, 128, 131, 132, 136, 137, 138, *139, 140,* 156, 165, *173*
Tsujimoto, R. N., 81, *88*
Tulving, E., 42, *59,* 70, 74, *88,* 94, *121,* 194, *219*
Turnbull, W., 126, *139*
Tversky, A., 2, 11, 14, *16,* 112, *121,* 131, *140,* 205, *219*
Tyler, R. B., 156, *170*

U

Uleman, J. S., 10, *17,* 42, *59,* 70, 71, 74, 81, 82, *87, 88,* 135, 138, *140,* 156, *173,* 211, *220*
Uranowitz, S. W., 196, *219*

V

Von Hendy, H., 148, 163, 166, *170*

W

Watkins, M. J., 10, *16,* 74, *88*
Watts, W. A., 2, *17*
Weary, G., 203, 204, *217*
Weber, R., 206, *218*
Wertheimer, M., 153, *169*
Whitten, W. B., 113, *118*
Wilkening, F., 199, *220*
Williams, C. J., 25, *36*
Wilson, T. D., 123, *140,* 162, *171*
Winter, L., 10, *17,* 42, *59,* 70, 71, 74, 7881, 82, *88,* 135, 138, *140,* 211, *220*
Wolman, C., 155, *173*
Wyer, R. S., Jr., 2, *15,* 23, 27, *37,* 55, *58,*

59, 62, 63, 64, 79, *88, 89,* 92, 97, *121,* 123, *140,* 147, *173,* 178, 179, 190, 203, 207, *217, 220*

Z

Zacks, R., 10, *15*
Zajonc, R. B., 93, 97, *121*
Zalinski, J., 187, 213, *220*
Zanna, M. P., 157, *169, 171*
Zarate, M. A., 33, 34, 35, *37*
Zehner, K. S., 96, 110, 112, *120*
Zukier, H., 73, *86,* 143, 150, *169, 172*

Subject Index

A

Anchoring, 131–132
Attention, 156–161, 163
Attitudes, 24–25
Attributes, *see* Inferences, trait
Attribution, *see also* Inferences 61, 83, 196–204
  causal, 197–198
  person, 61–65, 69, 74–85
  situation, 75–76, 126–139
Automaticity, *see also* Practice effects 70–71, 81–82
Averaging theory, 184–187

C

Categories, *see also* Schemas 33–35, 124–126, 134–136, 141–158
  accessibility, 27–29
  action, 62, 65–67, 69, 72–85
  confirmation, 143
Covariation, 76–77, 201–203

E

Encoding specificity, *see* Memory, representations
Evidence evaluation, 12–14

Expectancies, 12, 125–126, 134–135, 148, 154–155

F

Fan effect, 43–46, 48–51, 53, 55

I

Identification, *see* Memory, encoding
Impression formation, 1–2, 39–43, 47, 53, 56–57, 61–63, 71, 75, 82–84, 91–92, 96–97, 141–158
Incentives, 157
Inference-memory-based processes, *see also* Memory-based processes, On-line processes 7–8
Inferences, 6–11, 32–35, 46–49, 72–74, 77–78, 81–84, 159–161, 180–185, 193–194, 205–209
  causal, 68, 150, 201–203
  contextual effects, 123–130, 133–139, 147, 160–161
  correspondent, 67, 200–201
  trait, 10, 20–21, 23–32, 39–46, 48–53, 55–57, 61–85, 123–139, 147–154, 156, 183–185, 198–200
Information integration theory (IIT), 177–180, 210–211
Interference, 4–5, 49

227

SUBJECT INDEX

J

Judgments, *see* Inferences

K

Knowledge systems, 191

M

Memory,
  assemblage, 192
  availability, 205
  encoding, 124-125, 129-139, 151-154, 162-163
  episodic, 194-195
  functional, 176-187, 204-205, 207-211
  impression, *see* On-line processes
  long-term, 189-191
  person, 188-191
  recall, 69-74, 101-108, 112-114, 180-182, 184, 206-207
  representations in, 6, 41-43, 62-65, 70-73, 93-98, 100, 105, 108-112
  reproductive, 176, 178-179, 192-193, 205-207
  verbal, *see* Memory-based processes
Memory-based processes, *see also* Inference-memory-based processes, On-line processes 1-14, 108-112, 137-138, 175, 178-179, 205-206, 209-212

N

Need for cognition, 116-117

O

On-line processes, *see also* Inference-memory-based processes, Memory-based processes 1-14, 19-24, 39-44, 48-49, 55-57, 64, 92, 96-97, 109-112, 117-118, 138, 142-146, 175-176, 182-184, 189-191, 197, 209-212
Opinion formation, 91-98, 100-114
Order effects, 130-134, 137

P

Person perception, *see* Impression formation
Persuasion, 91-92, 114-117
Practice effects, 19-20, 23-36
Priming, 27-29, 84
Procedural efficiency, 24-36
Productions, 21-23
Protocols, 162-165

S

Salience, 131-132
Schemas, *see also* Categories 65-66, 73, 80-81, 195-196, 200-203, 213-214
Self-report measures, 165-167
Stereotyping, 32-35, 114-117

T

Traits, *see* Inferences, traits